MASSACHUSETTS BAY CONNECTIONS

Historical and Biographical Sketches
of the Towns and Communities of the
Massachusetts Bay Colony

Judy Jacobson

CLEARFIELD

Printed for
Clearfield Company, Inc. by
Genealogical Publishing Co., Inc.
Baltimore, Maryland
1992

Reprinted for
Clearfield Company, Inc. by
Genealogical Publishing Co., Inc.
Baltimore, Maryland
1994, 2004

International Standard Book Number: 0-8063-1330-7

Made in the United States of America

Table of Contents

Preface   v

In Explanation vii

A Map of the Massachusetts Bay Area   x

Massachusetts Bay Colony   1
    The Beginnings   1
    The Towns   6
        Beverly   6
        Boston   6
        Braintree   7
        Brookline   8
        Cambridge   10
        Charlestown   11
        Hingham   12
        Hull   13
        Roxbury   15
        Salem   16
        Weymouth   18
        Woburn   20

Families   22
    Aspinwall Family   22
        Peter Aspinwall Family   22
        William Aspinwall Family   29
    Baker Family   33
    Balch Family   36
    Collins Family   41
        Edward Collins Family   41
        John Collins Family   46
    Gardner Family   49
        Thomas Gardner Family of Roxbury   49
        Thomas Gardner Family of Salem   53
    Hull Family   61
        John Hull Family   61
        Joseph Hull Family   66
    Lobdell Family   70
    Maverick Family   75
    Nash Family   85
    Palfrey Family   88
    Payne / Paine Family   90
    Porter Family   94
        John Porter Family   94
        Richard Porter Family   98
    Preston Family 100
    Russell Family 103
        John Russell Family 103
        Richard Russell Family 105
        William Russell Family 108
    Sharp Family 111
    Stone Family 115
        Simon Stone Family 115
        Gregory Stone Family 117
    Stubbs Family 119
    Talmadge Family 123
    Ward Family 127
    Weston Family 131

Appendix 136
    Towns 136
    Aspinwall 139
        Ambrose/Aspinwall Family 139
        Will of Thomas Aspinwall 140
    Balch 141
        Will of John Balch 141
    Gardner 142
        Will of Thomas Gardner 142
    Hull 143
        Will of Robert Hull 143
    Maverick 144
        Will of Radford Maverick 144
        Will of Moses Maverick 145
        Genealogy of Mary (Gye) Maverick 145
    Payne 147
        Payne Family of "ffrythenden" 147
    Sharp 148
        Inventory of Robert Sharp's Estate 148
        John Sharp's Agreement to Abide by Father's
            Will 148
    Ward 149
        Ward Family Genealogy Circa 1500 149
    Miscellanous 150
        Freeman's Oath 150
        Allerton - Maverick - Tuttle - Ward Families 150
        Winthrop / Dudley Feud 150
        Colonists 151
            Roger Conant 151
            Matthew Craddock 151
            John Harvard 152
            Peter Hobart 153
            Thomas Hooker, Jr. 153
            Isaac Johnson 154
            Thomas Morton 154
            William Pynchon 154
            Richard Saltonstall 154
            Samuel Sewall 155
            Thomas Shepard 155
            John Tilley 156
            Henry Vane 156

Literature Cited 157
Index of Proper Names 161

Preface

While researching my family tree I discovered a number of curious coincidences, including ancestors of mine from completely different branches of my family tree living on adjoining lots in the same town. These were people who fought together in the French and Indian Wars whose descendants would later become my ancestors. They did not connect at those points to create an ancestor of mine. Thomas Gardner, John Balch and Peter Palfrey arrived together in the spring of 1624 aboard the "Zouch Phenix". John Balch was my great-grandfather's ancestor: Palfrey and Gardner were my great-grandmother's. It seemed odd that after being so close, it wouldn't be until a century or more later that their descendants would come together. These coincidences led me to name this volume "Massachusetts Bay Connections".

Symbols Used

aft	after
b.	born
betw	between
bpt.	baptized
br	brother of
bur.	buried
c.	approximately
ca	approximately
circa	approximately
d.	died
dau	daughter of
Dea	Deacon
eng.	engagement announced
est inv.	estate inventoried
grad.	graduated from college
Lt.	Lieutenant
m.	married
mthr	mother of
nd	no date
np	no place
pos	possibly
prob	probably
repr	reprint
Sgt.	Sergeant
sis	sister of
son	son of
vol	volume
wid	widow or widower of
wll dtd.	will dated
wll pro.	will proven

In 45 B.C. the Julian Calendar, in an attempt to correct earlier errors, assigned every fourth year with one additional (leap) year. In reality, the error had only required an adding 7 days every 900 years instead of 25 every 100 years. So more changes were needed.

In an attempt to further correct the problem a calendar was released during Pope Gregory XIII's reign which omitted ten days. So October 5, 1582 became October 15th. While Roman Catholic nations adopted the new calendar immediately, the Gregorian Calendar was not adopted in England until 1752. Because of the delay, when it was finally adopted in England, eleven rather than ten days had to be skipped. The day after September 2, 1752 became September 14th.

The legislation that required the omission of eleven days, also shortened the previous year. So 1752 began with what would have been January 1, 1751 instead of March 25, 1752.

When an event in this book occurred in a January, February or March prior to 1752, the double-year date (i.e. February 3, 1682/3) will be used to denote both the old and new calendar. If a date appears as "1682-83", the event being discussed happened between those two dates.

And lastly, the initials NEHGR were used as an abbreviation for <u>The New England Historical and Genealogical Register</u>.

Names and Titles in New England

"Anglo-Saxon" can be used to describe the general period
when Germanic tribes invaded the British Isles circa 500 A.D.
establishing their own language. Anglo-Saxon is also frequently referred to as Old English. The Normans conquered the
British Isles in 1066 with William the Conqueror. Most of the
names given by the New England settlers originated from one of
the two groups - Anglo-Saxon or Norman.

There were 452 English freemen in Boston between 1630 and
1634. The six leading men's names were John, William, Thomas,
Richard, Robert, and Edward. All were of Norman origin with
little religious connotation. While there were some, like
Isaac and Samuel, that were Old Testament, most were not.

However, according to Stewart in <u>American Given Names</u>,
there was a "revolution" when those Puritans began naming
their children in the New World. Ninety percent of the
children of those Boston freemen had biblical names. The top
ten names of Boston's children were John, Thomas, Samuel,
Joseph, James, Nathaniel, William, Ebenezer, Isaac, and
Jonathan.

Among women, 21% of those born in the Massachusetts Bay
Colony between 1630 and 1670 were named Mary, 17% were named
Elizabeth, and 15% were named Sarah.

Prior to 1731, scarcely anyone had a middle name.
However, by 1783, they had become very popular.

Surnames developed in a completely different way. The
examples below may have all been the sons of someone named
Richard of Kingsly Hall. The names the sons adopted as their
surnames came from a variety of characteristics.

Given Name	Surname	Reason for Name
David	LeClerke	a scholar
William	DeMalpas	the name of his estate
Phillip	Gogh	"Red" because of his hair
Daniel	Goodman	received from others of excellence of his character
Richard	Little	from his diminutive stature
William	Kenclarke	"knowing scholar"
John	Richardson	from father's baptismal

In this study of Massachusetts Bay families, a single
spelling of each name will be used. Even though differing

spellings might have appeared for a person's surname in assorted records, only one spelling will be used in this text. Any variation will appear between quotation marks. For example, Payne / Paine / Pain / Payn are all variations of a single surname. "Payne" will be the spelling used in this book.

In New England "Mr." was a title applied to sea and military captains, eminent merchants, doctors, school masters, magistrates, clergymen, and freemen with two college degrees. The females of their families were referred to as "Mrs." Those who were not of the "Mr." or "Mrs." status were referred to as "Goodman" or "Goodwife".

Maps of the Massachusetts Bay Area

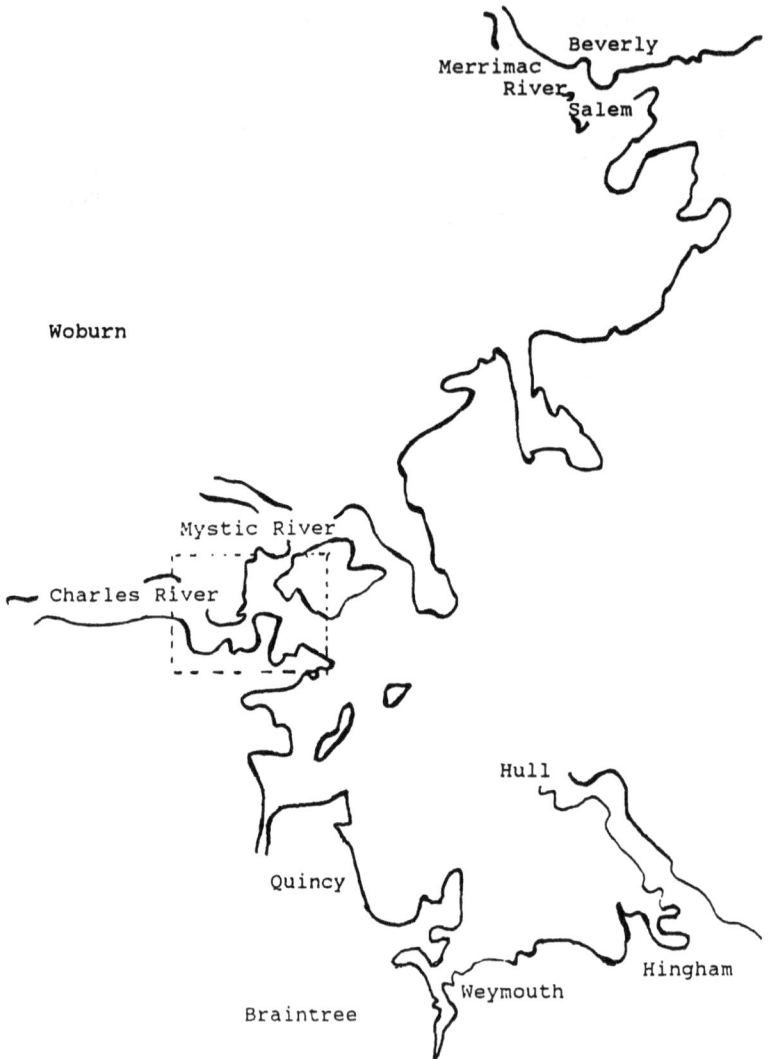

Beverly

Merrimac
River

Salem

Woburn

Mystic River

Charles River

Hull

Quincy

Hingham

Weymouth

Braintree

Massachusetts Bay Colony

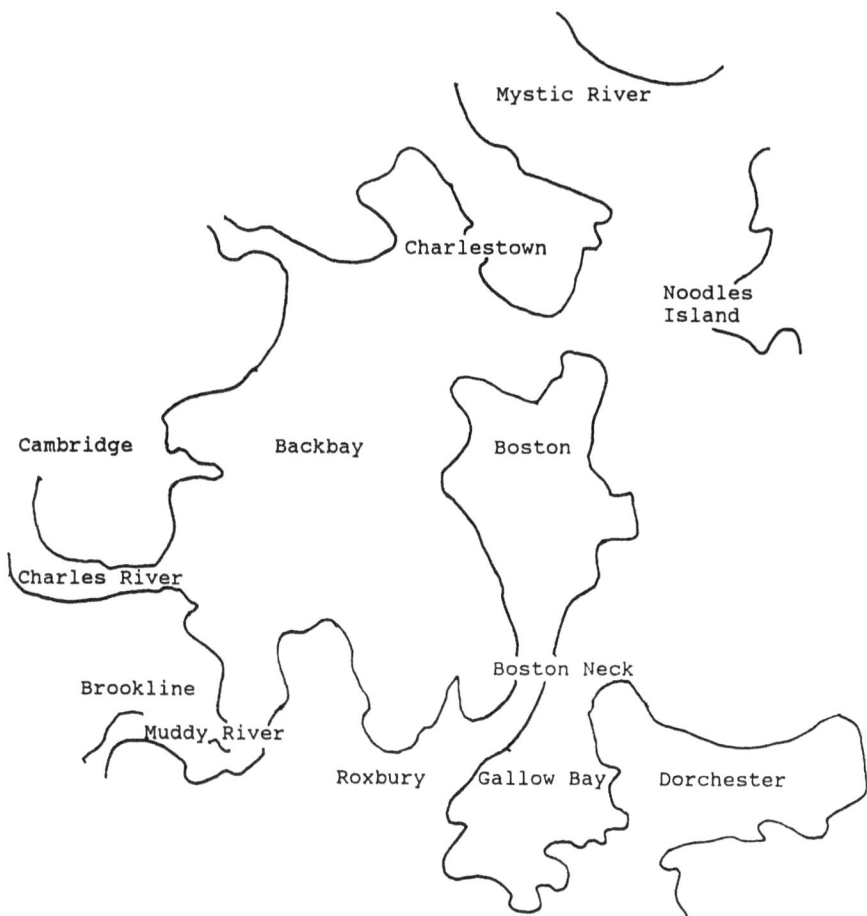

Area Within the Box

Massachusetts Bay Colony

The Beginnings

When Henry VIII started a non-Protestant, non-Catholic hybrid church in the 1500's affairs really became perplexing for the English. Henry's son Edward VI, who died in 1553, was a Protestant: his half-sister Mary Tudor, who ruled until her death in 1558, was Catholic. Another half-sister, Elizabeth I, a Protestant, followed Mary as Queen. With each change of monarch, the English were expected to conform to the religion of that monarch. As Charles Banks wrote in The Winthrop Fleet of 1630, England was being torn apart while "Catholic Mary and Protestant Elizabeth were engaged in killing off each others heretics."

Religion was in chaos. "Heretics" (persons who disagreed with the established religion) were burned at the stake. Clerics were unlearned or "popish" or in danger of losing their positions. Other clerics were fleeing the country. Separatist leaders were being executed.

One of the centers of discontent in England was Cambridge University which had educated a number of the rebel clergy. Seventy-one percent of the university graduates who emigrated to the Massachusetts Bay Colony before 1646 had attended Cambridge. In addition, certain English counties were erupting. Of those who later traveled with the Winthrop Fleet, 46% were from Suffolk County, 25% from Essex, 16% from London, and another 5% from Northampshire. The remaining 8% were divided among citizens of Yorkshire, Kent, Leicestershire, Lancashire, Hampshire, Norfolk, Oxfordshire, Buckinghamshire, Hertfordshire, Nottinghamshire, Rutlandshire, Chester and Holland.

Most of the discontented were yeoman fated to work for the landed gentry: serfdom, not much different from slavery, was condoned by the church and the government. A very few people owned most of the land and those without land had little hope of acquiring any. The cost of living and the birth rates soared while the economy became more depressed. Bad harvests meant starvation for many as the price of food outran wages. There was a severe slump in the cloth trade. The Black Death hit England. Piracy was affecting imports and safety. And, finally, Prince Henry who was thought to be sympathetic to reform died suddenly in 1612 and Prince Charles became heir to the throne.

English religious extremists known as "Pilgrims" left their country in 1608 for the religious freedom of Holland. However, expectations of unlimited land, control of their own destiny, and use of the language of their parents influenced them to leave Holland and sail to the New World. With nearly intolerable conditions aboard the "Mayflower", those who made it to the New World were certainly a bold and hearty breed of people.

In <u>Chronicles of Old Salem</u>, Robotti wrote that there were approximately 100,000 Indians representing seven tribes already living in New England when the English began to arrive. But wars and plagues killed thousands and the Pawtucket Indians alone dropped from 3,000 to only a few hundred by 1626. Frances Jennings wrote that the Massachusett Indians had declined from 3,000 to only 300 by 1674. The influx of new colonists aggravated the situation.

The Dorchester Company was formed to promote commercial fishing in New England. Six shipwrights and supplies were sent to the Massachusetts Bay Colony in 1629 to build small fishing boats for expected settlers. In fact, their profession was considered so important in 1639 that shipbuilders, along with some fishermen, were exempted from military training. Dow claimed that by 1665 New England had 300 trading vessels and over 1300 smaller fishing vessels at Cape Sable.

As the predecessor of the Massachusetts Bay Company, the London Company had been formed for the same commercial reasons. Like members of the Dorchester Company, the members of the London Company saw the New World as a supply house. These large English corporations were formed to run the companies separately from the King.

The French had managed to establish themselves in Canada and the Spanish in Florida. So the English were anxious to establish themselves on the continent too. Even though early colonies had proven unsuccessful, persistent groups continued to leave each year, undaunted by failures or by prospects of a hazardous passage. A trading post was established at Wessagusset in 1622 and settlements were established in Weymouth and Braintree in 1623, in Winnesimmet (Chelsea) and Naumkeag (Salem), Shawmet (Boston) and Nantasket in 1624, and Mishawum (Charlestown) in 1625 followed. These settlements stimulated the large migrations of the 1630's.

John Endicott and five others working for the New England Company had received a royal patent which dictated the boundary of the colony as a north line from the Atlantic to the "South Sea, three English myles to the northward of the said riuer called Monomack, alias Merrymack (Merrimac River)." The southern boundary was "three Englishe Myles on the south porte of the saide river called Charles riuer." Much of the land had already been granted to Robert Gorges of the Wessagusset settlement. But Gorges agreed to Endicott's grant because he thought it would not effect his own grant to establish a fishing venture. Endicott's royal patent stated that the primary purpose of the colony was to "wynn and incite the natives of country, to the knowledge and obedience of the onlie true God and Savior of mankinde and the Christian Fayth."

Sixty colonists, with Endicott as their governor, settled a colony at Salem and made it clear they intended to control the entire area in their patent, including Gorges' fishing plantation. They were able to secure the Crown's backing for

their successful ouster of Gorges. Endicott's charter creating
the Massachusetts Bay Colony was issued March 4, 1629.

It was not until 1632 that Gorges realized he had been
outwitted. He fought the Massachusetts Colony's grant for
another seven years but he lost and, in the end, he received
a grant in Maine in its place.

In John Winthrop's case, when parliament was sent home
and autocratic royal rule began he was removed from his office
as attorney in the Court of Wards. Barred from his job, dis-
illusioned by his government, and faced with financial
difficulties, Winthrop looked to the New World for hope.

By September, 1629, John Winthrop had decided to leave
England and had joined the Massachusetts Bay Company. On March
29, 1630; Winthrop and his band left.

Many of those who finally settled to the Boston area
arrived with the Winthrop Fleet. Eleven vessels were officially part of the Fleet. The 350 ton "Arbella" was the flagship.
The ships arrived in Salem from June 13th into July, 1630 with
approximately 500 of the original 700 passengers surviving. On
August 23, 1630, they had their first official meeting on
land. That same year, the first church of Boston was founded
in Charlestown.

Winthrop originally planned to settle the group in one
large community. However, according to Wall, "sickness, lack
of good food and water, and fear of French pirates forced the
settlers to disperse." Sir Richard Saltonstall (see Appendix
X) took a group up the Charles River to settle Watertown,
William Pynchon (see Appendix X) settled Roxbury, Winthrop
established Boston, Roger Ludlow began Dorchester, Deputy
Governor Dudley settled New Towne (Cambridge), and Increase
Nowell remained at Charlestown as its leader.

The first temporary homes in the Bay area were cone-
shaped huts of branches and earth. Later the settlers' houses
were of sawn timber erected around a central brick chimney.
Straw, clay and gravel were used to fill in between boards.
Clapboards protected the outside while wide perpendicular
boards covered the inside.

Since younger sons of wealthier English gentry were
unable to inherit family lands, many went to New England to
make their fortunes. According to The English Origins of the
"Mary & John" Passengers, in 1650, nineteen descendants of
Edward I lived in New England.

But the group was made up of all classes of people, from
nobility like Lady Arbella, the wife of Isaac Johnson (see
Appendix X), and Sir Richard Saltonstall; to Esquires like
Winthrop; to gentlemen like Pynchon and Feake; to yeomen.
While they were primarily English Protestants, a few were
Irish, Jewish, Dutch, Catholic, and West Indian.

On the whole, early colonists were not adventurers. They
were older in years and more stable in character. Many were
college educated. Not surprisingly, sixty-six percent were
ministers. All the necessary professions were represented;

including bakers, masons, blacksmiths, herdsmen, butchers, fishermen, carpenters, coopers, tanners, military officers, physicians, and weavers.

Slaves arrived as early as the 1630's and several Massachusetts merchants became active traders. Even though, several Blacks managed to become free and accumulate property, Blacks also were the only two people - the first in 1681 in Roxbury and the second in 1755 in Cambridge - burned alive at the stake in the colony.

Andrews reported that in 1630, 17 ships with 2000 settlers arrived. By 1641 over 300 vessels with 20,000 passengers had arrived. And in 1643, Winthrop wrote that "near half of the commonwealth for number of people and substance" had settled in the Boston area."

The influx came about because in the 17th century the English government had begun to consider how expansion could help the country grow financially. In Historical Sketch of the Town of Weymouth, Gilbert Nash wrote that "the great companies were..looking to the men and the places by whom and where they could carry out their grand schemes, accumulate the fortunes and seize the honors." Nash called them "not more scrupulous than some of their modern successors." Since the rightful owners (the Indians) of the land were "few, ignorant, and of not fixed abode," their projects seemed secure.

Although profit had been the initial purpose for the colony, religion soon replaced it. The Puritans did not want to separate from the Church of England. They only wanted to separate themselves from what they perceived as the church's corruption and sought to "purify" the State church.

Robert Wall, Jr., in Massachusetts Bay: The Crucial Decade 1640-50, wrote that the word "Separatist" usually held the connotation of "enthusiasm with overtones of horrors." Unfortunately that was what the Puritans eventually became like.

The fundamental source of authority in the Colony was the Royal Charter. When Winthrop arrived he took the governorship from Endicott. According to Robert Wall, Jr. in Massachusetts Bay: The Crucial Decade, 1640-50, Winthrop firmly believed "that men of birth, wealth, and social standing had been blessed by God and given command to rule" and that it was his followers' obligation "to obey and be ruled". His followers accepted that idea because it was not very different from their lord-of-the-manor experience in England.

There was no New England Church: no central organization existed. Following Plymouth's lead, each plantation in the Bay Colony set up an ecclesiastical type of government and worship. And they became radicals. Plantations, which later became towns, were governed by religion with little difference between the religious and the civil communities.

By 1646, the Colony considered itself independent from the British Parliament. But the clergy and magistrates feared democracy and made certain that only church members could vote or hold office and that clergy determined who could join the church. As late as 1670 only 20 to 25 percent of the adult male population could vote.

According to Andrews, clergy were dominant and "political order was determined according to a rigid interpretation of theology", making the government intolerant and oppressive. The church did all censuring, discipling, expelling and excommunicating. Dissenters were fined, thrown into irons, or banished. Bartholomew Hill was whipped for stealing a loaf of bread and John Baker for shooting at wild birds on the Sabbath. The pillory and stocks were common modes of punishment. Some people were forced to sit for months with one end of a rope tied to their neck and the other end to a gallows. A few towns used a cage to embarrass Sabbath-breakers while other towns used ducking and gagging for various "crimes". Daniel Blake was fined five pounds for addressing Edmund Bridge's daughter without the consent of her parents. A drunkard was sentenced to wear a red "D" around his neck in Boston. Servants were flogged for leaving their masters. Winthrop wrote that "Philip Ratliff, a servant of Mr Cradock (see Appendix X), being convict, ore tenus, of most foul, scandalous invectives against our churches and government was censured to be whipped, lose his ears, and be banished from the plantation." Slitting noses, branding, whipping, cutting off ears, and other such punishments were not outlawed until 1813.

When Quakerism arrived in Salem, some of its members were banished. In the late 1650's, the General Court approved the death penalty for Quakers. Many who had fled England to escape just such conditions were suddenly faced with the same intolerance and harshness in New England.

By 1661, public opinion had turned against clerical violence and Charles II ordered jailed Quakers released. But the colony continued to be strict in their laws. In 1675, according to Andrews, among the things considered crimes were "immodest wearing of hair by men," new fashions of dress, and "tippling". It was considered evil for a merchant to overcharge and for men and women to participate in the "loose and sinful habit of riding from town to town...under pretence of going to lectures, but really to drink and revel in taverns." A law forbidding celebrating Christmas was finally repealed in 1681.

At the same time, persecution in England was at its height. With the British government bankrupt, and civil war looming, the king was far too busy to be concerned about a colony thousands of miles away. With Cromwell's 1653 victory in England the strict regime in the Massachusetts Bay Colony was reinforced.

Later, with the restoration of the monarchy, things did change for the Massachusetts Bay Colony. Charles II had heard too many complaints of the Puritans trampling the rights of those who did not believe the same as them. In addition, the colony had gotten too independent and powerful. So, in an attempt curb this trend, the King made Massachusetts Bay a royal colony under firmer control of the governor.

The Towns

The Town of Beverly

In the summer of 1623, the Dorchester Company sent fishermen and planters in the "Fellowship" from Weymouth, England to a base camp in the New World named Cape Ann after Prince Charles' mother. Roger Conant (see Appendix X) was named manager of the Cape Ann group because it was thought he could avoid bloodshed with the Plymouth Pilgrim's over fishing rights. He not only managed to settle the dispute, he got the old timers of Cape Ann to agree to help the Plymouth Pilgrims build another camp. But Cape Ann still failed. After the fall of Cape Ann, Roger Conant and several dozen others from his company followed an Indian trail along the north shore to a more suitable location in the Naumkeag (Salem) area. Conant's group became known as the "Old Planters" of Naumkeag.

Before leaving England, Governor Endicott had been warned to be kind to the "Old Planters" of Conant's company. But instead, Endicott dismantled their "great house" at Cape Ann and seized their homes and gardens in Salem. In exchange, Conant was given an inferior area which prior to that time had been a part of Salem called "Basse Riuer (Bass River). In 1638 Winthrop was given permission to set up a salt works there, but it did not succeed.

Beverly, in Essex County, was established as a town in 1668. The entry in the Beverly First Church Records read "The Bass River is made a distinct towne the 3d November, 1668: called Beverly." On May 28, 1679, the bounds between Beverly, "the village" and Wenham were established.

Early family names of Beverly included the Conant, Palfrey, Morgan, Wolfe, Black, Hill, Dodge, Lathrop, Root, Ellingwood, Stone, Bishop, Herrick, Corning, Woodbury, Balch, Gray, and Gardner. Rev. Jeremiah Hobart was minister at Beverly for a-while. But unlike the Hobarts of Hingham, Jeremiah had trouble getting along with his parishioners. He was fiery and was accused of cursing and swearing; and of reproaching fellow ministers. He had trouble getting paid his salary and was constantly in court. Finally Hobart was dismissed and replaced by Rev. Joseph Capen.

The Town of Boston

St. Botolph was the namesake of a town in Lincolnshire, England. Originally named Botolph's Stone, it then became Botulvestan, and finally, Boston (see Appendix I). The Puritans, thinking of the prosperous town, named the area on Massachusetts Bay after the Lincolnshire town.

When Winthrop and his followers arrived in 1630, the area eventually called Boston was the home of William Blaxton, sole survivor of Gorges colony. Blaxton invited the Winthrop group to settle in Shawmut (Boston) when Charlestown proved to be unsuitable. The name Shawmutt/Shawmut/Shaumut has been translated to mean "a spring of water", "peninsula", "Fountain of living water", "free land", "ferry", and "the neck".

The first English name for Shawmut at the mouth of the Charles River was Tramountain / Trimountaine, named for the three area hills in the area. Shortened to Tremont, it became the name of a main Boston Street. According to Massachusetts Bay Colony Records, on September 7, 1630 the name was officially changed to Boston. Winthrop first used the name in his journal on September 30th of that year. On many early maps the spelling was "Baston".

Samuel Maverick described it as "lying pleasantly on a plaine and the ascending of a High Mount which lyes about the midle of ye plaine. The wholl Towne is an Island except two Hundred paces of land at one place on the southside." At the time the town had "fouer fill companys of ffoote and a Troope of horse On the Southeast side of the Towne on a little Hill there is a Fort."

"The Neck" was the name used for the Boston peninsula, to be distinguished from Rumney Marsh (Chelsea), Noodles Island (South Boston) and Muddy River (Brookline). Most of the early settlers were East Anglican, West countrymen, with others from Devon, Dorset, and London. In addition to Robert Hull, early family names in Boston included Newgate, Collins, Stubbs, Leverett, Hutchinson, Keayne and Oliver.

Boston was the center for defense for the colony. Colonial records from 1633 indicated that each man in each plantation in the colony was required to do two days work on the fort at Boston. Then in 1634, the towns were required to send men "for a ward in Boston, while any ships ride there."

Boston also became the center of justice where, on September 28, 1637, John Williams, a ship's carpenter, was hanged for the murder of John Hoddy and William Schooler for the murder of Mary Sholy.

In 1630 Mattapan, founded by Roger Ludlow, was renamed Dorchester (see Appendix I) after the town in Dorset, England. Early settlers were divided into two groups - those who followed Rev. John Maverick from the Dorset area and those who followed Rev. Richard Mather from the Lancashire area. It was annexed by Boston in bits and pieces between 1804 and 1869. James Blake and William Preston were leading settlers of Dorchester.

"Powder Horne Hill" and "Pullen Poynte" were annexed to Boston in 1632; "Wynetsemt", "Rumney Mashe" in 1634; and "Deere Iland, Hogg Iland, Longe Island, and Spetakle Island" in 1635. Eventually Charlestown, parts of Braintree, and Roxbury were also annexed.

The Town of Braintree
Thomas Morton (see Appendix X) and companions settled at Mount Wooleston/ Wollaston which he renamed Ma-re Mount

7

(Merrymount). Morton was carefree and spent his days dickering with the Indians, hunting, and fishing. In 1627 Morton set-up a Maypole and his group spent days dancing, drinking, and entertaining Indian women. According to <u>Builders of the Bay Colony</u>, he purchased firearms and even taught the Indians how to use them.

In June, 1628, Plymouth's Miles Standish marched to Merrymount and arrested Morton for selling arms and liquor to the Indians, which caused problems for Plymouth's fur trade. Several Massachusetts Bay settlements, including Nantasket (Hull) supported the action.

Morton was banished but returned to Merrymount with more liquor and merriment. Again he was arrested, the Maypole was torn down, his home was burned in front of him, and he was banished.

A patent was granted in 1632, but in order to control the area, Boston annexed it in 1634. During 1635 and 1636, boundaries were set between Mount Wollaston and Weymouth. On May 13, 1640, it was established as a town named Braintree / Brantry (see Appendix I). Part of it later became a section of Quincy.

Thomas Hooker, Jr. and Moses Paine arrived early. Most early settlers came from East Anglia, but some emigrated from Gloucestershire, Northamptonshire, and Somersetshire.

It took Morton another 10 years to get back to the area. Even though time had mellowed him, he was still imprisoned by the Massachusetts Bay Colony. Maverick wrote that Morton was "keept in the Comon Goale a whole winter" for writing a book Maverick called "the truest description of New England as then it was that ever I saw. The offence was he touched them too neare they not proveing the charge he was sett loose, but soone after dyed, haveing as he said and most believed received his bane by harfd lodging and fare in prison." In reality he was released after paying a large fine, and eventually made his was to Maine where he died a broken man.

The Town of Brookline

Muddy River was settled to the south of Cambridge, Massachusetts and the Charles River. The town of Muddy River was named after a tributary of the Charles River.

In the beginning, it was the area where colonists went to cut wood for their homes and ships. Because of the area's good pasture and meadow land, early Boston inhabitants kept their cattle and swine there during the summer. That practice continued for many years.

The area first officially appeared in records in 1632 when Gov. Winthrop referred to the knoll in the center of the "great swamp" where the Sagamore Indians had created a stronghold. He wrote -
"Notice being given of ten Sagamores and many Indians being assembled at Muddy River, the Governor

8

sent Captain Underhill with twenty musketeers to make discoveries, but at Roxbury they heard that they were broken up."

The next year, a cart bridge was constructed over the Muddy River to the spot which would eventually become the town of Muddy River, and later Brookline (see Appendix I).

Boston records dated November 10, 1634, showed a constable had been assigned to assess a rate "for the cowes keeping, a rate for the goates keeping, and other charges in rambe goats about them and the cloes in common and make a rate for the young cattle and cows keeper at Muddy River."

Land grants were given out to induce settlement. In 1635, at a Boston General Meeting; William Colborne, William Aspinwall, John Sampford, William Balson and Richard Wright were assigned to lay out farms at Muddy River. According to Harriet Wood's Historical Sketches of Brookline, Mass., the poor of the area were given four acres per person for land near the head of the Muddy River and five acres per person for land farther from the river. The on December 30, 1639, Town Clerk Joseph Prout recorded that the inhabitants of Muddy River had decided to set aside 500 acres for "perpetual commage".

Early settlers included the Robert Sharp, Peter Aspinwall, Robert Hull and Thomas Gardner families.

In 1638, Winthrop described an "operation of the Devil" which had occurred along the Muddy River. Three people, including James Everett, had reported a 3-yards square light which "contracted into the figure of a swine" and ran "up and down about two or three hours".

By 1640, the boundary between Cambridge and Muddy River had been fixed. However, the Roxbury - Muddy River boundary changed so many times over the next years that at times the two towns seemed to be one. In fact, many early Muddy River settlers were buried in the old Roxbury cemetery and most early records were kept in Roxbury. Someone listed as being born or dying in Roxbury may have, in reality, been a resident of Muddy River.

By 1686, although the area was being called Brookline, it was still part of Boston. The residents of Muddy River began to assert their independence and established a school separate from Boston's. The first teacher was paid 12 pounds a year. It was a small wooden structure near the center of town, which eventually served the area for more than 100 years.

Then in August, 1704, the town leaders; including Thomas and several other Gardners, Samuel and Eleazer Aspinwall, and William Sharp; petitioned the General Court and Governor Dudley to establish the area as a separate village. On November 13, 1705, court records read that
        "the prayer of the petition be granted; and the
    powers and privileges of a Township, be given to the
    inhabitants of the lands commonly known by the name
    of Muddy River, the Town to be called Brookline; who
    are hereby enjoined to build a meeting-house, and

obtain an able Orthodox minister...within the space
of three years next coming."

However, it wasn't until March 2, 1713, that they were
able to stop worshipping in Roxbury and begin organizing a
church of their own. Samuel Aspinwall, John Druce and Peter
Boylston were appointed to manage "the affair relating to the
meeting-house. Caleb Gardner, Jr. donated land next to his
home lot, near the middle of town. The building went up in
1714 and held 14 pews and a number of benches. The steeple was
not erected until 1771.

In 1793, Brookline with over 500 inhabitants, became part
of Norfolk County. By 1796 there were 72 houses. By 1844 the
number had risen to 212 houses.

The Town of Cambridge

Simon Bradstreet established New Towne, later known as
Cambridge (see Appendix I) on a level plain across the Charles
River from Boston. But its early years were filled with
political uncertainties in addition to the usual hardships of
establishing a community in the New World. Governor Winthrop
intended to form a fortified capital with his entire group at
New Towne. The General Court even employed John Masters to dig
a 6-foot deep, 12-foot wide channel to accommodate vessels.
But others had different ideas. In 1631, when a sixty pound
tax was levied on the colony to be used to fortify New Towne;
the citizens of Watertown, upset that they had not been
allowed to vote on the tax, refused to pay. The General Court
had to be called upon to settle the dispute.

A group of settlers from Braintree; including Rev. Thomas
Hooker (see Appendix I), Samuel Stone and John Haynes; settled
in New Towne in 1632. The town had grown to 60 families by
1634, but their problems continued.

In 1632, Deputy Governor Thomas Dudley generated a rift
(see Appendix X) when he reminded everyone that Governor
Winthrop had failed to keep his promise to move his home to
New Towne. Dudley had built an extravagant home there. But
shortly after Governor Winthrop built his home in New Towne,
he had it dismantled and moved to Boston.

Another battle occurred when in 1634 most of the settlers
of the town petitioned the General Court for permission to
move to the Connecticut Valley. They felt New Towne did not
have enough land and was squeezed with Charlestown and
Watertown on either side. The court granted them more land but
it turned out to be too far away to pasture cattle and the
soil there would not grow wheat. The deputies approved their
petition: the magistrates rejected it. Dudley agreed with it:
Winthrop did not.

According to Builders of the Bay Colony, the members of
the Church of New Towne were lucky to be able to sell their
property on the installment plan to new settlers. Thomas
Hooker and his congregation not only carried their household
goods to Connecticut, but also their livestock and domestic
animals. So when Harvard College was established, only eight
of the original one hundred families remained.

The newcomers established their own church and "called to the Office of Pastor, that gratious sweet Heavenly minded, and soule-ravishing minister, Master Thomas Shepheard." Shepard (see Appendix X) was also described as a "little, weak pale-complectioned man" with "intense rapport" with his congregation. And Shepard had ties with the original New Towne settlers. He was a former classmate of Samuel Stone. And, in 1637, Rev. Shepard took as his second wife, the daughter of original church minister Thomas Hooker. Shepard's church was a primitive meeting house where he preached of love and compassion. The old meeting house stood until 1650 when a new, forty-foot square church was built.

Cambridge was laid out in a square. House lots in New Towne were assigned to the new settlers and a local government was started. Houses were to be roofed with slate or shingle for safety. All homes had to be at least six feet from the road.

The General Court moved from New Towne to Boston in 1636, returned in 1637 to escape Anne Hutchinson, and 18 months later returned to Boston.

Happily, conditions improved with a name change. In 1636 the name "Cambridge" first appeared in the Massachusetts Bay records. And on May, 1638, records read "Newetowne shall henceforward be called Cambridge."

Along with the name change, the town was given the 400 pounds originally set aside to build a college in Salem. Cambridge had been abandoned by its residents and then by the magistrates. So it was desperate for something to pour some life back into the town. The college promised to bring artisans, shopkeepers, intellectuals, and a market for goods.

According to Chronicles of Old Salem, John Harvard (see Appendix X) left 400 books and an additional 780 pounds to the college when he died on September 14, 1638. So the General Court decided to name the college Harvard after its benefactor. Like the old English towns, the citizens of Cambridge had reserved a square for a market place which eventually became Harvard Square. The first university class graduated in 1642. In 1644 every family in the colony was asked to give one peck of corn or twelve shillings to the university.

In October, 1641, the boundary between Cambridge and Boston was established. Cambridge finally became incorporated into a city in 1846.

The Town of Charlestown

Charlestown has been called "the mother of Boston" for good reason. Mishuwam (Charlestown) was founded by Winthrop. When Winthrop arrived, he found a solitary settler, a blacksmith named Thomas Wolford living in a stockaded enclosure on the hill overlooking the Charles River. But the only stream was low and available only when the tide was out. Certainly it was not enough fresh water to support a town the size Winthrop had in mind. So many, including Winthrop, moved to what would eventually become Boston.

Charlestown was presided over by Increase Nowell after most of the Puritans moved on to other areas. And, like Boston, Charlestown was on a peninsula with three main hills and connected to the mainland by a narrow neck. Maverick described its location as "one mile from Winnisme crossing Mistick River ... on the Northside of the Mouth of Charles River." Early records indicated that in 1637 it had grown to 150 homes and that boundaries went beyond the "Neck" to where the settlers pastured their cattle. It had a "Great House" which was inhabited by Governor Winthrop for a time, a large square, and the colony's first tavern. Maverick said it had "considerable Merchants in it and many usefull handicrafts and many good farmers belonging to it."

Charlestown was eventually annexed by Boston. Among its early pioneers were Rev Zechariah Symmes, Rev. Thomas James, William Aspinwall, Richard Russell, Capt. Robert Sedgewick (later a Major-General under Cromwell), George Bunker (for whom Bunker Hill was named) and William Stilson (who became deacon and General Court Deputy).

John Harvard (see Appendix X) settled there in 1637 and built a large home. Harvard, who died in Charlestown on September 14, 1638 at the age of 31, left half of his estate and all of his library toward building a college in the colony.

The Town of Hingham

Like other communities of the Bay Colony, Bare/Bear Cove (Hingham) was settled without a legal grant or bill of sale from the owners, the Massachusett Indians. Nor were the Indians paid for the land. Even though The Invasion of America gave the year of settlement as 1634; The Massachusetts Bay: The Crucial Decade gave 1633 as the year it was settled by a group of men from Norfolk, England.

Twenty-nine people including the Hobart family (see Appendix X), arrived in the settlement and officially changed its name to Hingham in September, 1635. It was settled on land an equal distance between Weymouth and Hull. Land from "Conihasset" was annexed in 1640. Maverick called it "a hand-some Towne supplying Boston also with wood, timber, leather, and board. Some Masts are had ther and store of provisions."

The Hobarts were from Old Hingham in England and dominat-ed the new town. Peter Hobart; a Cambridge graduate and former Bishop of Norwich, England; served as pastor of Hingham Church from his arrival until his death in January, 1679. His father Edmund Sr. and brothers Joshua, Edmund Jr., and Thomas held a number of important elected offices. Edmund Hobart Sr. was a deputy five times and Joshua was deputy twenty-six times.

Bozoan Allen, a friend of the Hobarts, served as deputy from 1643 until his death in 1652. Joseph Peck, Nicholas Jacob, and Daniel Cushing from Hingham, England, were also residents of the new Hingham. While others in the town, like Thomas Burton, were not from Hingham, England; they did not have anywhere near the power as those who were.

12

Lt. Anthony Eames was not from Old Hingham. But on the surface, it did not appear to be a problem: he was a freeman who served as a deputy to the General Court. However, in 1645, Lt. Eames was elected captain of the militia company and his name was sent to the magistrates. But before the magistrates could vote approval and with no explanation, the town withdrew Eames' name and replaced it with Bozoan Allen's.

Allen's primary qualification seemed to be that he was a close friend of the Hobarts and a former ship's captain. Because of Allen's lack of qualifications, the magistrates directed Eames to train the military company. The town of Hingham was outraged that the magistrates did not follow their wishes.

At training sessions the band refused to obey Eames. Rumors ran rampant. In church meetings the Hobarts accused Eames of lying. Petitions were signed. Eames resigned. From the view-point of the citizens of Hingham, Deputy Governor Winthrop was siding with Eames. There were court cases and Hingham citizens were jailed. Complaints were registered against the deputy governor. The lower house of the General Court battled the upper house over the issue.

In the end, Eames was returned as the commander of the military troops, but was admonished for quitting in the middle of the commotion. Joshua Hobart who was found to have lied was fined 20 pounds. According to Massachusetts Bay: The Crucial Decade, Joshua Hobart, Daniel Cushing, Thomas Hobart, Edmund Hobart, William Hersey and Bozoan Allen were declared "chief actors and occasoners of this disorderly and mutinous carriage, though some more guilty therefore than others" and fined. Edmund Gold was censured and fined. The Hingham militia was found to be mutinous. All petitioners except for John Tower, who had been jailed during the disturbance, were ordered to pay equal portions of a 53 pound, 10 shilling fine. Winthrop was found to be innocent of any wrong doing.

The Town of Hull

There were few records for early Hull. It was situated on a narrow strip of wooded land that separated Massachusetts Bay from the Atlantic Ocean. Samuel Maverick wrote that the town was not above 7 miles from Boston "by water tho neare 20 by land." Although it was only 3 miles north of the southern bounds of the Massachusetts Bay Colony, they had not gone beyond the boundary "although they have gone soe farr beyond them to the Northward."

Although in those early years, Natasket/Nantascot, as it was called, was not within the Plymouth Colony; the Massachusetts Bay Colony was not yet established. It became party of Suffolk county in 1643, but was included in Plymouth County in 1803.

The original village was a Massachusett Indian summer camp. Then, in 1621 the Plymouth Plantation established a trading post in the area. Ethel Farrington Smith suggested that the first permanent building was a storehouse erected in 1622 as part of the trading post.

Also in 1622, Chikataubut, Sachem of the Massachusetts, was in trouble. His tribe had been ravaged by plague. He agreed to sell the peninsula to Englishmen Thomas and John Gray and Walter Knight. But they did not remain long and in 1656, another sachem sold the same land to Thomas Loring, John Stone, Nicholas Baker, Benjamin Bosworth and other Hull inhabitants.

After Knight and the Grays left, outcasts from Plymouth arrived. While in Plymouth, John Lyford had been outspoken and had written a critical letter to England. John Oldham had represented anti-Separatist investors in Plymouth. Both Lyford and Oldham were banished from the Plantation and removed to Nantasket.

Roger Conant (see Appendix X) of Devonshire, England accompanied them, but had not been banished. Instead, he moved there in order to oversee the fisheries industry. Later he was chosen manager of the fishing settlement in Cape Ann before founding Salem in 1626.

Lyford, Oldham, and several others in their group eventually moved on also. Those left behind did not survive well. The "Plough" arrived in Nantasket in 1631 but only a few of the passengers remained. A number of them moved elsewhere in the colony.

Winthrop investigated fortifying the area for defense but decided against it. Other settlers came and went. It wasn't until June 2, 1641 that Nantasket and "all the neck to the end of the furthest beach towards Hingham, where the tide over floweth" was officially designated a fishing plantation.

In 1642 Hull planters named in a General Court document included "Jerrimiah Ballamy, John Colljer, Nathanj: Baker, Edmond Bosworth, John Prince, Nathani: Bosworth, Edward Bunn, Thomas Colljer, Richard Stubbs, Thomas Chaffey, William Kerley and John Stodder."

It was named Nantasket until May 29, 1644, at which time Winthrop wrote that the town had twenty homes and fishing was the primary industry. In 1659 Hull still had only twenty families and paid its minister forty pounds a year. The town may have been named after Rev. Joseph Hull. But more likely it was named after Hull, England.

In 1662, "Bruisters"/ "Breusters" Island was judged by the court to belong to the "toune of Hull". In 1673 the citizens asked for a lessening of taxes to offset the expenditures they had made while building a beacon at the entrance to the harbor.

On March 3, 1675, the inhabitants of Hull, referring to themselves as "your poore petitioners" wrote to the General Court requesting an exemption from the order to prepare themselves to fight the Indians during King Philip's War. They wrote that the "whole Country is Exposed to the wastinge ffury of the most barbarous heathen" and that they are "ffreely willinge to spend our care, our strength, yea, Wee hope our very lives in...defense off this place." However they had been ordered to not go fishing and to remain in town. But since

the men of Hull were fisherman and had "noe lands, nor Cattle
to mayntayne ourselves;" they asked their "sadd Condission" be
considered and asked that they be provided for by the other
towns and be given the "liberty to follow our imploy."

The Town of Roxbury

Roxbury (see Appendix X) first appeared as "Rocbury" in
the Massachusetts Bay records on September 28, 1630. According
to Builders of the Bay Colony the name was originally "Rocks-
borough", thus called because of a rock outcrop in the narrow
neck leading to Boston. Morison reported that the fields and
woods in the area were strewn with these rocks and that an
Indian legend blamed on an angry giant with bad table manners.

William Pynchon (see Appendix X) settled the area two
miles south of Boston. Pynchon was from Springfield, Essex
County, England. Most of the early settlers were followers of
Rev. John Elliot from northwestern Essex, southwestern Suffolk
and eastern Herefordshire.

John Elliot of Nazing, Essex County, England, was chosen
minister of the Boston Church when Rev. John Wilson left to
visit England. Eliot had attended Cambridge. But when friends
of Eliot settled in Roxbury, he moved there and, in 1632, became the first permanent minister in Roxbury. He served as
minister there for nearly sixty years and Thomas Dudley moved
to Roxbury in order to join Eliot's church.

Although Eliot was by no means an intellectual, his early
church records gave a good account of the town's early
history. In church records dated August 29, 1643, Eliot related the story of his niece, daughter of Jacob Eliot. John
called it "a strange p'rvudence if God" when his 8-year old
neice was playing near a wagon when a "piece of Iron" fell off
and "smote into her head and brains." According to Winthrop
who also discussed the accident, seven surgeons from around
the countryside and the ships in the harbor determined nothing
could be done to save the child. But another surgeon "applied
only plasters to it; and withal earnest prayers were made by
the church...and in six weeks...the child recovered perfectly;
nor did it lose the senses at anytime."

Rev. Eliot also discussed the excommunication of William
Franklin in his church records. Franklin had purchased a
pauper boy, Nathaniel Sewall, who had arrived aboard the
"Seabridge" in 1643. Franklin treated the boy terribly. Eliot
called Franklin "cruel and fierce" and wrote that the "boy
dyed vnder his rigorous hand." During a court trial it was
learned that Franklin had hung the boy in his chimney. Then,
it was testified, the boy was dragged five miles hanging from
a horse. Magistrates found Franklin guilty of murder and
ordered his execution.

Between 1638 and 1640, Roxbury had 69 men living in it.
Fifty-eight of them, or approximately 84 percent, were church
members and voters. By 1652 the town had grown to 120 houses,
but only about 50 percent of the adult males were church

members. Early settlers included Deputy Governor Dudley, the Thomas Gardner family, and William Denison and his sons Edward and Daniel. William and Edward Denison represented Roxbury in the General Court.

On February 24, 1844, portions of Roxbury were annexed to Brookline. The town of Roxbury was incorporated as a city on March 12, 1846. Different portions of Roxbury were annexed by Boston between 1860 and 1867.

The Town of Salem

In the early 1620's merchants from Dorchester, England began sending fishing ships into coastal waters of the New World. They sent fourteen men on board the <u>Fellowship</u> to establish a settlement at Cape Ann to organize work between fishing trips. Everything went well for two years until former Plymouth colonists who wanted their own settlement in the area got into a disagreement with the Cape Ann settlers over fishing rights. Governor Bradford sent Plymouth's Captain Miles Standish and his men to defend the Plymouth men. The dispute got heated. Roger Conant was made manager of the Cape Ann group and negotiated a settlement whereby his people would help the former Plymouth settlers set up their own fishing camp. However both Cape Ann and the Plymouth camp failed. The Dorchester group became discouraged. Several returned to England while a few remained behind to care for the cattle.

Some of those left behind thought they should settle a new location. Scouts recommended a "fruitful neck of land" just west of Cape Ann. The North River and South River on either side of the peninsula gave added outlets to the ocean. The settlers, led by Roger Conant, named it after the Indian name of Nahum-Keeke. The Cape Ann transplants became the "Old Planters" of the plantation of Naumkeag and built thatched cottages there in 1626.

Meanwhile, in England in 1628, a group of Puritans were securing a patent from the New England Council. At least one of the six grantees, John Humphrey, had been part of the Cape Ann settlement. They received a charter in 1629.

Winthrop arrived on Saturday, June 12, 1630. In his journal he wrote,
> "we that were of the assistants, and some other gentlemen, and some of the women and out captain, returned with them (John Endicott and others) to Nahumkeck (Salem) Where we supped with a good venison pasty and good beer, and at night we returned to our ship, but some of the women stayed behind. In the mean time most of our people went on shore upon the land of Cape Ann, which lay very near us, and gathered store of fine strawberries."

When Winthrop arrived, over 80 settlers had already died and there was only a two-week supply of food. Indians were a problem in those early days of the town. John Tilly (see Appendix X) of Salem had been tortured to death. John Oldham had been murdered by Indians.

Before Winthrop's arrival in the New World, Salem (see Appendix X) had been settled by an interesting mixture of people. Many were staunch supporters of the Anglican Church, which the Puritans mistrusted. And, according to Jennings in The Invasion of America, there were also pure separatists in Salem.

Roger Williams had become pastor in Salem after leaving Boston for religious reasons. In addition to his Separatist views, magistrates were displeased by his belief that Indians should be paid for their land. In those early years, Salem attempted to isolate itself from the rest of the colony which it saw as being filled with strict conformists. Williams and his followers refused to take the oath of allegiance to the colony. And as Jennings wrote, the magistrates and orthodox clergy were "outraged by the town that wanted autonomy and the minister who wanted liberty."

In May, 1635, in retaliation, the General Court ordered Salem to sell its Marblehead territory at cost. Salem's deputies were expelled from the General Court for a short period. At that point, Salem's General Court was "reduced to the rank of a committee." When Salem appointed "Mr. Sharpe", a Williams' supporter, as town land recorder, the General Court installed Emanuel Downing in his place. At one point Governor Winthrop managed to banish Williams from the community, although Williams did return in defiance.

In 1636 Salem bid to have a college built there. A tract of 300 acres at the neck of Marblehead just south of Salem, was proposed as site for the college. However, the 400 pounds set aside to establish the college were given to New Towne (Cambridge). Since New Towne was in dire straights with its loss of population and the General Court, the decision to place the college there may have been more a vote for New Towne rather then a vote against Salem. But it was still a loss for Salem.

Salem Population in 1637. (Includes Danvers, Beverly, Manchester, Wenham, and portions of several other communities.

No. of Families	Inhabitants in Each Family	Total population by No. of Members per Family
40	1	40
8	1-3 (16 uncertain)	8
34	2	68
23	3	69
29	4	116
1	4-5 (uncertain)	4
34	5	170
25	6	150
16	7	112
5	8	40
6	9	54
3	10	30
1	11	11
1	12	12
226		884-901

In 1635, Hugh Peters arrived and became pastor of the First Church in Salem as Roger William's successor. In later years, Peters would return to England, become Chaplain of Cromwell's Parliamentary Army, and be put to death when Cromwell's rule collapsed. When he was in Salem, Peters was an influential leader who urged development of commerce and, in particular, development of the Salem fisheries industry. A brick yard had been established as early as 1629. Shipbuilding began and salt works were built. The first tannery opened and, in 1639, when the Salem village was officially established, a glass factory opened. Samuel Maverick described the town as "very commodious for fishing, and many Vessells have been built there and (except Boston) it hath as much Trade as any place in New England both inland and abroad."

Simon Bradstreet, who arrived with Winthrop in 1630, became another illustrious citizen and statesman of Salem. Thomas Gardner was also prominent. One of his sons married Governor Winthrop's niece. Another son married George Corwin's step-daughter. Corwin was another leading merchant and politician in the early days of Salem.

James Underwood was Salem's baker, Richard Lambert was the joyner, William Jones was the tailor and William Woodcocke was the apothecary in the mid-1600's. Richard Hollingsworth had a shipyard at Salem's Neck and in 1641 built a three-hundred ton ship.

But all the families were not so distinguished. Salem's Quarterly court Records for 1647 told the tale of the Penyon family. First, Nicholas Russell was fined for "keeping in Nicholas Penyon's house after he had ordered him to keep away, being jealous of his wife (she said If Nicholas Russell departs the house, I shall depart also)." Then the wife of Nicholas Penyon went to trial for "fighting three times with her husband in ye night since she was bound to keep the peace. He beat her, also, and caused a miscarrige." Ralph Russell was called as a witness in that trial. Finally, but sadly, Nicholas Penyon was "presented for killing five children, as his wife says, one of them being a year old."

During Salem's witchcraft trials, 162 people - 42 males and 120 females; 37 single, 76 married and 21 widowed - were accused of witchcraft. Mary Black, the Negro slave of Lt. Nathaniel Putnam of Salem Village, was tried, convicted and jailed for witchcraft. She was released the next year. In all of New England, only 38 people were executed as witches from 1647 on, with twenty of those executions taking place in Salem in 1692.

Salem was incorporated as a city on March 23, 1836.

The Town of Weymouth

In 1622 Thomas Weston, a London merchant, along with his motley crew of vagabonds and adventurers off the streets of London, established a settlement named Wessagusset/Wessaguscus on the shore of Massachusetts Bay. Weston had a positive opinion of the potential prosperity of the country. But in order to escape problems encountered by other colonies, Weston decided to establish his trading post north of Plymouth with sixty able-bodied men without families. They arrived aboard the "Charity" and "Swan" and set-up the post in the well-protected, wooded area of modern day Weymouth. A severe winter, lack of supplies and heartiness, difficulties with Indians, and other deprivations led the community to near starvation. What defeated them were the very things that Weston had omitted because he felt they would hinder their success. They lacked the religious faith which gave their Pilgrim counterparts' strength. They were not fleeing persecution and families did not depend upon them for support and survival. The commitment to success was not with them.

In addition, according to The Invasion of America, the Plymouth Colony viewed the settlement as a religious danger, a rival in the fur trade and a hazard to Indian relations. Historical Sketch of the Town of Weymouth reported that the Weston group had previously proven themselves to not be worthy of the Indians' trust. Nash stated that "they applied to Plymouth for assistance." Other authors disagreed.

Whether asked or not, Captain Miles Standish took Plymouth troops to Wessagusset, excusing the action by saying it was necessary to protect the colonists and ended up by slaughtering several Indians.

Those Wessagusset colonists who were not killed in the Indian retaliation, fled to England. In the end, "ten of the colony (had) died of famine, two had been killed and one wounded by the savages..., and at the close of the spring, after the visit of Captain Standish, three of their number, the last of the company, were cruelly tortured to death by their Indian neighbors with whom they had sought refuge." Within a year of arriving, the settlement had disappeared.

Governor-General Robert Gorges has been credited with founding Weymouth (see Appendix X) near the site of the old Weston trading post. As the second permanent settlement in New England and the first in the Massachusetts Bay Colony, Gorges' Weymouth was a commercial fishing venture and an attempt of the council to keep a monopoly over trade and fishing.

Gorges had been granted the land ten miles along the coast to thirty miles inland and received a commission giving authority over all civil and criminal matters.

The town was situated on the shores of Boston Harbor south-east of Boston, northwest of Plymouth. The rolling, hilly area was shielded by the beach and peninsula of Nantasket. Great Hill / Smith Hill near the Bay was a perfect landmark for early Massachusetts Bay voyagers. The town's easy access by land and water to other areas made it natural rendezvous point for fishermen and traders. The area contained numerous ponds.

But after famine and other difficulties arose, several Weymouth settlers, including Gorges, returned to England. Others went to Winnesimmet (Chelsea), Mishawum (Charlestown) and Shawmut (Boston), while a few settlers remained behind in Wessaguscus.

From 1630 on, the settlement was considered part of the Massachusetts Bay Colony and taxed as such. In 1633 records it was referred to as a "small village".

In 1635, Joseph Hull sailed from Weymouth, leading twenty-one families (approximately one hundred persons). Many early settlers had emigrated from Dorsetshire and Somersetshire. Among them were Lt. James and Jacob Nash and Richard Porter. Robert Lenthall arrived in 1638 from Oxfordshire after receiving an invitation to become the town's minister. But Lenthall was soon forced out because of his "Antinomian" (pro-Hutchinson) opinions.

The Wey River of Dorset lent its name to Weymouth, England. According to Massachusetts Bay records, the name of the town of "Wessaguscus" was changed to "Waymothe" on September 2, 1635 and the town was raised to plantation status. The bound-ary between Hingham and Weymouth was established on September 3, 1635. Joseph Hull served as minister and deputy of the General Court.

Ferries connected neighboring towns and roads towards Boston were constructed. Mills were erected on streams. In 1667 the meeting house needed to be enlarged because of the growing population.

Weymouth suffered during King Philip's War. In February, 1675 the town was attacked and several houses were burned. In separate incidents, several men were killed by Indians. In March, 1675 seven more houses and barns were burned. In April, 1676 Sgt. Thomas Pratt was killed. Part of the townsmen were off fighting in the war. Others at home were being killed and few were left to protect the town when the town finally petitioned for help.

Weymouth was part of Suffolk County until 1793 when Norfolk County was established with Weymouth as part of it. The people of Weymouth attempted to have the town returned to Suffolk County, but the movement was unsuccessful.

The Town of Woburn

Charlestown might be called "the mother of Woburn". The town was first settled as Charlestown Village in 1640 by settlers from Charlestown. The General Court had granted seven freemen four square miles and the seven gave those grants to those who agreed to settle in the area. Most of the early settlers were East Anglican - with some Kent County and Worcestershire natives. The closer they lived to the meeting house, the less land they were allotted for their home lot. The poorest received 6 to 7 acres of meadow and 25 acres of upland.

The name was changed to "Wooborne" on September 27, 1642 and it was incorporated as a separate township. "Woh" was Old English for crooked and "bourns" were sources of water for Anglo-Saxons. So Woburn meant "winding stream."The name probably came from Woburn in Bedfordshire, England. Rev.

Thomas Carter was ordained pastor that year and remained in that post until his death in 1684.

In 1647 the town had 55 male residents over the age of 21. In comparison, Salem had 246 males, Boston had 389, Roxbury had 94, Hingham had 55, Braintree had 87, Charlestown had 129, and Cambridge had 121. However, little Hull had only 9. Of the 55 males in Woburn, only 27 (49% percent) were freemen.

Perhaps because of its small size, Woburn did not appear in early records very often. However, between 1645 and 1653 it was recorded that the town donated nearly six pounds to Harvard College. Early Woburn inhabitants only paid a small percentage of their taxes in cash. The rest was paid in produce or cattle.

Maverick wrote that they lived "by ffurnishing the Sea Townes with Provisions as Corne and Flesh, and also they ffurnish the Merchants with such goods to be exported."

Edward Johnson and John Russell were among the early settlers. The town was the birthplace of Benjamin Thompson (1780-1838) a well-known scientist; and Loammi Baldwin Junior (1780-1814) and Senior (1745-1807). Baldwin Junior was known as the father of civil engineering while his father was a famous horticulturist.

The town was granted an additional 2000 acres in 1664. Woburn, Middlesex County, was incorporated as a city on May 18, 1888.

Families

Aspinwall Family

The Aspinwall (Aspinall, Aspinell, Aspinwell, Haspineall) name may originated with the Saxon word meaning "Aspen vale" or "dwelling near the Aspen tree." The Aspinwalls in this genealogy may have been named for the locale of Aspinall in the parish of Aughton, Lancaster County, England.

Lancaster was overflowing with Aspinwalls. Gilbert de Aspenwall was there as early as 1332. Katherine of Aspenall died there in 1596. James Aspenall died in Aspenall in 1591. A clothier named William Aspinwall from Blackwell Hall, Standinge, Lancaster, was uncle of Edmond Aspinwall of Merley, Lancaster County.

Part I
Peter Aspinwall Family

William Aspinwall
    Children
        Thomas (see below)
        Elizabeth - bpt June 24, 1570
            m. Ellis (b.c. 1564), son of Ellis (1535-1609)
            and Anne (Ormeshaw) Ambrose Sr. of Ormskirk,
            England; August 29, 1587
            d. pos 1623
            Children
                William - b. March 15, 1598/9; Ormskirk,
                    England
                    m. Cecely
                    d. 1638; Stepney, England
                Peter - m. Judith, wid of ____ Bird of
                    Chester, mthr of John Bird
        Edward - d. aft 1624
        ? Peter

Thomas Aspinwall
    m. Mary, sis of James Horrocks
    d. December, 1624; Toxteth, Lancaster County, England
    Children
        Peter (see below)
        Elizabeth - m. Horrocks
        Samuel - b. by 1612
            m. Jane (d. aft 1672)
            wll dtd October 17, 1672
            Children
                Timothy
                Margaret - m. Graner
                Isaac
                Josiah
                Thomas
                dau - m. Fazackerly
                    Children
                        Edward
                dau - m. John Ellison

Peter Aspinwall
    b.c. 1612, Toxteth Park near Liverpool, Lancaster County,
    England

m1 Elizabeth Merrill/Morrell (m. 16 years)
m2 Alice (d. 1654) sis of Robert Sharp; by October 9,
1642
m3 Remember (1638-1701), dau of Peter and Edith Palfrey;
February 12, 1661/2;
d. December 1, 1687; Brookline, Massachusetts.
wll dtd. November 29, 1687
est inv. December 9, 1687
wll pro. January 20, 1691/2
Children by Remember
     Eleazer (see below)
     Samuel (Capt.) - b. November 4 or 10, 1662; Brook-
          line, Massachusetts
          m. Sarah (March 6, 1667-April 1, 1710), dau of
          Timothy and Sarah (Davis) Stevens; c. 1689
          d. September 6, 1727
          Children
               Sarah - b. September 17, 1690; Brookline,
                    Massachusetts
                    d. young
               Elizabeth - b. March 25, 1693
                    m. Peter Gardner of Brookline,
                    Massachusetts
                    d. in childbirth
                    Children
                         Nathaniel - d. young
               Samuel - b. February 13, 1696
               Thomas (Lt.) - b. May 21, 1698
                    m. Johannah, dau of Caleb Gardner
                    Children
                         William (Dr.)
                              Children
                                   William
                                   Thomas (Lt. Col.)
                                   Augustus
               Mary - b. January 3, 1700
                    m. Benjamin Gardner (c. 1697-1762);
                    December, 1725
                    Children
                         Samuel   Sarah
                         Elizabeth   Hannah
                         Mehitable
               Sarah - b. November 21, 1707
                    m. Benjamin White (d. October 19,
                    1777); Brookline, Massachusetts
                    d. September 11, 1801
     Peter - b. June 4, 1664
          bpt. 1673; Roxbury, Massachusetts
          m. Elizabeth (b. 1655), wid of John Leavens,
          dau of Edward Preston; March 24, 1689/90;
          Woodstock, Connecticut
          d. aft June 4, 1749
          Children
               daughter
     Nathaniel - b. June 5, 1666; Brookline, Massachu-
          setts
          bpt. June 10, 1666; Roxbury, Massachusetts
          m. Abigail (1670-1736), dau of Henry and
          Elizabeth (Johnson) Bowen
          wll dtd February 15, 1711/12; Woodstock,
          Massachusetts

wll pro June 4, 1713; Boston, Massachusetts
Children
    Abigail - b. October 5, 1701
        m. John Child of Woodstock; December
        7, 1721
    Elizabeth - b. March 12, 1703/04
        eng. to James Horsmer; February 5,
        1725/26; Woodstock
    Peter - b. February 16, 1706/07
    Nathaniel - b. September 7, 1709
Thomas - b. January 21, 1667/68
    bpt. January 26, 1667/68; Roxbury, Massachu-
    setts
    d.c. 1690; Barn Island Canada
Mehitable - b. September 14, 1669
    bpt. December 19, 1669; Roxbury, Massachusetts
    m. never
    d. Brookline, Massachusetts
Elizabeth - b. November 21 or 24, 1671
    bpt. November 26, 1671; Roxbury, Massachusetts
    m1 Stevens; Salem, Massachusetts
    m2 Daniel Draper of Dedham, Massachusetts
    Children
        Betty - m Kingsbury; Wrentham, Massachu
            setts
Joseph (twin) - b. October or November 9, 1673;
    Brookline, Massachusetts
    m1 Hannah Dean, niece of Lord Bellomont; July
    13, 1700; New York
    m2 wid of Samuel Smith
    d.c. 1743; Brookline, Massachusetts
    Children
        John
        Joseph of Dedham and Stoughton,
            Massachusetts
Mary - b. August 4, 1677
    m. Samuel Baker; June 5, 1710
Timothy - b. April 19, 1682
    d. Boston, Massachusetts

Eleazer Aspinwall (twin)
    b. October or November 9, 1673; Brookline, Massachusetts
    bpt. 1673
    m. pos Mary
    d. 1742; Farmington, Connecticut
    Children
        Aaron (see below)
        Mary - m. Thomas Adkins of Farmington, Connecticut;
            February 8, 1738/39
        Ann/Anna/Hannah - m. Charles Nott of Middletown,
            Connecticut; June 17, 1742
        Huldah - m. Ebenezer Cotton of Middletown,
            Connecticut
        Hamatter

Aaron Aspinwall
    b. June 6, 1711; Roxbury, Massachusetts
    m. Sarah Collins (c.1702-1769); October 20, 1732
    d. poss 1769; Bristol, Connecticut
    Children
        Dorothy - b. November 10, 1733; Wallingford,

bpt. November 11, 1733
m. James, son of Samuel and Mary Hotchkiss

Children
Cyrus	Phebe	Samuel
Levi	Sarah	David
James	Ira	Charlotte
Josiah	Mary	Rebecca
Asenath		

Caleb - b. May 4, 1736
bpt. May 7, 1736
d. by 1747
Sarah - b. December 8, 1739
Caleb - bpt. June 28, 1747
eng. to Betsy, wid of Freeman; March 13, 1675;
Roxbury, Massachusetts
? Aaron

The William Aspinwall of this genealogy was from Lancaster and had a son Thomas and a daughter Elizabeth. Elizabeth was recorded as being baptized on June 24, 1570 and married to Ellis (b.c. 1564) son of Ellis and Anne (Ormeshaw) Ambrose, Sr. (see Appendix II). Elizabeth and Ellis Ambrose had, at least, William eventually of Stepney; and Peter, later of Chester.

The line of William Aspinwall (see Appendix II) through Thomas and Elizabeth was easily determined through a series of Aspinwall and Ambrose wills. For example, William Ambrose of Stepney listed his uncle Thomas Aspinwall and cousin Peter Aspinwall of Toxteth Park, Lancaster in his February 10, 1637 will. In 1653 Peter Ambrose mentioned Peter Aspinwall in his will.

In Edward Augustus Bowen's Aspinwall genealogy in the July, 1893, NEHGR, appeared the suggestion that Peter Aspinwall of the Massachusetts Bay Colony may have been the son of Edward Aspinwall of Toxteth. In reality, Edward was Peter's uncle, and the brother of Thomas, as determined by Thomas' will and estate inventory.

The parentage of Peter Aspinwall can also be traced through the 1624 will (see Appendix II) of his father Thomas and the 1672 will of his brother Samuel . In English Origins of New England Families, G. Andrew Moriarty, editor of "Some Aspinwall Wills" agreed that Samuel and Peter were the sons of Thomas Aspinwall of Toxteth Park, Lancashire. Moriarty added that "there was evidently an earlier Peter who married as early as 1620, probably a brother of Thomas."

In Thomas' will, he appointed his cousin "Jirehjah" Aspinwall and brother-in-law James Horrocks as executors. He willed his estate and house in Toxteth to his children. He wrote that Samuel was his eldest child and that as of his 1624 will, Samuel had not had any children. The will was proven December 22, 1624. The inventory of household furniture and farm implement totaled 312 pounds 12 shilling and 8 pence. As of the June 28, 1624 inventory, Thomas owed a great deal of money. The following notation was added to the inventory -
"The whole Tacks of yeares in Rose Grounde, Edwd
Aspinwall his brother being allowed 1/4 part for

6 of the last yeares according to their bargain.
80 pounds"

When Rev. Richard Mather first taught in Toxteth Park, he was a roomer in the home of Edward Aspinwall. Thomas' son Peter probably met Reverend Mather at the time.

The will of Thomas' son Samuel was probated in Chester after his 1672 death. His estate was valued at 2268 pounds 13 shillings 6 pence.

Thomas Aspinwall's son Peter was probably born in Toxteth Park, Lancashire County, near Liverpool, the same year as the Lancashire Witch Trials in 1612. The trials were based on 1604 English law forbidding the practice of the "devilish art of witchcraft" and harming neighbors or their cattle with its use. Hanging was the mandatory punishment. The trials took place in late April with the last executions taking place on November 16th.

Before emigrating to New England circa 1630, Peter married his first wife. Although they were married for sixteen years they had no children. Her maiden name was Morrell.

He emigrated to the New England area circa 1630 and took as his second wife, Alice Sharp who Savage said was one of "brother Mr. William Tyng's maid servants." When she was admitted to Cotton Mather's church on October 9, 1642, she was listed as Peter Aspinwall's wife and they were living in Dorchester, Massachusetts at the time. He joined the First Church of Boston in 1645.

The deed to his Brookline, Massachusetts homelot was dated 1650 and; curiously, was recorded by William Aspinwall of the other Aspinwall genealogy in this book. It was witnessed by Major General Humphrey Atherton. Peter built the Brookline house in 1660 on what would become Aspinwall Avenue. He bought 150 acres with Robert Sharp, probably the brother of his second wife. They purchased the land from William Colburn / Coleborne. Then in 1663 the colony granted him land in Roxbury.

He was married to Remember Palfrey on February 12, 1662 by Governor John Endicott. Peter was about fifty years old at the time. Remember was the daughter of Peter Palfrey of Reading, Massachusetts and was the mother of all ten of Peter's children. The children were baptized at the First Religious Society (Unitarian) and appear in those church records.

After becoming a freeman in May, 1645, Peter held a number of public offices, including surveyor from 1651-2 and from 1661-2 and constable in 1667. According to Brookline records, in 1661 Peter Aspinwall and Peter Oliver were "deputed to joyne with Cambridge men to lay outt a high way from muddy river to Cambridge." In 1667 Peter, Thomas Gardner, and several others were chosen "perambulators for the bounds betw Muddy River and Roxbury; and Cambridge." Peter and two others were appointed on April 24, 1676 to a committee for "preventinge of excessive drinkinge & disorder in private houses." On March 25, 1677/78, Peter was elected "to oversee & regulate the ffences about the comon ffield at Muddy River."

His will was dated November 27, 1687. The December 9, 1687 estate inventory was filed on January 20, 1691/92 as case #1911 in the Suffolk County Probate Court Records, Boston Massachusetts. According to gravestone records of Eliot Cemetery, Roxbury, he died on December 1, 1687, at age 75. His widow died by April 4, 1701.

In 1706 Eleazer Aspinwall, son of Peter, served as Brookline's assessor and in 1707 was highway surveyor. It has been suggested that Eleazer was sent by his father to settle at New Roxbury (Woodstock). In 1720 he took charge of Governor Belcher's farm between Hartford and New Haven, Connecticut. Eleazer died in Farmington, Connecticut before the July 2, 1742 inventory of his estate.

According to <u>Historic Sketches of Brookline</u>, Samuel had been a lieutenant in the militia when Sir William Phipps took possession of the fort at Port Royal and the coast to the Penobscott River. He later became a captain of Brookline's militia and held that rank until his death on September 6, 1725. He drowned in the Charles River near his farm.

Samuel, sometimes called Captain Aspinwall, was the eldest of Peter's children. He married Sarah Stevens, daughter of Timothy and Sarah (Davis) Stevens who buried in Eliot Cemetery like her father-in-law.

Samuel was a farmer and office holder. At various times he was elected Surveyor, Constable, Fence-Viewer, Tythingman, Assessor, Selectman and Treasurer of Brookline, in addition to sitting on numerous committees, including one in 1712 to "agree with Mr. Cotton for a burying Place." According to Bowen's Aspinwall genealogy in NEHGR, he was also appointed guardian to minor orphans. He even made the bricks of the old meeting house and built a schoolhouse. In March, 1700; Samuel signed a petition to have Brookline set off as a town separate from Boston. The petition was refused, but Brookline was allowed to hire a school teacher. He signed the 1705 petition for separation which in November, 1705 was finally granted. His brother Eleazer also signed the 1705 petition.

Eleazer's twin brother Joseph went to sea young. He owned vessels which he sailed to such different locales as France and South America. According to Dr. William Aspinwall, Joseph's ship was captured and taken to Port Royal at the same time his brother Samuel was taking part in the siege there. Joseph's ship was destroyed by fire during the winter at "Seabrook" and he was jailed as a debtor. Later he became a lieutenant for Spain in the West Indies' slave trade. And then he was master of a large ship for several years until, because of lost business, he returned to Boston.

Joseph first married Hannah Dean, the niece of Lord Bellomont, in New York. He was made a freeman in New York City on June 6, 1710. His second wife was the widow of Samuel Smith. Dr. William Aspinwall said Joseph was supposedly "exceedingly careless of his children's affaires."

Peter's sons Nathaniel and Thomas were in the disastrous expedition of Sir William Phipps against Canada. Like Capt. Andrew Gardner, Thomas was killed during that expedition. He was "cast out" from a ship at Barn Island in the Canadian River before April 4, 1701.

In numerous sources, Mehitable was referred to as a "Doctress". She never married but did reside with Dr. Oliver of Cambridge for twenty years. Later, she lived with Dr. Williams of Boston. But whether she was a university-trained doctor or a doctor's apprentice has not been ascertained. Mehitable died at her father's home.

Peter's son Timothy was admitted to Old South Church on January 25, 1701. He died while an apprentice in Boston, Massachusetts.

Peter Aspinwall, Jr. seldom appeared in early records; but he was probably Peter's son. He, along with his brother Eleazer, was an early settler of New Roxbury (Woodstock) Plantation. Later he was a founder of Killingly, Connecticut and became a benefactor of the primitive church there.

In describing is March 24, 1689/90 marriage to widow Elizabeth (Preston) Leavens, Genealogies of Connecticut Families from NEHGR referred to Peter as "a bachelor some years younger then herself (Elizabeth)." She was nine years older than her second husband. Dr. William Aspinwall wrote that "she always kept him low,...was no so meek as her husband," and was fined during her first marriage for libel ... but she seems to have been a faithful wife and he was a man of versatile power and eminent usefulness."

Aaron, Peter's grandson by son Eleazer, may have received certificate #41394 (sort of an IOU) for $45.73 for service during the Revolutionary War. An Aaron and Caleb Aspinwall of Norfolk were on the Connecticut line from 1777 through 1781 and on a list of married officers or soldiers. The same Aaron fought in Col. Sam Webb's Third Connecticut Regiment. Since Eleazer's son would have been 66 years old in 1777; more likely, Caleb and Aaron were sons of Aaron. An Aaron and Abigail Aspinwall were listed in Father Nash's 1797-1827 records of baptisms for central New York as the parents of Matteus, Zebina, Bourne, and Caleb Aspinwall.

An Aaron Aspinwall supposedly died in Bristol, Connecticut in 1769 at the age of 67. Although our Aaron would have been 57 or 58 years old, not 67; the one who died in 1768 still might have been Eleazer's son.

The Dr. William Aspinwall (Thomas 5, Samuel 4, Peter 3, Thomas 2, William 1) who put together a genealogy of the Aspinwall family in 1767 was the same William Aspinwall who had a private smallpox hospital in Brookline. He "had made a fortune through the old inoculation", according to the Concise Dictionary of American History. In July 8, 1800, Benjamin Waterhouse, a professor at Harvard, obtained the smallpox vaccine and vaccinated his children. Then, at Aspinwall's hospital, Waterhouse exposed his children by passing smallpox infected thread through their punctured skin. None came down with smallpox and Aspinwall "acknowledged the superiority of the inoculation." William Aspinwall retired when he went blind.

During the War of 1812, William's son Thomas became a colonel and, on September 17, 1814, lost his left arm storming British entrenchments. Later, he served as U.S. Consul in London for thirty-seven years and was a well-known historian.

Part 2
William Aspinwall Family

William
   b. by 1620; prob Manchester, Lancashire, England
   m. Elizabeth, prob sis of Christopher or his wife Susana
   Stanley
   d. aft 1662
   Children
         Edward - b. September 26, 1630; Manchester,
               Lancashire, England
               d. 1630
         Hannah - b. December 25, 1631; Charlestown,
               Massachusetts
               m. John Angier
         Elizabeth - bpt September 22, 1633
         Samuel - bpt September 20, 1635; Massachusetts
         Ethlannah - b. March 12, 1637; Boston, Massachusetts
         Dorcas - b. February 14, 1640; Massachusetts
         ? Mary - b.c. 1635
               d. 1667; Cambridge, Massachusetts

William Aspinwall was a rebel, or an independent thinker or maybe just a jinx. Whatever the cause, even though he held a number of responsible positions, he was in constant in trouble with the authorities.

William may have been born in Manchester, Lancashire, England; since that was the area listed as home when William, his wife Elizabeth, and his new-born son Edward emigrated with the Winthrop Fleet in 1630.

Also in the Winthrop Fleet was Robert Parker, supposedly a servant of William Aspinwall's. Parker was admitted to the church and became a freeman in 1634. He eventually moved to Cambridge and married Judith, the widow of Richard Bugby.

The William Aspinwall family went to Charlestown and became one of the thirteen families that remained when the other members of the group removed to other settlements in the colony. At some point he may have purchased property in Watertown, but never resided there.

In September, 1630, William was chosen for the jury looking into the death of Austin Bratcher on Mr. Cradock's plantation. Then on August 27, 1632, William was tenth and his wife was sixteenth on the list of original members of the First Church of Boston and William was elected one of two deacons.

On October 19, 1630 he listed as desiring "to be made ffreeman." William took the oath of freeman on April 3, 1632/33. Records dated "14th 10m, 1635" revealed that "It is agreed yt Mr. Wm. Coleburn, Mr. Wm. Aspinwall, Mr Jno. Sanford, Wm Balstone & Richard Wright, or four of them, shall lay out at Muddy River, a sufficients Allottment for a farm for or Teacher, Mr. John Cotton." He became one of the Selectmen of Boston in 1636 and 1637. But then his troubles began.

Andrews wrote that in 1637 "an epidemic of heresy struck the colony." Anne Hutchinson and Rev. John Wheelwright were upsetting life in the Boston area.

It was ironic. The non-conformists who had fled what they called "popish" aspects of England had become intolerant conformists in the New World. Among those who disagreed with the Puritan Church were Anne Hutchinson and John Wheelwright who were forced from the colony for their beliefs. In November, 1637, William Aspinwall drew up a petition to the General Court for sixty others to sign supporting Mr. Wheelwright in religious matters.

The Colony was in such an uproar that the General Court was dissolved and a new election was called to rid the colony "of the fettaries who would not be dragooned into the abandonment of their convictions." It was hoped that the Wheelwright-Hutchinson council members from Boston, like Henry Vane (see Appendix X), would be replaced. But Coggeshall and Aspinwall, who were great supporters of Wheelwright and Hutchinson in the "Antinomian Controversy," were elected and Coddington, another supporter, was re-elected.

When the General Court was reconvened in 1637, Aspinwall was questioned about his part in the petition and asked if he fully "adhered to its fentiments." Even though he justified his actions and maintained the petition was perfectly legal; the Court deposed him of membership, and eventually disfranchised and banished him. When Coggeshall objected, he received the same fate. According to a volume of Aspinwall Notarial Records, Aspinwall had been "seduced & led into dangerous errors" by the "opinion & revelations of Mr Wheelwright & Mrs Hutchinson" and was disarmed by a General Court order on November 20, 1637.

According to Unafraid: a Life of Anne Hutchinson, those that signed the petition knew they might have to eventually leave the colony. On March 7, 1637/8, nineteen of them signed an agreement incorporating themselves into a "Bodie Politick." Roger Williams persuaded Aspinwall, William Hutchinson, William Coddington, and others to go to Rhode Island. And, in early 1638, Aspinwall signed the compact at Portsmouth. Rev. John Wheelwright bounded Exeter, New Hampshire.

By 1639 William Aspinwall was in trouble again. Early Rhode Island Colony records indicated in 1638/39, Aspinwall was suspected of "sedition against the state." Because of the suspicions it was decided that "a stay of the building of his Bote should be made; whereupon ye workman was forbidden to proceed any further." Then in 1639 his boat was attached for debt. At the same time, William Coddington split with Anne Hutchinson and founded Newport, Rhode Island.

During his banishment, he wrote <u>An Abstract or the Lawes of New-England, as they are now established</u>. It was published in London in 1641 by F. Coules and W. Ley. Even though in 1642 William Aspinwall was in New Haven as witness in the trial of George Spencer in General Court, he had already been granted safe passage to Boston to "come and satisfy the counsell."

According to Winthrop, on March 27, 1642/43, Aspinwall was

"reconciled to the church of Boston. He made a
very free and full acknowledgment of his errour
and seducement, and that with much detestation of
his sin. They like he did after, before the magistrates,
who were appointed by the court to take his submission,
and upon their certificate thereof at the next general
court, his sentence of banishment was released."

The turn around was quick. On September 7, 1643, Aspinwall was appointed Clerk of Writs for the town of Boston and he joined the Artillery Company that same year. In 1644 he became the second to hold the office of Recorder of the Suffolk Co. Court after Stephen Winthrop and was also made "Publique notary". Things were looking up.

In 1644 Aspinwall and six others petitioned for a monopoly of the Indian trade. According to Winthrop,
"merchants of Boston being desirous to discover the
great lake (Lake Champlain, also known as Lake of
the Iroquois), supposing it to lie in the north west
part of our patent, and finding that the great trade
of beaver which came to all the eastern and southern
parts, came from thence, petitioned the court to be
a company for that design, and to have the trade which
they should discover, to themselves for twenty-one
years." The court claimed they should not grant a monopoly because monopolies where prohibited by the Body of Liberties, the code of laws drawn up by Nathaniel Ward in 1641. But the General Court granted the group a monopoly anyway.

The group outfitted an expedition and, under the command of Aspinwall who Winthrop reported was "a good artist & one who had been in those parts." They set sail up the Delaware River which they thought flowed into Lake Champlain. However, the Swedes and Dutch higher up the river refused to let them pass.

And more troubles were to follow Aspinwall. On October 14, 1651, William was suspended as recorder and fined after being accused of coercing a jury "to go against the lawe and conscience, making the landlord to pay rent to the tennant." Edward Rawson replaced him as recorder. Later, Aspinwall was replaced as notary and was ordered to turn in all of his record books.

At that point Aspinwall sent a letter to the General Court in which he complained that
"manifould haue beene the afflictions I haue suffered

since I came into theis Country & it adds vnto them
the late order you made that I should deliver vp my
bookes vnto the secretary, but most of all afflictiue
is, that my late troubles haue sprung from brethren...
I justify not my selfe, but condemne my folly...I haue
desired to be faithfull, & my aime hath beene the Honor
of God & his vice-genents, the publick good of the
Country, & private of pticular psons."

Following his supposed apology, William wrote that he had
not given over the books as the court had requested because
"they are no publick Records." He said they were all "privt
Records of my owne Acts" purchased "at my owne chardge" and
that "no man can safely & effectually attest any thing out of
my privat writeings but myselfe, nor shall I be able to attest
to any thing when my bookes are taken away." And since most
of the things in the records related to England and since he
intended to go there, they should be of more use with him in
England.

William Aspinwall did indeed leave for England shortly
after his letter and was still living there in 1662. William
wrote seven more books published between <u>A briefe Description
of the Fifth Monarch, or Kingdome that shortley is to come
into the World the Monarch, Subjects, Officers and Lawes
thereof</u> in 1653 to <u>Abrogation of the Christian Sabbath</u> in
1657. All were published in London.

The lines of his male issue became extinct. However, his
numerous daughters married and their lines have survived in
New England.

Baker Family

John Baker
    Children
        Nicholas (see below)
        Nathaniel - m. dau of William Lane of Dorchester,
            Massachusetts
            r. 1635, Hingham, Massachusetts
            wll dtd. May 11, 1682
            d. June 3, 1682; Hingham, Massachusetts
            Children
                    Mary - bpt July or August, 1639; Hingham;
                        Massachusetts
                        m. John Loring; December 16, 1657
                        d. July 13, 1679; Hull, Massachu
                        setts

Nicholas Baker (Rev.)
    b.c. 1610; Hingham, Norfolk County, England
    m1 Unknown (d. April 23, 1661; Scituate, Massachusetts)
    m2 Grace prob Dipple, (d. April 29, 1662; Braintree,
    Massachusetts); Scituate, Massachusetts
    r. 1635, Hingham, Massachusetts
    d. August 22 or 29, 1678; Scituate, Massachusetts
    Children
        Samuel - b. October 2, 1638; Hingham, Massachusetts
            m1 Fear (1645-aft 1703), dau of Isaac and
            Margaret (Hanford) Robinson; December 16, 1666
            d.c. 1714; Windsor, Connecticut
        Mary - bpt. December, 1641; prob Hingham,
            Massachusetts
            m. Stephen Vinal; February 26, 1661/62;
            Scituate, Massachusetts
            d. aft 1678
        Elizabeth - bpt. November 10, 1644 or 1645; Hingham,
            Massachusetts
            m. John Vinal, February 2, 1664; Scituate,
            Massachusetts
            d. aft 1678
        Nicholas - b. 1650
            m. Experience (d. January 24, 1694/95), dau of
            Lt. Thomas and Jane (Curtis) Collier of Hull,
            Massachusetts
            d. 1695, prob at sea
            Children
                Jane
                Elizabeth
        Deborah - bpt June 6, 1652
            m. Israel Chittenden, 1679
        Sarah - m. Josiah Litchfield (1647/48-1707/08);
            February 22, 1671; Scituate, Massachusetts
            d. betw 1715-1722; Scituate, Massachusetts
        ? John

    The Baker name is an occupation surname possibly stemming
from the Saxon word "bacon" which meant "to dry by heat". In
Old English, "baechus" meant "a bakery" and "baecere" meant "a
man who bakes." "Baccestre" meant "a woman who bakes". In
later years, the female form "bakester" became the names
Bagster, Baxster, and Backster. However, Baxter became the
Scottish form. The name Baker was strictly of English origin.

33

Frequently English peasants were fined if they did not
bake in the community or lord's oven under the charge of the
public baker. The baker would ring a bell to notify villagers
when they could bring their goods to bake. In 1177, William le
Bakere (William the Baker) had an occupation name.

Nathaniel and Nicholas of this genealogy were the sons of
John Baker, probably from Hingham, Norfolk County, England.
Nathaniel was residing in Hingham, Massachusetts in 1635 and
married the daughter of William Lane of Dorchester,
Massachusetts. Her name may have been Sarah. In 1648 Nathaniel
purchased land from John Porter described as "house and all
lands in Hingham, bought by said Porter, or granted by the
town." Only one child, a daughter named Mary who later married
John Loring, was chronicled in early records as being a child
of Nathaniel. Mary was baptized in July, 1639. Nathaniel's
will dated May 11, 1682 provided for his widow and two Indian
slaves. Most of his property was bequeathed to his grandchildren and a mention of his brother Nicholas' six children
was made. Nathaniel died on June 3, 1682.

The life of "Honest Nicholas Baker," as Cotton Mather
later referred to him, was better recorded. He probably was
born to John Baker circa 1610 in Hingham, Norfolk County,
England. He attended St. John's College at Cambridge University and received his B.A. in 1631/2 and him M.A. in 1635.

Nicholas emigrated to the New World in 1635 and settled
in Hingham, Massachusetts. According to Homes in Directory of
the Heads of New England Families, Nicholas removed to
Scituate, Massachusetts in 1636. However, Nicholas remained
in Hingham much later, since he was made a freeman there in
1636 and was representative to the General Court from 1636
through 1638. And, according to Ethel Farrington Smith's
"Seventeenth Century Hull, Massachusetts, and Her People" in
NEHGR, Nicholas and other Hingham men were refused lands in
"Seekonk".

The 1659 inventory for the estate of Thomas Marsh
mentioned "5 acres planting Land vpon Bakers hill" in Hingham.
Possibly the hill was named after Nathaniel or Nicholas.

He had married the mother of all of his children before
1638, the year his son Samuel was born. Samuel was followed
by Mary; Nicholas, Jr.; Sarah; Elizabeth and Deborah.

Sometime between his residency in Hingham and moving to
Scituate, Nicholas may have lived in Roxbury for a short
period of time. In addition, Nicholas Baker of Hull was one of
many debtors listed in Captain Bozoan Allen's September 22,
1652 will. That coincides with Samuel Eliot Morison's The
Founding of Harvard College in which he referred to Nicholas
Baker who emigrated to Hingham as a large land owner in Hull.
Morison also wrote that Nicholas Baker moved from Hull circa
1644. Ethel Farrington Smith's history of Hull listed Nicholas
as receiving two two-acre lots on Further Hill in 1644. She
also related that Nicholas, along with a John Baker who Smith
believed to be Nicholas' son, owned a lot on Town Hill in
Hull, in addition to eleven other islands and hills.

Whatever his stay in Hull, Nicholas was in Scituate, Massachusetts by 1660 when he was ordained as the third minister of the First Church of Scituate. Savage reported that Baker was such a good-tempered minister that he managed to reconcile two churches which had been quarreling for over thirty years.

On July 16, 1663 Nicholas witnessed the will of Thomas Ensign of Scituate. Then on February 17, 1663/64 he conducted the inventory of Ensign's estate.

Nicholas' wife died on April 23, 1661 in Scituate and he married for the second time, a woman named Grace in 1662. She probably was Grace Dipple Baker who later died in Samuel Baker's Barnstable, Massachusetts home.

Although Nicholas was still the minister in Scituate at his death in August, 1678, he still owned a homelot in Hull. In his will he made his wife executrix of his estate and mentioned his brother Nathaniel. His wife and his son Samuel divided the Hull home lot. Son Nicholas received his father's Hingham property; daughters Mary, Elizabeth, Sarah and Deborah each received 10 pounds and the land in Scituate. He bequeathed 10 pounds to granddaughter Mercy Baker.

His son Samuel, who had been baptized by Rev. Hobart in Hingham, married Fear Robinson in 1666 in Scituate. He may have taken Abigail Lathrop, widow of John Huntington, as his second wife. Samuel became a selectman in Hull in 1675 and, along with John and Nicholas Baker, Jr., signed a petition for a tavern license. While in Hull, Samuel had a disagreement with his neighbor Richard Stubbs in 1671. Stubbs had no access to his land except by crossing Baker's land. The court ruled that Stubbs had to get Baker's permission before crossing his land.

After his father's death, Samuel removed to Barnstable, Massachusetts where he was admitted to the church along with his wife on May 12, 1687. They eventually moved to Connecticut.

Nicholas Baker's son Nicholas, Jr. and daughter-in-law Experience both died in 1695 leaving two young daughters. Experience's mother, Jane Collier, a widow, was appointed their legal guardian.

There are a number of other possible but unproven relatives of these brothers. Hobart's Journal, which chronicled the births of most of Nathaniel's and Nicholas' children, included the entry, "___ Baker", who died on September 2, 1677. That Baker was probably a relation of the brothers.

John Baker; who married Charity, had Nathaniel, and resided in Hingham in 1635; could be another relative. Another John Baker was baptized in Hingham in 1642. The Samuel Baker who was born in England circa 1630; married Eleanor and, Patience; and had eight children born between 1658 and 1671 was once thought to be the son of Nicholas Baker of Hingham and Scituate or of Nathaniel Baker of Hingham.

John Balch
    b. by 1600; Bridgewater, Somersetshire, England
    m1 Margaret (Margery), poss "Lovel" / "Lovett" / "Lea-
    vett"
    m2 Annis (Agnes) Patch; Salem, Massachusetts
    wll dtd. May 15, 1648
    wll pro. May/June, 1648
    Children
        Benjamin (see below)
        John - b.c. 1630
            m. Mary (b. Salem, Massachusetts), dau of Roger
            Conant
            d. June 16, 1662; Beverly, Massachusetts
            inquest June 24, 1662; Beverly, Massachusetts
            Children
                Mary - d. young
        Freeborn - b.c. 1631
            d.c. 1658

Benjamin Balch
    b.c. winter, 1628/29
    m1 Sarah (1631-1686), dau of Thomas Gardner; circa 1650;
    Beverly, Massachusetts
    m2 Abigail (Maverick) (1637-1690), wid of Matthew Clark;
    1688/89
    m3 Grace, wid of Hosea Mallott; 1691/2; Beverly,
    Massachusetts
    d. aft. January 31, 1714/15
    Children
        Samuel (Dea.) - b. 1651
            m. Mary Newmarsh, 1675
            d. 1723
            Children
                Martha - b. September 13, 1676
                Samuel - b. May 16, 1678
                    eng. to Mary Baker; 1710; Salem,
                    Massachusetts
                Joseph - b. April 26, 1680
                    eng. to Sarah Hart; March 21, 1697/8;
                    Beverly, Massachusetts
                Phebe - b. April, 1684
                Peter - b. May 6, 1685
                Cornelius - b. May, 1687
                Abigail - b. May 1689
                Thomas - b. April, 1692
        Benjamin - b.c. 1652
            m1 Elizabeth (b.c. 1654), sis of Abigail
            (Woodbury) Waldron; April 19, 1692
            m2 Grace Mallet Ware; March 15, 1691/2
            Children
                Joseph - b. September 20, 1677
                    Children by Elizabeth
                        Ebenezer   Abigail
                        Elizabeth   Caleb
                        Ruth
                    Children by Grace
                      Deborah
                      Lydia

```
John (Lt.) - b. 1654
    m. Hannah Denning; December 23, 1674
    d. 1738
    Children
        John - b.c. 1678
                 d. April 27, 1679
        Sarah - b. March 20, 1683
        Ruth - b. October 6, 1687
        Joshua - b. November, 1688
        Roger - b. July 14, 1693
        David - October, 1691
        Caleb
        Israel
Joseph - b.c. 1658
    d. September 18, 1675
Freeborn - b. August 9, 1660
    m1 Merriam Knowlton/(Moulton) Batchelder, c.
    1681
    m2 Elizabeth Fairfield by 1704
    d.c. 1706 or 1729
    Children by Merriam
        Merriam         Benjamin
        Freeborn        Skeper/Skipper
    Children by Elizabeth
        William - b. September 30, 1704; Beverly,
                 Massachusetts
                 m. Rebecca Stone, c. 1728
                 d. January 12, 1792; Bradford
                 Children
                     Benjamin        Rebecca
                     William         Hannah
                     Sarah           Daniel
                     Nathaniel
        Abigail - d. June 1, 1690
        Tabitha - m. Paul Rayment; Frbruary 3,
                 1716; Beverly, Massachusetts
        Mary
        Elizabeth
    Abigail - Cornelius Larkum; February 8, 1681;
        Beverly, Massachusetts
```

Although there were several possible origins for the name Balch, it most likely meant "the bald man". It also could be an abbreviation of Balchin, which meant "son of Balch" or "son of the bald man." It could have come from Balck in Germany, van der Balcht in Brussels and Flanders, Balchen in Norway, or Balloch in Scotland.

The name Balchman was in the Roll of Battle Abbey in 1066. Richard Balch's May 12, 1495 will directed he be buried next to his father in the church of St. Andres of Farnham. He mentions William and Matilda Balch and their children John, Margaret and Nicholas; Florence Balch Quynby; and Isabella Balch. John Balche was a Somerset sheriff in 1392.

William F. Balch, in his "A History of the Balche Family" in the July, 1855 NEHGR, suggested George Balch, born circa 1536, was the English ancestor of the Beverly, Massachusetts Balch family. While George Balch did have sons named George (b. 1577) and John (b. 1579) William provided no proof.

However, John Balch was born before 1600 in Bridgewater, Somersetshire. Bridgewater layed in Somerset, England; on the Parrett River; approximately across the Bristol Channel from the Cardiff, Wales area. In her book Somerset, Mrs. Hann called Bridgewater "the true capital of all the moors and marshes... between the Mendip and the Quantock Hills." St. Marys, the parish church in the center of town, had a "graceful spire and a curiously low tower."

The name Bridgewater supposedly came from "Burgh Walter" -burgh of Walter de Douai. At one time there was a large castle which was built in 1216. British Admiral Blake was born there in 1599 and attended Bridgewater's grammar school. He would have been there at the same time as John Balch.

John Balch, as head of the family, and his wife Agnes arrived aboard the "Zouch Phenix" - along with Thomas Gardner, Thomas Gray, Walter Knight and Peter Palfrey - in the spring of 1624, and joined the company of Captain Robert Gorges at Cape Ann. Along with Roger Conant, Balch searched for a better place to settle when Cape Ann failed.

Supposedly during that time, his son Benjamin was born (1629), becoming the first male born in the Massachusetts Bay Colony. However, Banks, in The Planters of the Commonwealth, listed Benjamin and John as accompanying their parents on the "Zouch Phenix" long before 1629.

On May 18, 1631, John "Balche" took the oath to become a freeman. He was a member of the jury in the trial of Walter Palmer for killing Austen Bratcher. John was also a member of the Grand Jury in 1645. While in Salem, as one of the "Old Planters" Balch held the post of selectman and collector of revenue. According to William Balch, John was one of thirteen "Executive Rulers of Salem" appointed on January 26, 1637.

Balch Genealogica claimed that John was a member of the Church of England, but "gave up Episcopacy and joined the local church" after arriving in Massachusetts. He became an original member of the First Church of Salem.

But when new arrivals drove the "Old Planters" across the Bass River to Beverly, John Balch received 200 acres of land there. He signed the deed for his home lot in November, 1635. The home he built in 1636 survived with the aid of the Balch Family Association and owned by the Beverly Historical Society as the oldest, standing, documented house in America. Margery Balch became a member of the church of Beverly before 1636.

William Balch, in his Balch family genealogy in an 1855 NEHGR, reported John was a man of perseverance, integrity and intelligence. When he died in 1648, Benjamin, Jr. inherited the bulk of his estate (see Appendix III).

Two of John's three sons died young. John II was only 32 years old and Freeborn was 27 when he died. John II, a mariner, married Mary Conant, daughter of the head of the "Old Planters". They had a daughter Mary who died young. John drowned while crossing to Beverly on a ferry or skiff during a fierce storm on June 16, 1662. A June 24th, 1662 inquest was

called to look into his death. The inquest records indicated
that
"being constrained to leave the canowe in which he was
bounde over the river at Salem ferrie, by reason of the
violence of the winde and vaues & indeavoringe to return
againe to the shore, died by the extremitie of the cold
with the violence of the winde and rage of the seas and
soe perished in the water."
His estate was appraised at 189 pounds 17 shillings. His widow
next married William Dodge.

In his family history, William Balch suggested that
Freeborn's name came about because he was born shortly after
his father became a freeman in 1630. Freeborn was next
mentioned in his father's 1648 will. John left him one-fourth
of his farm and household goods, among other bequests. Records
from 1658 stipulated that Walter Price had been appointed to
act as executor and administrator for Freeborn Balch. Freeborn's land was being disposed of, but the document mentioned
that the deal was void "if ye said Freeborn Balch appeare to
be alive." So there was obviously some question as to Freeborn's whereabouts and/or whether he was alive in 1658. It has
been suggested that Freeborn had emigrated to England and lost
contact with the family. He would have been approximately 27
years old at the time.

Depending upon the source, Benjamin either emigrated with
his parents or was born in Salem during the winter of 1628/29.
In addition to inheriting the larger share of his father's
estate, he inherited the home lot when his father's second
wife died. He lived there until his death in 1714/15. He also
inherited when his brother Freeborn disappeared. When his
brother John died, he received more land, leaving Benjamin
quite well-off.

Benjamin married Sarah, probably the daughter of Thomas
Gardner, and had at least five sons - Samuel, John, Joseph,
Freeborn and Benjamin.

Deacon Samuel Balch (born in 1651) was town clerk in
Beverly in the 1690's. He and his brother John (born in 1654)
inherited the majority of Benjamin's estate.

Joseph (born circa 1658) served as a soldier under
Captain Thomas Lothrop. On September 18, 1675 the Indians were
winning King Philip's War. Troops under Captains Lathrop,
Appleton, Mosely, and Beers had been gathered in the Deerfield
and Hadley area. Capt. Lathrop's troops, including Joseph
"Bolch", were appointed to deliver a large quantity of corn
safely from Deerfield to Hadley. Unknown to the English, a
large band of Indians waited to ambush the English five miles
from Deerfield where the Muddy Brook crossed the road.
According to Bodge, the soldiers had laid their guns in the
carts and were picking wild grapes when the Indians struck.
There were few English survivors. Approximations of numbers
killed ranged from sixty-one to eighty English. Among those
massacred was Joseph Balch. In 1835 a monument was erected
which read
"On this ground Capt. Thomas Lathrop and eighty men
under his command including eighteen teamsters from
Deerfield, conveying stores from that town to Hadley,

were ambushed by about 700 Indians, and the Captain
and seventy-six men slain Sept. 18th, 1675."
Nearby the grave of those killed was marked by a stone slab.
The name of the river was afterward changed from Muddy Brook
to Bloody Brook.

The Balch Family Association chart from <u>Balch Genealogica</u>
did not list Joseph as a Balch son. However, since Joseph died
when he was only about 17 years old, he did not appear in his
father's will and other records. He could easily have been
missed.

William F. Balch and Savage did not list Benjamin, Jr. as
a Balch son. But Benjamin did end up in early records. During
the Salem witchcraft trials, his wife Elizabeth testified
against Bridget Bishop. According to Elizabeth's deposition,
after George Corwin's funeral, Elizabeth and her sister,
Abigail (Woodbury) Waldron of Wenham were returning to Beverly
from Salem. Edward Bishop and his wife Bridget, both of whom
had been in jail on suspicion of witchcraft, overtook the
sisters, and the couple had some "words of Difference" about
how fast they were going. Edward Bishop said Bridget had been
a difficult wife and was getting worse. He told the sisters
that "the Devill did come bodily vnto her" and that she was
"familiar with the Deuil." When Elizabeth Balch castigated him
for talking about his wife that way, Bishop answered that he
was only speaking the truth.

Elizabeth was probably Benjamin Balch, Jr.'s second wife
since she was approximately 38 and he was approximately 40
years old when they were married.

Several of John Balch's descendants became rather renown
clergymen. Rev. William Balch, born in Beverly on September
30, 1704, was the son of Freeborn and Elizabeth Balch. He
attended Harvard and was ordained at Bradford, New Groveland.
He was pastor there until his death in 1792 and was buried in
the old Burying Ground in Bradford.

Rev. Thomas Balch was born on October 17, 1711 in
Charlestown, Massachusetts. After attending Harvard, he was
ordained at the Congregational Church in South Dedham on June
30, 1736. He was chaplin of the Cape Breton Expedition in
1744. He died at South Dedham on January 8, 1774.

Collins Family

The Collins name can stand for "the son of Cole," a pet name for Nicholas. It could also be from the Gaelic "Cuilein" which means "darling" and is used as a term of endearment for young animals. The Welsh "Collen" means "hazel" as in "a hazel grove."

There is a possible connection between the Edward and John Collins families. Families of Early Guilford Connecticut reported John and Edward might be brothers. Genealogies of Connecticut Families and Directory of Heads of New England Families 1620-1700 claimed they were, indeed, brothers. If they were correct; Edward and John had another brother named Daniel. However, with the absence of wills, church records and so forth. Using their information, the first generation would look like this:

```
                    Unknown
                    Children
                        Edward (see below)
                        Daniel
                        John
```

However, for this genealogy, Edward Collins and John Collins and their direct descendants will be treated separately.

Part 1
Edward Collins Family

Edward Collins (Dea.)
    b.c. 1603; poss Kent, Surrey, Suffolk, or Essex Counties, England
    m. Martha (1609-1700); Cambridge, Massachusetts
    d. April 9, 1689; Charlestown, Massachusetts
    Children
        Daniel - b. 1629, England
            r. Konigsberg, Prussia
        John (Rev.) - b. 1633, England
            grad 1649, Harvard
            d. December 3, 1687; London, England
            Children
                John - b.c. 1673; London, England
                    d. March 19, 1714
        Sibyl - b. 1638, England
            m. Rev. John Whiting (d. September 8, 1689; Hartford); 1654
            d. June, 1672
        Samuel - b. by 1639
            m. Mary (d. May 5, 1713/4)
            Children
                Edward - b. June 18, 1664; Cambridge, Massachusetts
                Martha - b. March 3, 1666; Middletown, Connecticut
                    m. William Harris; January 8, 1689/90
                Samuel - b. October 21, 1704
                    m. Martha; October, 26, 1704
                    Children
                        Samuel   Martha

41

```
                    Hannah          Jonathan
                    Daniel          Mary
                    John            Benjamin
                    James
          Sibyl (Sibella) - b. February 24, 1670;
               m1 Isaac Rice of Sudbury, Massachu-
               setts
               m2 George Reed of Woburn, Massachu-
               setts
          Mary - b. June 16, 1672
               m. Richard Moore of Needham and
               Oxford, Massachusetts
          Abigail - b. June 2, 1673
               m. Sgt. William Ward of Middletown,
               Connecticut
          Daniel - b. October 5, 1675
               d. June 6, 1689
Martha - b. September, 1639; Cambridge, Massachu
     setts
     m. Rev. Joshua Moody (d. July 4, 1697; Boston,
     Massachusetts) of Portsmouth, New Hampshire
Nathaniel (Rev.) - b. 1642; Cambridge, Massachusetts
     m. Mary (d. October 25, 1709), dau of William
     Whiting; August 3, 1664
     d. December 28, 1684
     Children
          Mary - b. May 11, 1666
               m. John (December 14, 1658 - January
               2, 1733), son of Giles Hamlin of
               Middletown, Connecticut; January,
               1684
               d. May 5, 1722
          John - b. January 31, 1667/8
               m. Mary, dau of Judge John Dixwell
               ("the regicide"); December 24, 1707
               Children
                    Nathaniel - b. November 17, 1708
                    Mary - b. September 23, 1710
                         m. John "Curruthers" of
                         Guilford, Connecticut; May
                         10, 1737
                    John - b. March 18, 1712
                         d. May 6, 1714
                    John (twin) - b. November 13,
                    1714
                         d. October 12, 1715
                    child (twin) - b. November 13,
                    1714
                         d. November 13, 1714
                    Sybil - b. August, 1716
                    Abigail - b. January 4, 1718/9
                    Susannah - b. November 26, 1669
                         m. William Hamlin (February
                         3, 1667 - May 22, 1733) of
                         Middletown, Connecticut;
                         May 25, 1692
                    Sybil (Sybill/Sibbil)  -  b.
                    August 20, 1672
                         d. young
                    Martha - b. December 26, 1674
                         m. Thomas Hurlburt (d. 1752
```

42

<pre>
                              or 1756) of Middletown,
                              Connecticut; December 15,
                              1705
                              d. June, 1748
                         Nathaniel - b. June 13, 1677
                              m. Alice (d. February 19,
                              1755), dau of Rev. William
                              Adams of Dedham,
                              Massachusetts
                              Children
                                   Ann - m. Ephraim Terry
                                   Nathaniel - m. Abigail
                                        Pease (b. 1708)
                              Abigail - b. July 13, 1681
                              m. Samuel Wolcott of
                              Wethersfield, Massachu-
                              setts;
                              December 27, 1706
                         Samuel - b. April 16, 1683
                              d. April 23, 1683
          Abigail - b. September 20, 1644; Cambridge,
               Massachusetts
               m. John, son of Capt. Thomas Willet; 1663
          Edward - bpt. June, 1646; Cambridge, Massachusetts
</pre>

Edward Collins was believed to have been born circa 1603.
Depending upon the source, he may have been born in Kent,
Surrey, Suffolk or Essex County, England. _Genealogical_
Gleanings in England reported a possible connection between
Edward and Samuel Collins, the Vicar of Braintree. Edward
Collins of Cambridge, New England; his sons Daniel, John and
Samuel; and his daughter Sybil were mentioned in the 1639 will
of Daniel Collins of "St. Peter le Poor, London and Braintree,
Essex" County. Daniel referred to Edward as his brother. So
whether or not there was a connection between Edward and John,
there was a definite relationship between Edward and Daniel.
In _Pioneers of Massachusetts_, Pope related that Edward
     "was brought up by godly parents, (and that) his father
     died and he was placed in a gentleman's house...(and)
     apprenticed in a wealthy family."

Whatever Edward's background, he appeared first at Cambridge, Massachusetts in 1638 and became a freeman on September 7, 1639. He had brought his wife Martha and several
children with him from England. On May 13, 1640 he was made a
deacon of the first church in Cambridge. In November, 1640,
"Edwrd Collings," Joseph Cook, and Robert Sanders were "chofen
to Recorde the towns landes & delivr in a Tranfcript to the
Genrall Court for this year enfuing." Then, in 1641, Edward
Collins and Edward Goff were chosen as constables. And from
1654 through 1670 he served as representative in the General
Court.

He was granted thirteen acres in 1645 and six acres in
1646. Then in 1653, the citizens of Cambridge met to divide
"the reminder of the wood Lotts." A "Mr, Collins" was allotted
1 1/2 acres in the first "Squardrant." In 1648 it was proposed
that Harvard's President Henry Dunster and Edward Collins be
given additional land because of their positions in the
community. The additional land was granted in 1649.

Holmes reported Edward may have lived in Medford for a time and Pope placed him there in 1656. Savage agreed that he lived for many years on Governor Cradock's plantation in Medford and, eventually, purchased it. He claimed Edward sold 1600 acres of it to Richard Russell and other considerable parcels to others. However,, 1670 Cambridge town records listed an Edward Collins as being appointed to "catichife the youth (teach catechism) beyond menotime".

In __Magnalia__, Cotton Mather referred to Edward as the "good old man, the deacon of the church of Cambridge, who is now gone to heaven; but before he went thither, had the satisfaction to see several most worthy sons become very famous persons in their generation." He died on April 9, 1689 in Charlestown, Massachusetts.

Daniel Collins was only nine years old when his parents emigrated. He was living in Konigsberg, Prussia in 1658.

John graduated from Harvard College in 1649. He moved to Edinburgh, Scotland, and became chaplain to General Monk. He was in Scotland in 1658. After the Restoration John returned to England and became pastor of an independent church at Pinner's Hall in London. He died in London on December 3, 1687. His son, John, Jr. succeed Nathaniel Mather as minister in London.

Edward Collins' son Samuel also emigrated with his father. After Samuel's marriage, he also went to Scotland circa 1658 or 1659, but returned to New England after a short time. He received full communion in Cambridge, Massachusetts on May 31, 1664 and may have still been at Cambridge in 1675. He was at Charlestown in 1678. However, from his first purchase of lands in Middletown, Connecticut, which was recorded on February 28, 1667; Samuel spent most of his time there. He was a representative for Middletown in 1672.

Sibyl also emigrated with her father. She married Rev. John Whiting who graduated from Harvard in 1653 and became the minister at Salem, Massachusetts and then at Hartford, Connecticut.

Martha was the first of Edward's children born in New England. She married Rev. Joshua Moody who, like his brother-in-law John Whiting, graduated from Harvard in 1653. He became the minister at Portsmouth, New Hampshire, where he was convicted of administering the sacraments contrary to the law, and refusing to administer them according to the rites and ceremonies of the Anglican Church. He spent thirteen weeks in jail before friends managed to have him freed. He later preached in Boston where he left ninety-three volumes of sermons that he had delivered. Moodey became well-known during the witchcraft trials when he told Philip English of Salem, who along with his wife was out on bail for witchcraft, to flee to another town. He married Ann Jacobs of Ipswich after Martha's death.

Edward Collins' son Nathaniel was born in Cambridge, Massachusetts on March 7, 1642. He graduated from Harvard in 1660 and appeared in Middletown, Connecticut land records as early as January 24, 1664. He was ordained there on November 4, 1664.

Nathaniel Collins died December 28, 1684. In **Magnalia**, Cotton Mather wrote "There were more wounds given (by his death) to the whole colony of Connecticut in our New England, than the body of Caesar did receive, when he fell wounded in the senate-house."

John Collins I
      m. Susannah
      d. March 29, 1670; poss Boston, Massachusetts
      Children
            John II (see below)
            Susannah - b. March 24, 1643
                  bpt. April 5, 1646; Boston, Massachusetts
                  m. Thomas Walker of Boston; March 25, 1662
            Thomas - b. September 5, 1645
                  bpt. April 5, 1646; Boston, Massachusetts
            Elizabeth - b. April 4, 1648
                  bpt. April 16, 1648; Boston, Massachusetts

John Collins II
      b. 1640, prob England
      m1 Mary (d. 1667 or 1669)
      m2 Mary, dau of John Stevens, wid of Henry Kingsworth;
      June 2, 1669
      m3 Dorcas (d. May, 1734), dau of Samuel Swain, wid of
      John Tainter/Taintor; March 6, 1699
      d. December 10, 1704
      w11 pro. January 1, 1704/5
      Children by Mary
            Mary - b. 1663
                  m. Dea. Nathaniel Chapman (d. April 5, 1726)
                  d. 1695 or 1697
            John III - b. 1665
                  m. Ann, dau of John Lette, granddau of Gov.
                  William Leete; July 23, 1691
                  Children
                        Ann - b. May 9, 1692
                              m. Daniel Bartlett, Jr. of Guilford,
                              Connecticut
                              d. October 11, 1745
                        Mary - b. April 11, 1694
                              d. February 2, 1729
                        John IV - b. February 23, 1697
                              m. Rachel Mix of New Haven, Connecti-
                              cut
                              Children
                                    John   Sybil
                                    Pitman   Hepzebah
                                    Asa   Ruhamah
                                    Leah   Uriah
                                    Nathan   Manassah
                                    Asenath   Tyrannus
                        Timothy - b. February 11, 1698
                              d. February 19, 1698/9
                        Timothy (Rev.) - April 13, 1699
                              m. Elizabeth, dau of Samuel Hyde of
                              Lebanon; January 6, 1723
                              d. February 7, 1777
                              Children
                                    Anne   Freelove
                                    Daniel   Ruth
                                    William   Avis
                                    Zerujah   Dimetrius
                                    Lorraine   Lois

                        Augustus
            ? Daniel - b. June 13, 1701
                    m. Lois Cornwell
            Susannah - b. September 25, 1703
                    d. October 5, 1703
            Samuel - b. November 2, 1704
                    m. Margaret (Margery), dau of William
                    Lette; October 20, 1734
                    d. December 6, 1784
                    Children
                            Margery   Samuel
                            Thomas   Anne
                            Gurdon/Gordon   Charles
                            Sarai/Sarah   John
            Mercy - b. January 19, 1707
                    m. Samuel Hopson of Wallingford
                    d. January 22, 1786
            Oliver - b. October 18, 1710
                    m1 Elizabeth, dau of Dea. Thomas
                    Hall; November 6, 1730
                    m2 Ann Smithson; June 11, 1752
                    d. February 20, 1788
            Avis - b. April 1, 1714
                    m. Peter Buell
                    d. November 1, 1754
    Robert - b. 1667
            m1 Lois Bennett (d. 1704) of Southampton, Long
            Island; June 24, 1689
            m2 Eunice, dau of Edward and Elizabeth Foster;
            June 3, 1707
            wll dtd. January 2, 1741
            wll pro. September 2, 1745
            Children
                    Robert - b. October 12, 1690
                            d. October 2, 1703
                    Mary - b. July 8, 1693
                            d. October 6, 1703
                    Thomas - b. June, 1695
                            d. November 20, 1700
                    Jonathan - b. April 28, 1698
                    Eunice - b. June 3, 1700
                            m. Horton
                    Lament - b. 1704
                            d. May 13, 1732; Middletown,
                            Connecticut
                    Mary - b. April 26, 1708; Middletown,
                            Connecticut
                            m. Andrews
                    Robert - b. February 7, 1710
                            d. October 4, 1757
                    Edward - b. August 7, 1711
                            d. January 2, 1802

A John Collins married Susanna Skinner in May, 1620 at
St. George, Dorsetshire, England. However, 1620 was probably
too early to be the John Collins of this genealogy.

If John I was indeed the brother of Dea. Edward Collins,
he probably came to New England prior to his brother. He was
a shoemaker and tanner. First John received a land grant at
Braintree. But then on April 4, 1646 John was admitted to the

church of Boston where, on May 6, 1646 he became a freeman. He belonged to the artillery company there in 1644.

His son John Collins II probably emigrated with his parents. He became a shoemaker and tanner like his father. In 1663, John II went to Middletown, Connecticut at the time his possible cousins - Samuel and Nathaniel, sons of Edward Collins - were there. He was in Saybrooke at the same time as his supposed cousin Samuel. He signed the covenant at Branford in 1668 and was made a freeman there in October, 1669. But he was in Guilford, Connecticut in December, 1669. In 1682 he began teaching at the grammar school.

His son John Collins III was a cordwainer and tanner at Guilford, Connecticut. His wife Ann was the granddaughter of Governor William Leete.

Gardner Family

Spelled a variety of ways including Gardner, Garner,
Gardiner, Gardener and Gardyner; the name might have come from
the French "Garnir" meaning "to summons, warn or call out."
The Italian form was "Gvarnier", the Norman was "Garner." The
Normans also used the name to mean "to fortify."

Or the name could have emanated from the occupation. The
Latin derivation for "a person who works in or tends a
garden," was "Gvrdianus." The Spanish was "Gardena," and the
German was "Gaertner." Perhaps William Garden in 1220 was
blessed with a green thumb or was a peasant farmer.

A knight named Des Jardine, the French derivative of
"Gardener," went to England with William the Conqueror. But as
an occupation name, there were Gardeners and its variations in
the British Isles long before 1066. Gardeners lived on the
Channel Island, Guernsey and Jersey. A Gardner was London's
Lord Mayor in the 1500's. Other Gardeners came from the Gordon
Clan of Scotland.

Part 1
Thomas Gardner Family of Roxbury

Thomas Gardner I
- b. England
- m. (bur. October 7, 1658)
- d. November, 1638; prob Roxbury, Massachusetts
- Children
    - Thomas II (see below)
    - Peter - b.c. 1617, England
        - m. Rebecca Crooke (1630-1675); May 9, 1646; Roxbury, Massachusetts
        - d. November 5, 1698; Roxbury, Massachusetts
        - Children
            - Rebecca - bpt. November 9, 1647; Roxbury, Massachusetts
            - Peter - b. June 24, 1648; Roxbury, Massachusetts
                - d. October 30, 1673
            - Peter - b. January 24, 1649
                - d. October 7, 1673; Roxbury, Massachusetts
            - Samuel - bpt. May 8, 1657
                - d. April 21, 1678
            - Thomas b. May 1, 1652
                - bpt. May 23, 1652
                - d. young
            - Sarah - bpt. January 29, 1654
                - d.c. 1660
            - John - b. December 6, 1655; Roxbury, Massachusetts
                - bpt. December 30, 1655
            - Joseph - bpt. January 16, 1659
            - Sarah - b. April 20, 1663; Roxbury, Massachusetts
                - bpt. June 8, 1668
                - m. John Gore; May 31, 1683
            - Benjamin - b. April 23, 1664; Roxbury, Massachusetts

49

```
                              bpt. May 22, 1664
                         Ebenezer - b. August 5, 1665; Roxbury,
                              Massachusetts
                              d. May 13, 1683; Roxbury, Massachu
                              setts
                         Jonathan - b. August 14, 1667; Roxbury,
                              Massachusetts

Thomas Gardner II
     b. England
     m. Lucy Smith (d. November 4, 1687; Roxbury, Massachu
     setts)
     of Roxbury, Massachusetts; July 4, 1641; Roxbury,
     Massachusetts
     d. aft. 1686
     Children
          Thomas III (see below)
          Andrew - b. March 5, 1642; Roxbury, Massachusetts
               m. Sarah, dau of Hugh Mason; May 20, 1668
               Children
                    Andrew - b. 1674
                         bpt. November 15, 1674; Roxbury,
                         Massachusetts
                         m. Mary, wid of Swan; November 12,
                         1702; Roxbury, Massachusetts
                         d. May 7, 1704; Roxbury, Massachu
                         setts
                    Abigail - bpt. October 31, 1680; Roxbury,
                         Massachusetts
                    Thomas - b. December 9, 1684; Roxbury,
                         Massachusetts
                         r. 1689; Muddy River (Brookline),
                         Massachusetts
                         d. 1690

Thomas Gardner III (Dea. or Lt.)
     b. August 24, 1645; Roxbury, Massachusetts
     m. Mary, dau of Elder John Bowles; November 17 or 19,
1673;
     Roxbury, Massachusetts
     Children
          Sarah - b. March 15, 1675; Roxbury, Massachusetts
          Thomas - b. April 18, 1676; Roxbury, Massachusetts
          Mary - b. March 11, 1678 or 1679
          John - b. January 9, 1679/80; Roxbury, Massachusetts
          Caleb - b. April 23, 1682; Roxbury, Massachusetts
          Peter - b. July 22, 1684; Roxbury, Massachusetts
               bpt. August 24, 1684; Roxbury, Massachusetts
          Isaac - b. August 18, 1686; Roxbury, Massachusetts
               bpt. August 25, 1686; Roxbury, Massachusetts
          Benjamin (Capt.) - d. 1797; Brookline, Massachusetts
               Children
                    Samuel - b.c. 1729
                         d.c. 1772
                    Elisha - d. 1797; Brookline, Massachusetts
          ? Solomon
```

The entire branch of this Gardner family settled in
Roxbury. The early Gardners were large land owners and, in the
first years, made up a significant percentage of the population.

The first Thomas Gardner of Roxbury, Massachusetts was
born in England. He may have emigrated aboard the Elizabeth
from London in 1635. Thomas I and his wife had at least two
sons, Peter and Thomas II. Although Holmes' Dictionary of the
Heads of New England Families called him the brother of Peter,
he was, in reality Peter's father. Frank Gardner, in his
genealogy, described Thomas Gardner of Roxbury as prominent
and reported that one of Thomas' granddaughters married an
Adams and became the mother of one President of the United
States (John Adams) and grandmother of another (John Quincy
Adams).

Thomas I died in November, 1638. Early Boston records of
his death referred to him as "a housekeeper". According to
early church records "our aged sister Gardne," probably Thomas
I's widow, was buried on October 7, 1658.

Their son Peter was born in 1617 and was aboard the
"Elizabeth" when it sailed from London in April, 1635. On May
9, 1646 he married Rebecca, settled in Roxbury, and had at
least thirteen children. His son Joseph was made surveyor in
1694 and 1698, fence viewer in 1695, and constable in 1699.
Peter's son Samuel was a soldier in Captain Johnson's Company
at a battle on December 19, 1675. He was killed along with
eight others from his company in April, 1676 while fighting
under Wadsworth at Sudbury. He was only nineteen years old.

Thomas II was a member of the Roxbury church in 1650 and
paid thirteen shillings tax to support the school. It would
have been the school in Roxbury, as the one at Muddy River
would not be established until the 1700's.

In 1672, Thomas Gardner II or III paid 10 pounds of the
104 pounds, 13 shillings raised to build " a nue metting-hous"
in Roxbury. At the same time, an Andrew Gardner paid 5 pounds.
In 1686, Thomas II signed the unsuccessful petition requesting
permission to begin a school in the Muddy River area.

Historical Sketches of Brookline, Massachusetts reported
that a Thomas Gardner who died in 1689, left sons named
Thomas, Joshua and four daughters, including one named Mary.
It also reported that the home of Joshua Gardner burnt on
January 11, 1691 and two of his children died in that fire.

It is unlikely that Joshua was the son of any of Peter's
(Thomas I) children. Mathematically it seems impossible. It
also appears impossible for Joshua to be one of Thomas III's
children. It is, however, possible that Joshua and his four
sisters were the children of Thomas II. Since Thomas II was in
early records until at least 1686, the Thomas who died in 1689
and was the father of Thomas, Joshua, Mary and 3 other
daughters could have been Thomas II.

Thomas II's son Andrew appeared in records when his 1641
birth was registered. He married Sarah, the daughter of Hugh
Mason on May 20, 1668.

One of Andrew's sons, probably Andrew Jr., was accidentally killed by a soldier in 1704. The "Boston News Letter"
gave an account of the "Death of the Rev. Mr. Gardner,
minister of Lancaster." Since three members of the garrison

51

were out of town and two others were very tired, Rev. Gardner decided to keep watch that night alone. As he approached a garrison building, a soldier sleeping by the fire was awakened. Startled, the soldier fired, thinking he was shooting at Indians.

Andrew Jr. was not the only one of Andrew's son to meet a violent and unexpected death. Thomas was a captain on the Canadian Expedition under Sir William Phipps when he lost his life in 1690.

Thomas III married Mary, the daughter of Elder John Bowles and had at least eight children. He was one of 32 who signed the 1705 petition renewing the request for establishment of separate village status and a school.

Frequently referred to as Lt. Thomas, he was one of six men along with Lt. Samuel Aspinwall assigned to negotiate with Caleb Gardner, Jr. when, on December 2, 1713, Caleb offered to give a piece of his land on which to build a "Meeting House for the Public Worship of God."

And when the new church was finished in 1718, Thomas III was assigned the pew "between (the) west door and men's gallery stairs" and was elected one of two first deacons. Joseph Gardner's pew was to the "left of (the) front door."

As an active citizen, Thomas III served as selectman numerous times in the early 1700's. In 1702 he was chosen along with Sgt. Benjamin White and Sgt. Samuel Aspinwall "to manage ye Affairs of the Hamlet" (selectman ?). He was elected to the Grand Jury in 1707, as representative in 1718, and to a committee to purchase land in 1722.

Historical Sketches of Brookline, Massachusetts, related that Thomas III also had a son named Solomon. There was a Solomon Gardner who, along with Nathaniel Gardner, was elected "Hogreaves" on March 6, 1737/8. He was elected "Surveyor of Highwayes March 5, 1738/9." If he was not Thomas III's son, he could have been from the next generation.

Part II
Thomas Gardner Family of Salem

Thomas Gardner
    b.c. 1592; poss Scotland or Sherborne, Dorset Co. England
    m1 Margaret Fryer/Tryer/Frier/Frayre
    m2 Damarius Shattuck (d. November 28, 1674), wid
    d. prob. December 29, 1674
    Children
        John (see below)
        Thomas II - b. by 1624, England
            m1 prob. Hannah, 1649
            m2 Elizabeth, pos Horne
            d. 1682
            Children
                Mary - bpt. 1643
                Thomas - bpt. June 25, 1645
                    m. Mary Porter; April 22, 1669
                    d. November 16, 1695
                Eliza/Elizabeth - bpt. 1649
                Abigail - bpt. 1651
                Bethiah - bpt. 1654
                    m. Samuel Gaskill
                Hannah - bpt. 1657
                Jonathan - bpt. 1664
                David
                Susannah - m. George Flint; March 2,
                    1698/9
                    d. March, 1720
                Dorcas - m. Robert Carver; June 19, 1688
        Richard - b. by 1624, England
            m. Sarah (c. 1632-1724), dau of Damarius
            Shattuck
            Children
                Richard - b. October 23, 1653
                    m. Mary, dau of Joseph Austin of
                    Dover, gr dau of Edward Starbuck
                    Children
                        Richard (Capt.) - m. Leah Folger
                        Patience   Benjamin
                        Joseph   Miriam
                        Solomon   Peter
                        Lydia (2)   William
                Deborah - b. February 12, 1658
                    m1 John, son of Thomas and Sarah Macy
                    m2 Stephen Pease
                    d. 1712
                Demaris (Damorice) - b. November 21, 1662;
                    Salem, Massachusetts
                    d. 1662
                James - b. May 19, 1664; Salem,
                    Massachusetts
                    m1 Mary, dau of Nathaniel and Mary
                    (Coffin) Starbuck
                    m2 Rachel, his cousin, dau of John
                    Gardner, wid of John Browne
                    m3 Patience, wid of Ebenezer Harker,
                    dau of Peter and Mary (Morrell)
                    Folger of Nantucket
                    d. 1723
                    Children

```
              Samuel            Jonathan
              Jethro            Elizabeth
              Barnabas          Mehitable
              James
     Nathaniel - b. November 16, 1669
          m. Abigail, dau of James and Mary
          (Severance) Coffin
          d. 1713, England
          Children
              Hannah            Judith
              Ebenezer          Margaret
              Peleg             Nathaniel
              Andrew            Abel
              Susannah
     Love - b. May 2, 1672; Nantucket,
          Massachusetts
          m. James Coffin Jr.
     Hope - b. November 16, 1669; Nantucket,
          Massachusetts
          m. John, son of James and Mary
          (Severance) Coffin
     Sarah - m. Eleazer, son of Peter and Mary
          (Morrell) Folger, Nantucket,
          Massachusetts; uncle of Benjamin
          Franklin
     Miriam - m. John, son of William Worth;
          September 22, 1684
     Joseph - m. Bethia (b.c. 1650, Salsbury,
          Massachusetts), dau of Thomas and
          Sarah (Hopcott) Macy; March 30, 1670
          d. 1701
          Children
              Bethia - b. August, 18, 1676
                   m. Eleazer Folger Jr.; her
                   cousin
              Sarah - m. Joseph Paddock of
                   Barnstable, Massachusetts
              Damaris - m. Stephen, son of
                   Nathaniel Barnard
              Deborah
              Hope - m. Peter, son of Lt. John
                   and Deborah (Austin) Coffin
                   Children
                        Mary - m. Matthew
                             Jenkins
                        Abiel - m. William
                             Clasby
Joseph - b. by 1624, England
     m. Anne (c. 1634 - April 19, 1713), dau of
     Emanuel Downing (niece of Gov. Winthrop);
     August, 1656
     d. December 19, 1675
George - b. by 1624, England
     m. Elizabeth Allen (d. 1681), wid of Rev.
     Samuel Stone of Hartford, Connecticut
     d. August 20, 1679
     Children
          Hannah - b. December 5, 1644
               m. John "Buttolph"
          Samuel (Capt.) - b. May 14, 1648
               m. Elizabeth (Browne) Grafton
```

```
                    d. 1724
                    Children
                         John - b. 1681
                               m. Elizabeth Weld
                               d. 1722
                    Marrey - b. July 10, 1653
                         m. Turner
                    George - b. September 24, 1654
                    Ebenezer - b. August 16, 1657
                    Ruth - bpt. April 2, 1665
                         m. Hathorne
                    Mehitable - b. April 20, 1660
                         d. May, 1660
          Samuel - b.c. 1629; prob. Salem, Massachusetts
               m. Mary White (d. September 12, 1675)
               d. October, 1689
               Children
                    Mary - b. August 5, 1658
                         d. by 1663
                    Elizabeth - b. May 30, 1660
                         d.c. 1678
                    Marey - b. June 29, 1663
                         m. Joseph Henfield
                    Margaret - b. July, 1664
                         m. Deliverance Parkman
                         d. March, 1689
                    George - b. January 15, 1668
                         d. by 1669
                    Jonathan (twin) - b. July 18, 1669
                    Hannah (twin) - b. July 18, 1669
                    Abel - b. September 1, 1673
                         m. Sarah (b. 1675), dau of Israel and
                         Elizabeth (Hathorne) Porter
          Sarah - m. Benjamin Balch (1629-1715); c. 1650;
               Beverly, Massachusetts
               d. April 5, 1686
               Children
                    (see Balch)
          Miriam - m. Hill
               Children
                    Miriam
                    Susanna
          Seeth - bpt. December 1636
               m. Grafton

John Gardner (Capt.)
     b.c. 1624; pos Cape Ann, Massachusetts or aboard ship
     m. Priscilla Sanders or Grafton; February 20, 1654;
     Salem, Massachusetts
     d. May 6, 1706; Nantucket, Massachusetts
     Children
          John - b. March 20, 1653/4
               m. Susannah, dau of Nathaniel and Mary (Hon
               chine) Green
               Children
                    John - m. Priscilla, dau of Jethro and
                         Mary (Gardner) Coffin
                         d. July 6,, 1759
                    Jeremiah - m1 Sarah, dau of James and Ruth
                         (Gardner) Coffin, Jr.
```

                    m2 Lois, wid of Grindal
                       d. May 5, 1768
                    Nathaniel - m. Jemima Coffin, 1722
                    Priscilla - m. John Lovell
          Priscilla - b. December 6, 1656
              m. John Arthur
              Children
                  John   Elizabeth   Joseph
                  Margaret   Mary
          Benjamin - b. March 3, 1658; Salem, Massachusetts
              d. young
          Rachel - b. August 3, 1662; Salem, Massachusetts
              m1 John, son of John and Hannah (Hubbard)
              Brown
              m2 James Gardner, her cousin
          Benjamin - b. May 17, 1664; Salem, Massachusetts
          Ann - b. February 30, 1667; Salem, Massachusetts
              m. Edward Coffin
          Nathaniel - b. September 24, 1668; Salem,
              Massachusetts
          Mary - b. May 27, 1670
              m. Jethro Coffin
          Mehitable - b. November 24, 1674; Nantucket
              Massachusetts
          Ruth - b. January 26, 1667; Nantucket, Massachusetts
              m2 James Coffin
          ? Joseph
          ? George

     This Thomas Gardner probably emigrated from Sherborne,
Dorset County, England; or, less likely, from Scotland.
"Sherborne" meant "bright or shining stream" in Old English.
His wife and sons George, Richard and Joseph emigrated in 1624
aboard the "Zouch Phenix" with Peter Palfrey and John Balch.

     Thomas may have been related to Rev. John White; one of
the main motivators in Cape Ann. Rev. John's sister first
married a Thomas Gardner. Possibly he was Thomas' father.

     The Gardners settled with the Dorchester Company in Cape
Ann. But he did not become a freeman when most of his fellow
Cape Ann settlers did. Some sources have referred to Thomas as
overseer of the plantation there while John Tilley, a rather
disreputable man, was overseer of the fisheries and Roger
Conant was governor. However, Savage claimed Thomas was
employed to oversee the fisheries. However, the rocky, un-
productive soil made farming nearly impossible.

     When the Cape Ann settlement collapsed in 1626, Gardner
removed with Conant to Naumkeag (Salem) where he resided until
his death. While in Salem, he may have been the Thomas Gardner
who became a freeman on May 17, 1637. He did become a representative that same year. Thomas was on the Grand Jury in 1647
and on a regular jury in 1648. Thomas signed a grant of 300
acres farmland to Thomas Scruggs. In 1637 and 1640, he was
appointed to survey fences. He was listed as "cunstable" in
1639 Salem records. He layed out George Wright's land in 1642,
Francis Johnson's in 1643, and Michael Shaflin's in 1644. In
1645 Salem records noted that Thomas Gardner was discharged
from military training when his sixth son joined the militia.
But his service to the town continued through the years,

including fence repairs, contract writing, estate appraisals, and land surveys. In 1662 he was even granted permission to sell "what strong waters he hath in his hands" (see Appendix IV).

Frank Gardner, in his genealogy of Thomas, related that the second Mrs. Thomas Gardner, Damarias, chose to attend Quaker meetings, even though she had been admitted to the Salem church in 1641. She was taken to court a number of times and was fined at least once because of her absence for her church.

The John Spencer Gardner whose 1637 English will was proven in Salem in 1648, may have been of some relationship to Thomas. So may have been a Nicholas Gardner in Salem about the same time.

Lt. Thomas Gardner was eldest son of Thomas. When the Gardner family emigrated, the passenger list on the "Zouch Phenix" included Thomas Senior, his wife and sons Richard, Joseph, and George. Thomas II was not listed. Either he was accidentally left off the list, or he emigrated separately from his parents. During those early years, a number of older male children emigrated alone, many as bonded servants.

Whatever way Thomas II arrived, he first appeared in Salem records, supposedly as an adult, in July 18, 1637, when "Tho. Garner Junor" was granted five acres of land. Then in November, 1637; "Thomas Gardiner and George Gardiner bretherin haue eyther or them tenn acres alowed." Thomas II joined the First Church in Salem in 1639 and became a freeman in 1641. Although not as civicly active as his father had been, Thomas II appeared in a number of land deeds through the years. Frank Gardner, in his family genealogy, reported that Thomas II was a shoemaker, cordwainer, and also owned a "ketch" used for cod fishing.

Thomas I's son George was born before 1624 in England and emigrated with his parents. His first mention in Salem records was in 1637 when he was granted ten acres of land. He became a member of the church in 1641, a freeman on December 27, 1642 and a jury member in 1648. According to Savage, his wife, Elizabeth also was indicted for favoring Quakers, and Savage suggested that George's children Ebenezer and Ruth may not have been baptized until after their mother's death because of this. Early records seemed to indicate his youngest child, Mehitable, was never baptized. Frank Gardner quoted 1658 court records which demonstrated George's wife had attended

"a diforderly quaking meeting & alfoe of her frequent abfenting her felfe from publike worship of God upon the Lord's Day: to pay 5 sh. costs."
Frank Gardner suggested that both the second Mrs. Thomas Gardner I and Mrs. George Gardner went to court and were fined for favoring Quakers and missing church. However, it would seem to be far more likely that all the event concerned only one Mrs. Gardner.

Thomas' son Capt. Joseph Gardner married in 1656. In 1648, Joseph was taken to court to answer charges of trespassing. He did not become a freeman until 1672. In <u>Soldiers in</u>

King Philip's War, Bodge indicated Joseph was "a man of energy and ability" who "held many positions of honor and importance in Salem." In May, 1672 the General Court appointed him lieutenant and on May 12, 1675 he was appointed captain of the foot company of Salem.

In November of that year, Capt. Gardner took ninety-five members of the First Company of Salem on an expedition against Narraganset. Bodge quoted from Church's "Entertaining History" in describing the death of Gardner.
"Mr Church spying Capt. Gardner of Salem amidst the wigwams in the East end of the Fort, made towards him;...they were looking at each other in the face, Capt. Gardner settled down, Mr. Church stepped to him, and seeing the blood run down his cheek...he (Gardner) looked up in his face but spake not a word, being mortally shot through the head."

After his death, the company command fell to Gardner's lieutenant, William Hathorn. On June 6, 1676, Gardner's widow married Gov. Simon Bradstreet.

According to Bodge, since Gardner had not children, his Narraganset claim went to the eldest
"male heir of his eldest brother Thomas. This heir was Habakkuk Gardiner, son of the Captains nephew Thomas who in the list of claimants claims in the 'right of his uncle, Capt. Joseph Gardiner'."

Thomas I's son Samuel was born circa 1629, probably in Salem. In 1663 Samuel and his brother John were granted permission to build a mill over the South River provided it was built within two years.

Thomas I's son Richard was living in Salem until 1666. In 1667 his family and he removed to Nantucket. His brother John followed several years later. In 1673 Richard and his brother John received permission to purchase seaside land from the Indians on which to establish a fishing business. In 1683 the brothers received another deed. Richard's son James married Mary Starbuck, the first Anglo-Saxon child born on Nantucket. Richard supposedly died on "1st mo. 23d 1688". Sarah Gardner, his widow, was made executor of his estate.

Thomas' son John first appeared in early records on December 5, 1639 when the General Court ordered the treasurer to "pay John Gardner 20s for witness charge & carrying Goodman Woodward his instruments to Ipswich." John was approximately 15 years old at the time.

On February 23, 1642/3, he was granted land along with his brother Richard "nere Mackrell Cove". He was approximately 18 years old. Later he sold that land and, on September 6, 1656, he bought a dwelling and half acre of land from John Ingersol. Even after he removed from Salem, John kept his property there. Upon his death, John left the Salem home and 1/8 of a mill to his grandson John.

The mill was probably the one John and Samuel Gardner were given permission to build on South River. About the same time, John was granted the estate of John Cornings as long as

Gardner paid all of Cornings' debts. However, John was primarily a mariner and was frequently referred to as Capt. Gardner.

John Gardner was a very public man. He served as juror from 1658 through 1661 and then again in 1672, appraiser in 1659, attorney for Henry Bartholomew in 1661, inquest juror in 1662, and surveyor in 1669. Sometime between 1660 and 1667, he probably was the John Gardner who plotted a map of the Merrimac River. He served on committees to purchase a house for Pastor Higginson in 1659; and to set boundaries between Boston, Charlestown and Lynn in 1660.

Nantucket, Massachusetts records indicated that on August 5, 1672,

"a grant was made by the town unto Mr. John Gardner of Salem, marrener, a seamans accommodation, with all appurtinances belonging unto it as fully as the other seamen and tradesmen have in their former grants, upon condition that he com to Inhabit and fet up the Trade of fifhing with a sufficient vafsel fit for the taking of Codfish...and that the aforefayd John Gardner shall use his best endeavor to prosecute the fifhing trade... and if he see caufe to depart from the Island within Three years after the time that he shal return into the hands of the aforesayd grantters..."

According to the agreement, John Gardner and his family were to be in Nantucket by the end of April, 1674. He was also granted the "liberty to set a house upon the hy-way at Wefko going down to the landing place."

After a trip to New York with his brother Richard in 1673, John returned, commissioned by the Governor as captain of the foot company of Nantucket. The brothers also requested permission to purchase more land from the Indians to use in their fishing business. Permission was granted but it upset all of Nantucket.

John got into a number of misunderstandings with others on the island. One battle pitted Peter Folger and John versus Tristram Coffin, Sr. and others, and included threats, accusations, fines, and injunctions.

In the end, John Gardner was commissioned Chief Magistrate of Nantucket in 1680, in 1682, and again in 1684; and was elected to a number of other offices and committees. In 1692 he was chosen representative to the General Court from Nantucket and was Tax Commissioner for Martha's Vineyard and Nantucket in 1692 and 1693. In 1692 he was appointed Probate Judge, a position he held until his death in 1706.

John had a number of connections with the Indians. According to Frank Gardner's genealogy, he purchased a great deal of land from the Indians, including land on Martha's Vineyard. His 1694 letter to the governor complained about the physical condition of the Indians. In the early 1700's, an Indian girl accused of stealing 5 pounds worth of items was condemned to return the items, pay a 10 pound fine, be whipped 10 lashes and serve John Gardner for four years. John was also Special Justice in an Indian murder trial.

John was probably back in Salem in 1678 to witness a deed involving his brother George and again in July, 1682 to settle the estate of Joseph Grafton, possibly his father-in-law. On the same 1682 visit he appointed Samuel Gardner, Jr. of Salem as his attorney.

Hull Family

Hull was one of many English names; such as Downs Heap, and Knowles; for hills or mounds. Hull was an early spelling of "Hill" and was frequently written as "Hulls". Cornhull was written as "Cornhulle" in early records. Hull might have also stemmed from a word for "hollow". A person with the name Hull might also have been descended from someone who originally lived near the Hull River in Yorkshire; or came from Hull in Cheshire County, England.

John de Hulls appeared in English records in the late 1300's. Andrew Hulls was Keeper of the King's Privy Seal in the 1450's. A John Hull married Mary Graye on November 21, 1545 at South Perrott and Mosterton Parrish, Dorsetshire, England. And an Arnold Hulls was a patentee of the Virginia Charter in 1606.

Part 1
John Hull Family

Robert Hull
    m2/3 Judith (d. March 29, 1654), dau of Pares, wid of
    Edmund Quincy and Moses Paine; aft. 1643
    d. Brookline, Massachusetts; aft 1657
    wll dtd. December 15, 1646
    est inv. September 4, 1666
    Children
        John (see below)
        Edward - d. by 1657
        dau m. Richard Storer

John Hull (Capt.)
    b. December, 1624; Market Harborough, Leicestershire,
    England
    m. Judith (b.c. 1626 d. June 22, 1695; Boston,
    Massachusetts); dau of Edmund Quincy and step-sis of John
    Hull (husband)
    d. September 30, 1683; Brookline, Massachusetts
    bur. October 5, 1683; Boston, Massachusetts
    Children
        Hannah - b.c. 1658
            m. Chief Justice Samuel Sewall (March 28, 1652 -
            January 8, 1729/30); February 28, 1675/76
            d. October 19, 1717
            Children
                Samuel Jr. - b.c. 1678
                    m. Rebecca, dau of Gov. and Mrs. J.
                    Dudley
                    Children
                        Mary - b. July 20, 1711
                        Henry - b. March 8, 1719/20
                John - b. April 2, 1679
                Elizabeth - b.c. 1680
                    m. Grove Hirst (d. 1717)
                    d. July 13, 1716
                    Children
                      Mary   Samuel
                      Elizabeth Hannah
                      Jane
                Joseph - b. August 15, 1688

```
Judith - m. Cooper
Sarah - d. December 23, 1696
Hannah - d. August 15, 1671
Henry - d. yound
Hull - d. young
Rebecca
Stephen
3 more children
```

In Pioneers of Massachusetts, Charles Henry described
Robert Hull as a blacksmith and chandler in Boston. He was
admitted to the church in 1636 and became a freeman on March
9, 1636/7, when he was only 12 years old. According to Builders of the Bay Colony, Robert emigrated with his son John
aboard the "George". Banks, in Planters of the Commonwealth,
reported that Robert Hull "of Market Harborough, county
Leicester, chandler" emigrated with John and "Mrs." Elizabeth
Hull; arriving in Boston. Winslow recorded that Robert and
John arrived in 1635.

He gave his son John a house and land in Boston to become
his at age 21, but which Robert would be able to live in for
life. John enlarged it, purchased more land, and landscaped
it.

Robert's will was dated December 15, 1646 (see Appendix
V), but was not proven until February 12, 1666. His son Edward
appeared in the original 1646 will, but was not mentioned in
the 1657 codicil. His son John was made administrator being
"his Eldest & now only sonn."

In both the will and the codicil Robert referred to "my
sonne, Richard Storer." Storer was probably the husband of
Robert's daughter. In the original will he referred to "my
sonne, Edmund Quinney (Quincy) that porsson which is due to me
by my wife." Robert's wife Judith had previously been married
to Edmund Quincy. This was probably a son from that marriage,
Robert's step-son.

Pope related that in 1653 Robert's son Edward commanded
Rhode Island forces against the Dutch. Edward pre-deceased his
father. An Enos Hull listed as residing in Brookline, Massachusetts in 1657 may have been another of Robert's sons.

According to Builders of the Bay Colony, John Hull was
born in December, 1624 at Market Harborough, Leicestershire,
England. His father and he arrived off Sable Island in 1634
aboard the "George".

After working the fields with his father, John finally
settled down to work as a goldsmith and did very well. When he
married Judith Quincy, Governor Winthrop performed the
ceremony.

He joined the church on October 15, 1648. Winslow wrote
that John "was not only a church member... he could translate
godliness into business integrity." He probably was the John
Hull who took the oath for freeman on May 2, 1649. He was
accepted into the military band as a corporal under Major

Gibbons, a repentant member of Thomas Morton's group at
Merrymount.

His journal became a useful historical source. He
described Endicott's attempt to raise forces against the
Dutch.
"Few volunteers presented themselves, though the
drums beat up and proclamation made in the several
towns for them."
But it did not matter since New Amsterdam surrendered to Col.
Nicholls with little effort on August 29, 1664. Then on March
15, 1664/5, he wrote in his diary
"Our honored Governor, Mr. John Endicott, departed
this life, - a man of pious and zealous spirit, who
had very faithfully endeavored the suppression of
a pestilent generation, the troubles of our peace,
civil and ecclesiastical, called Quakers. He died
poor, as most of our rullers do, having more attended
the public than their own private interests. It is
our shame: though we are indeed a poor people, yet
might better maintain our rulers that we do. However,
they have a good God to reward them."

In 1652, because money had become limited and counter-
feiting had become prevalent, the General Court decided to
begin coining money. According to Every Day Life in the
Massachusetts Bay Colony a sixteen-foot square mint house was
built behind John Hull's home. Silver was brought in from
South America. Tools for melting, refining, and coining silver
were furnished; and John Hull was appointed Master of the
Mint. Robert Sanderson joined Hull as a partner and, together
coined money in the same alloy as the English. They received
1 shilling 6 pence for each 20 shillings minted. Over the year
they minted over $5 million worth of pine tree coins.

It wasn't until after the Restoration that the English
government realized the Colony was coining its own money. Sir
Thomas Temple was assigned to placate the King. Temple
explained the colonists had had to coin their own money
because the King had not been able to do it. After he told the
King that the pine tree on the coin was a "royal oak" to show
their loyalty to the king during Cromwell's reign, the King
allowed the Boston mint to continue.

In 1654 John's brother Edward wrote from London offering
to send him a die-cutter. But it appeared that Hull or
Sanderson did their own die cutting. The mint took little time
and their goldsmith / silversmith business flourished. Hull
took on a number of apprentices. Sanderson's three sons went
into the business. Together they had a major influence on
silver work of New England.

Hull was a cautious businessman who spread his interest
around. In Rhode Island, he discovered a coal deposit which he
exported to England and Holland. In addition to being a smith,
Hull imported English goods; owned farms, such as the one at
Cotton's Hill and another one at Point Judith; purchased large
tracts of land, such as the Pettaguamsett Purchase in Narrangansett territory; bred horses, like the Narrangansett pacers;
built and operated a mill; and, during King Philip's War,

"sustained the public credit by his own" as Treasurer of the Colony.

He also owned ketches - the "Friendship", "Society", "Hopewell", and "Tryall" - built in Massachusetts Bay. His shipmaster for the sloop the "Endeavor" was instructed to not allow "Sabbath-breaking and swearing" aboard ship. Briganteens and pirates were a problem. In 1653 he lost three ships to the Dutch and one to the Spanish. Twice he had to send money to save his seamen from "Algerine" slavery.

But even after becoming a prosperous merchant and colony treasurer, he still signed legal documents "John Hull of Boston, goldsmith." That was what he was most proud of. The Hobart Journal contained the notation "Capt. John Hull Esq daceased on the sabbath day" on September 30, 1683. He was buried in Boston's Granary Burying Ground on October 5th.

His daughter Hannah was made infamous in "Grandfather's Chair" by Hawthorne about her father dowering her by placing her plumb body on one side of the mint's scales while servants heaped coins on the other side until the scale was balanced. Watching the action, her groom began to imagine his father-in-law had all the money in the treasury. While the story was not true, her dowry was a hefty 30,000 pounds.

Hannah and Samuel Sewall (see Appendix X) were married by Governor Bradstreet in the "Old Hall" of the Hull home. Samuel became the equally infamous Judge Sewall of witchcraft fame. Like his father-in-law, Samuel also kept a journal which gave a fascinating look at colonial life. In it he described the birth of his child.
"April 1. About two of the Clock at night I waked and perceived my wife ill: asked her to call Mother. She said I should goe to prayer, then she would tell me. Then I rose, lighted a Candle at Father's fire, that had been raked up from Saturday night, kindled a Fire in the chamber, and after 5 when our folks up, went and gave Mother warning. She came and had me call the midwife, Goodwife Weeden, which I did. But my wives pains went aeay in great measure after she was up: toward night came on again, and about a quarter of an hour after ten at night, April 2, Father and I sitting in the great Hall, heard the child cry, whereas we were afraid 'twould have been 12 before she would have been brought to bed. Went home with the midwife about 2 o'clock, carrying her stool, whose parts were included in a bagg. Met with the watch at Mr. Rocks brew house, who bad us stand, enquired what we were. I told the woman's occupation, so they bad God bless our labours, and let us pass."
Sewall also wrote that he named his daughters Judith "for the sake of her grandmother and great-grandmother...and the signification of it very good" and Sarah for her "standing in the scripture."

Hannah Hull Sewall died on October 19, 1717. In 1721, Samuel Sewall set out a "stone post in (the) Elm pasture in Remembrance" of his wife. Most of her fourteen children died before adulthood. Her son Rev. Joseph Sewall served as President of Harvard University, after being chosen on August 12, 1671. Samuel, Jr. had marital difficulties. On December

64

20, 1716, his wife, the daughter of Gov. Dudley, gave birth to a son. On August 29, 1717, Samuel, Jr.'s father noted in his journal that his son insisted "that the infant lately born should not be chargeable to his estate."

Part 2
Joseph Hull Family

Thomas Hull
    b. Crewkerne, Somersetshire, England
    m. Joan Peson (prob Person); January 11, 1572/3; Crew-
    kerne, Somersetshire, England
    Children
        Joseph (see below)
        George - b.c. 1595; prob Crewkerne, Somersetshire,
            England
            m1 Thamzen, dau of Robert Mitchell of Stock-
            land, Devon, England; September 27, 1614
            m2 Sarah, wid of David Phippen of Boston,
            Massachusetts
            d. 1659; Fairfield, Connecticut
            Children
                Joshua - bpt. 1630; Crewkerne,
                    Somersetshire, England
                    d. 1658
                Mary - bpt. July 27, 1618
                    m. Humphrey Pinney
                    d. August 18, 1685; Windsor,
                    Connecticut
                Josiah - bpt. November 5, 1620
                    m. Elizabeth, dau of Joseph Loomis;
                    May 20, 1641
                    d. 1675
                    Children
                        Joseph - m. Mary Merwin
                Elizabeth - bpt. October 16, 1625
                    m. Samuel Gaylord
                    d. 1646
                Cornelius - b. 1627
                    m. Rebecca (1633-1695), dau of Rev.
                    John Jones; November 19, 1653
                    d. 1659
                    Children

                        Samuel   Theophilus
                        Cornelius   Rebecca
                        Sarah   Martha
            Naomi
            Martha

Joseph Hull (Rev.)
    b.c. 1595; Crewkerne, Somersetshire, England
    m1 ? Joanne
    m2 Agnes (b.c. 1610); by March 20, 1634
    d. November 10, 1665; Isle of Shoals, New Hampshire
    Children
        Joane - b.c. 1619, England
            m1 Capt. John Bursley; November 28, 1639;
            Barnstable, Massachusetts
            m2 Dolar Daves of Barnstable and Concord,
            Massachusetts
         Joseph - b.c. 1621, England
            m. Elizabeth Harper, step-daughter of Dea.
            Henry Farnham of Roxbury, Massachusetts
            Children
                Tristam - b. Barnstable, Massachusetts
                John (Capt.) - b. 1654

```
                      m. Alice Tiddeman
                      d. December 1, 1732; Rhode Island
                      Children
                            John - m. Dumaris Cory
        Tristam - b.c. 1623, England
              m. Blanche
              wll dtd December 20, 1666
              Children
                    John        Sarah
                    Mary        Hannah
        Temperance - b.c. 1625, England
              m. John Bickford of Oyster River, New Hampshire
        Elizabeth - b.c. 1627, England
              m. Capt. John Heard of Dover, New Hampshire
        Grissell - b.c. 1629, England
        Dorothy - b.c. 1631, England
              m1 Oliver Kent
              m2 Benjamin Matthews
        Hopewell - b.c. 1635; Weymouth, Massachusetts
        Benjamin - bpt. March 24, 1639; Hingham, Massachu-
              setts
        Naomi - bpt. March 23, 1640; Barnstable, Massachu-
              setts
        Ruth bpt. May 9, 1642; Barnstable, Massachusetts
        ? Reuben - b.c. 1644, York
        ? Samuel - m. 1677, Mary Manning
        ? Sarah m. 1677
```

According to <u>Genealogies of the Early Families of Weymouth, Massachusetts</u>, Thomas Hull and Johane Peson (Joan Person) were married in Crewkerne, Somersetshire, England on January 11, 1572/3. "Crewkerne" may have originated with the Celtic word "crewe" meaning "stepping stones."

When Thomas died in Crewkerne in 1636, his estate was worth only 17 pounds 7 shillings 6 pence and he owed 9 pounds 2 shillings 6 pence in debts. After funeral expenses, he left only 2 pounds cash. Ann Hansen, in <u>The English Origins of the "Mary & John" Passengers</u> speculated that his home "must have been hardly more than a hovel since, according to the inventory, it contained only a bed, two table boards, one chest, two coffers, one chair, one other item of furniture, one skillet, and one pewter dish."

George and Joseph Hull were born into that poor Somerset family. So if should not have been surprising that they both looked to the New World for an improved economical life.

Hansen proposed that George emigrated with six of his children while his wife Thamzen remained in England until after their son Joshua was born in 1630. But George's family listed as four the number aboard the "Mary & John" in 1630. Obviously more of the family remained behind because seven and one-half months after George emigrated, his son Joshua was baptized in Crewkerne.

Although the "Mary & John" was not actually part of the Winthrop Fleet, it went with the advanced knowledge of John Winthrop and its destination was the same. The ship was owned by Roger Ludlow, as assistant of the Massachusetts Bay Company. Edward Rossiter, another assistant was also on board.

In the New World, George Hull became a freeman on March 4, 1632/3 and served as selectman, surveyor, and representative to the General Court for Dorchester, Massachusetts. In 1637 he moved to Windsor, Connecticut, where, according to The "Mary and John", he helped lay out that town and neighboring Wethersfield.

In 1647 he sold that home to Governor John Haynes and accompanied Roger Ludlow to Fairfield, Connecticut. He was a representative and Ludlow's assistant of military operation in 1649. As assistant magistrate in 1651, 1653, and 1654 he was authorized to marry persons and "press horses for the public welfare." George died in Fairfield in 1659.

On May 22, 1612 Thomas and Joan's son Joseph went to study at St. Mary's Hall, Oxford. He received a B.A. on November 14, 1614. In Oxford records he was referred to as "son of a commoner."

John Warham, later one of two clerics chosen ministers of the Dorchester Company, had also been born in Crewkerne and attended St. Mary's Hall, Oxford. In 1629, according to The English Origins of the "Mary & John" Passengers, John Warham, John Cox and Joseph Hull preached in Crewkerne "without showing any license to do so" and the church wardens got into serious trouble for allowing it.

Joseph had been the rector of North Leigh, Devon, from April 4, 1621 until 1632 when he gathered 106 persons from the Crewkerne, Somerset area to emigrate to the New World. In addition to his family, Rev. Joseph took three persons listed on the ship's manifest as his servants. They were Judith French (age 20), John Wood (age 20), and Robert Dabyn (age 28). The company sailed from Weymouth, Dorset circa March, 1634/5. They arrived in Dorchester, Massachusetts on June 7, 1635 and went on to Weymouth. Winthrop wrote that on July 8, 1635 "Wessaguscus was made a plantation and Mr. Hull a minister of England and twenty-one families with him allowed to set down there."

On September 2, 1635 he became a freeman of Weymouth and on June 12, 1636, as the town's minister, he received a land grant there.

According to Chamberlain, he left Weymouth and was granted a home lot in Hingham for which he served as deputy to the General Court in 1638 and 1639. The Hobart Journal listed his son Benjamin's baptism in Hingham on March 1638/9 and his farewell sermon on May 5, 1639.

At Braintree he was made a freeman of the Plymouth Colony on December 3, 1639. Chamberlain wrote that Rev. Joseph was in Yarmouth in 1641; Barnstable in 1642 and 1643; and York, Maine in 1643. In his history of Weymouth, Nash wrote that Joseph and his wife were excommunicated for going to Yarmouth but were later restored to the church.

Winthrop also wrote that Plymouth Colony "took a different course from us..." and added that they had made "Acomenticus (a poor village) a corporation...had entertained one Hvll, an excommunicated person and very contentious, for their minister."

Chamberlain added that Joseph Hull had not been liked by either the Massachusetts Bay or Plymouth Colony. As an Episcopalian minister, he was at odds with the Puritan clergy. And early Weymouth records bore that out. In 1637 and 1638 four different persons representing four different groups claimed the Weymouth pulpit. Hull's Episcopalian services were met by a number of dissenters and he became aligned with the moderate dissenters and independents.

In 1662 he could be found in Oyster River (Durham), New Hampshire. But Nash claimed that Joseph was "driven" from there by the Quakers. He died at Isle of Shoals, New Hampshire in 1665.

Three children; Reuben, Samuel, and Sarah; who were listed as children of Rev. Joseph Hull, were more likely his grandchildren.

Lobdell Family

Nicholas Lobdell
    b. 1605; Devonshire or Kent County, England
    m1 Jane, England
    m2 Bridget Price, Pierce or Belamy (d. March, 1641)
    d. aft 1645
    est inv. June 5, 1662
    Children
        Isaac (see below)
        Elizabeth - bpt. August 21, 1631; Northam, Devon
            shire, England
            m. Jonathan Burt; October 20, 1651
            d. November 11, 1684; Springfield, Connecticut
        James - d. September 23, 1632; Northam, Devonshire,
            England
        Simon - bpt. December 23, 1632; Northam, Devonshire,
            England
        Ann - bpt. March 8, 1634/5
            m. Samuel Terry
            d. May 16, 1684; Springfield
        John - b.c. 1639; Hingham, Massachusetts
            m1 Hannah (d. April 23, 1662), dau of John
            Leavett; July 19 or 29, 1659; Hingham,
            Massachusetts
            m2 Mary; February 5 or 21, 1664; Hull,
            Massachusetts
            Children
                Hannah - b. May 27, 1660
                Elizabeth - b. April 23 or 30, 1662
                    d. April 30, 1662
                John - m. Hannah Vickers (bpt. May 1660,
                    Hingham, Massachusetts; d. January
                    31, 1681; Hingham, Massachusetts);
                    May 23, 1704
                    Children
                        Hannah - b. June 19, 1706
                Sarah - d. 1697
                Nathaniel
                Mercy
        Mary - b. 1663
            m. Jonathan (1661-1722), son of Samuel and Mary
            Pierce
            d. December 18, 1744
        Sarah
        ? Nathan

Isaac Lobdell
    b.c. 1637; Hingham, Massachusetts
    m. Martha (1636/7-May 4, 1708), dau of Samuel Ward; circa
    1656; Dedham, Massachusetts
    d. May 5, 1710 or by 1718
    Children
        Isaac Jr. - b. June 28, 1657
            m1 Sarah (January 31, 1666 - March 27, 1697),
            dau of Samuel King of Plymouth, Massachusetts
            m2 Hannah Bishop; August 12, 1697
            d. by 1718
            Children
                dau - b. February 13, 1680; Plymouth,
                    Massachusetts

70

```
          d. February 22, 1680
     Sarah - b. September 27, 1682; Plymouth,
          Massachusetts
          m. Nathaniel, son of Thomas and Mary
          (Rudd) Bingham; July 25, 1705
     Mary / Martha - b. February 24, 1684;
          Plymouth, Massachusetts
          d. April 13, 1686
     Samuel - b. February 17, 1686/7; Plymouth,
          Massachusetts
          Children
               Sarah - b. November 19, 1710
               Isaac - b. July 6, 1715
     Ebenezer - bpt. November 1, 1694; Hull,
          Massachusetts
          m1 Lydia (b. November 2, 1697),dau of
          Benoni and Lydia (Waterman) Shaw of
          Plymton; July 12, 1715
          m2 Mercy, dau of Ebenezer and Hannah
          (Sturtevant) Standish; December 18,
          1745
          Children
               Isaac          Sarah
               Lydia          Ezekiel
Samuel - b. April 28, 1661
     Children
          Sarah - b. November 19, 1710
          Isaac - b. July 6, 1715
Nicholas - b. October, 1663
     m. Elizabeth, dau of Luke Perkins of Charles
     town, Massachusetts; August 18, 1687
     d. 1698
     Children
          Nicholas - b. 1688
               d. 1689
          Elizabeth - b. 1689
               m. Jeremiah Wright of Boston,
               Massachusetts
Joseph - m. Elizabeth (b. 1664, Boston,
     Massachusetts), dau of Richard and Elizabeth
     (Cromwell) Price, wid of James Townsend;
     December 1, 1692
     wll dtd. January 21, 1724; Hull, Massachusetts
     wll pro. June 3, 1725
     Children
          Cromwell - b. June 12, 1693
               d. June 23, 1696
          Elizabeth - b. July 19, 1695
               d. 1706
          Joseph - b. March 18, 1697
          Benjamin - b. December 27, 1698
               d. by September, 1747
          Cromwell - b. December 3, 1700
               m. Judith Collier (d. aft 1774);
               October 21, 1726
               d. aft April 17, 1740 by 1774
          Rebecca - m. Caleb Loring (d. September
               15, 1756); January 6, 1731/2
               d. 1766
Mary - b. 1663
     m. Jonathan Pierce (1661-1722) of Charlestown,
```

Massachusetts; December 4, 1683
d. December 18, 1744
Children

Mary	Samuel	Joseph
Sarah	Jonathan	Martha
Elizabeth	Thomas	Benjamin
Isaac	John	Jacob
John		

Abigail - m. John Steele; May 15, 1696
Rebecca - b.c. 1670; Hull, Massachusetts
  m1 Richard, son of Richard and Margaret (Read)
  Stubbs
  m2 John Cox (b.c. 1658 d. November 23, 1742;
  Dorchester, Massachusetts)
  d. August 6, 1743
  Children
    see Stubbs
Elizabeth - m. William, son of Thomas and Sarah
  (Stedman) Perry; 1681
? dau - m. poss Lendall

In England the "-dell" and "-den" were interchangeable. The name has appeared a Lobdell, Lobden, Lopdell, Lobdoll, Lobel, Lobdon, and other variations.

A "lobdell" was "a dweller of a deep hollow infested with spiders." "Lub" came from the Gaelic and meant "bending or curving" and "dail" meant "a narrow vale or meadow." The name also could have originated with "lobel" meaning "one who flatters of deceives another."

One possible ancestor of these Lobdells was physician Matthew Lobel (Mattias de L'Obel) who was born in 1538 in Lille, son of a distinguished lawyer. After practicing medicine in Germany, Italy, and Switzerland, he emigrated to London where he became physician to James I and discovered the medicinal qualities of the plant Lobelia. He died in St. Michael's in "Cornhill" and was buried in London on March 2, 1616. He had a daughter named Mary.

Early records of the French Church of London described the marriage of other possible ancestors on December 16, 1605. "Jacques Coole native of Anuers, and Louye, (married the) daughter of Mestre Mitias de Lobel, native also of Anuers." On May 21, 1609, "Mathias Lobell, stranger" was buried at St. Diones in London.

James Sargis married Annis Lobdell on August 25, 1600 in Maidstrom in Kent, England. There was even a Count Nicholas Lobdell. And in 1644 a Simon Lobdell was given a house and a one-half acre of land to lease in Milford, Connecticut.

Julia Harrison Lobdell placed the origin of the Nicholas Lobdell of this genealogy as Kent County, England. She reported that Nicholas Lobden, a retainer of Capt. James Lasher, Baron to Parliament, was arrested because of debts on September 22, 1621. Sir Thomas Richardson secured his pardon on October 3, 1621. James Lasher was also Mayor of Hastings, Kent County, England.

However, using parish records, Douglas Richardson, in "Nicholas Lobdell, Founder of the New England Lobdell Family" made a good case for the family origin being Northam, Devonshire, England. He found christening records of four children of Nicholas and Jane Lobdell. Elizabeth was christened August 21, 1631, Symon on December 23, 1632 and an unnamed daughter he assumed was Ann on March, 1634. A son named James was buried on September 23, 1632. All of the children would have been born before the Nicholas of this genealogy would have emigrated to the New World. So the dates matched.

Several other children - Nathan, Mary and Sarah - were accepted by Julia Harrison Lobdell, but eliminated by more recent genealogists like Richardson. Everyone has agreed that John and Isaac were the sons of Nicholas Lobdell.

Born circa 1639 Hingham, John Lobdell was mentioned in the estate inventory of Thomas Marsh of Hingham in 1658. The estate included "Part of a home Lott bought of John Lobden." He had moved his family to Hull by June 5, 1662 when William Chamberlyne (Chamberlain) and John inventoried the estate of Thomas Loring of Hull. On a March 9, 1673 list, John was listed as having "warded" the beacon at Hull.

John's October 26, 1673 will was witnessed by his brother Isaac. It was number 7-339 of the Suffolk County Probate Records. He left all his "sollid" estate to his sons John and Nathaniel Lobdell and he dictated that his sons were "to be brought up at trades at the disposal of father Bosworth (his step-father)." Deacon John Leverett renounced executorship. The inventory valued his estate at 229 pounds 19 shillings. Nathaniel Bosworth paid 1 pound 12 shillings for John's burial.

Isaac Lobdell was listed as a resident of Hull in 1658. On May 12, 1670 Isaac sold a parcel of land for 39 pounds. On May 17, 1670 he deeded the land to his son John. At sometime he resided on the Samuel Ward (Isaac's father-in-law) lot between Richard Stubbs and John Benson at Town Hill in Hull. On April 22, 1679 George Vickars of Hull deeded land to his son Isaac that was bounded on the northwest by Isaac Lobdell, Sr. and on the south by George Vickars Jr.'s lot.

Isaac became a freeman on May 7, 1673. He was a petitioner in 1681 to give Nathaniel Bosworth, his step-father, the power to administer oaths and marry couples.

In 1696, Isaac "et als...proprietors of Further's Hill at Hull," sold land to Israel Nicholas. In 1697 Isaac's brother John was also listed as a proprietor.

According to Julia Harrison Lobdell on March 15, 1702 Isaac deeded to his son Joseph, as mariner of Boston "a messuage in Hull with balance of a lease for 18 years of Bumpers Island, a Negro Slave Sambo, and other items..."

In his 1710 will, which was proven in 1718, Isaac again left his house to his son Joseph. He wrote that he had five children - Joseph, "dau. Perry", Marah Pierce, Abigail Street, and Rebecca Stubbs. He left "Grand children, Ann and Lydia Lendall, each 5 pounds."

The identity of those grandchildren have caused a number of confusions and mis-assumptions through the years. However, the mistakes were seldom made by Lobdell genealogists. Descendants of Daniel Landon of Bristol, Massachusetts in a search of his descendants seem to have stumbled upon Isaac Lobdell's will and assumed that the Ann and Lydia Lendall mentioned in it were Ann and Lydia Landon, two of seven children of Daniel Landon. Why Isaac would name only two of Daniel's seven children has never beensatisfyingly explained by the Landon genealogists. From their first assumption, they further assumed that Ann, the mother of the Landon children, must have been Isaac Lobdell's daughter.

There was little evidence upon which to base the conjecture. No serious Lobdell genealogist has suggested that Isaac had a daughter named Ann. Directory of the Ancestral Heads of New England Families mentioned the Lindall, Lyndall, Lindale name which stemmed from "lin" meaning "a brook or lake" and "dai" meaning "dale". Henry Lindall was listed as a resident of New Haven, Connecticut in 1646 and James Lindall as a proprietor at Duxbury, Massachusetts in 1640. At any rate, the "Lendall" in Isaac's will could easily have been a mis-spelling or mis-reading of the word "Lobdell".

The marriage of Isaac Lobdell, Jr. to Hannah Bishop in 1697 was presided over by Cotton Mather.

Isaac Lobdell, Sr.'s daughter married John Steele on May 15, 1695. A deed dated September 29, 1699 and acknowledged on April 28, 1701 sold to John Steele the Hull home lot of Jonathan "Vickary" for 25 pounds.

Isaac's son Joseph resided in Boston in 1695. In early records Joseph, listed as a mariner, and his wife "Eliy'b" of Hull sold land to William Brown of Boston in March, 1712. Elizabeth Lobdell was the granddaughter of Captain Thomas Cromwell, and the Lobdells named two of their children Cromwell after him. Joseph and Elizabeth were listed as heirs of Capt. Cromwell in 1704.

In his January 21, 1724 will Joseph bequeathed to his wife Elizabeth his
"whole estate for life, if she marry not again; if she marry, my negro slaves Cose and Kate and 200 pounds in full of her dower.

Maverick Family

Robert Maverick (Rev.)
    bur. November 14, 1573; Awliscombe, Devonshire, England
    Children
        Peter (see below)
        Alexander - b.c. 1552
            m. Alice Crabbe; November 6, 1575; Awliscombe,
            Devonshire, England
            Children
                William - bpt. November 4, 1576; Awlis
                    combe, Devonshire, England
                    bur. February 4, 1576/7; Awliscombe,
                    Devonshire, England
                Robert - bpt. July 18, 1578
                Wilemott - bpt. February 6, 1579/80;
                    Awliscombe, Devonshire, England
        John (Rev.) - d. by 1622
            Children
                Cicely - bpt. April 18, 1591; Honiton,
                    Devonshire, England
                    m. John Choram; May 5, 1619; Ottery
                    St. Mary, Devonshire, England
                John - bpt. February 4, 1593/4; Honiton,
                    Devonshire, England
                    d. aft. November 27, 1622
                Elizabeth - bpt. February 6, 1587/8;
                    Awliscombe, Devonshire, England
                    d. April 3, 1598
                Radford - d. aft November 16, 1622
        Radford (Rev) - bpt. June 18, 1561; Awliscombe,
            Devonshire, England
            m. Awdrye (bur. June 18, 1561), sis of Mary

            Eastcott
            wll dtd July 20, 1622; Exeter, England
            bur. December 26, 1622; St. Mary Major, Exeter,
            England
        Elizabeth - bpt. April 19, 1564; Awliscombe,
            Devonshire, England
            m. Thomas Brewer; July 4, 1584; Awliscombe,
            Devonshire, England
            Children
                Mary
                Thomas
        William - bpt. November 5, 1567; Awliscombe,
            Devonshire, England
            bur. January 3, 1567/8
        Edward - bur. May 3, 1598; Honiton, Devonshire,
            England
            Children
                Nodiah - bpt. October 18, 1590
                    bur. 1598
                Henry - m. Sarah; Honiton, Devonshire,
                    England
                    d. by May 21, 1656
                    Children
                        Edward - m. Jane
                            wll dtd February 1, 1675/6;
                          Honiton, Devonshire,
                            England

```
                    Elias           Elizabeth
                    Johane          Rebecca
                    Henry           Samuel
            Elizabeth - d. aft July 20, 1622
```

Peter Maverick (Rev.)
    b.c. 1550
    m. Dorothy Tucke; November 7, 1577; Awliscombe, Devon-
    shire, England
    d. by February 3, 1616/7
    Children
        John (see below)
        Judith (tw) - bpt. June 24, 1580; Awliscombe,
            Devonshire, England
            bur. October 10, 1580; Awliscombe, Devonshire,
            England
        Rebecca (tw) - bpt. June 24, 1580; Awliscombe,
            Devonshire, England
            bur. October 10, 1580; Awliscombe, Devonshire,
            England
        Nathaniel - bpt. June 24, 1583; Awliscombe,
            Devonshire, England
            m. Mary, wid of _____ Langley
            d. November 24, 1630; London, England
        Daniel (tw) - bpt. June 11, 1585; Awliscombe,
            Devonshire, England
            bur. June 12, 1585; Awliscombe, Devonshire,
            England
        Elizabeth (tw) - June 11, 1585; Awliscombe,
            Devonshire, England
            bur. June 13, 1585; Awliscombe, Devonshire,
            England
        Marie - bpt. July 24, 1586; Awliscombe, Devonshire,
            England
            bur. November 21, 1586; Awliscombe, Devonshire,
            England
        Marie - bpt. August 4, 1588; Awliscombe, Devonshire,
            England
            bur. August 21, 1604; Awliscombe, Devonshire,
            England

John Maverick (Rev.)
    bpt. December 28, 1578; Awliscombe, Devonshire, England
    m. Mary (b.c. 1580, d. aft 1666), dau of Robert (d. by
    1608) and Grace (Dowrish) Gye; October 28, 1600; Ilsing-
    ton, Devonshire, England
    d. February 3, 1635/6; Dorchester, Massachusetts
    Children
        Samuel (see below)
        Elias - b.c. 1604, England
            m. Ann / Anna (b.c. 1613, d. September 7,
            1697), dau of Thomas (d. by 1633) and Elizabeth
            Harris; c. 1633; Charlestown, Massachusetts
            d. September 8, 1684
            Children
                John - b. February 3, 1635/6; Massachu-
                setts
                bpt. February 27, 1635/6; Massachu-
                setts
                m. Catherine Skipper; April 9, 1656
                d. by April 27, 1680; Boston,

Massachusetts
Abigail - b. August 10, 1637
    m. Matthew Clark of Winnessemet; June
    4, 1655
Elizabeth - b. June 2, 1639
    m. Lt. John Johnson of Charlestown,
    Massachusetts
    d. March 22, 1673/4; Haverhill,
    Massachusetts
Sarah - b. February 20, 1640/1
    m. Samuel (b. June 5, 1639; Marble
    head, Massachusetts), son of Samuel
    and Elizabeth Walton
    d. June 10, 1714; Reading,
    Massachusetts
Elias - b. March 17, 1643
    m. Margaret Sherwood; December 8,
    1669; Charlestown, Massachusetts
    d. betw. January, 1695/6 and November
    2, 1696
Peter - m. Martha (d. by September 29,
    1681; Boston, Massachusetts), dau of
    Robert Bradford
James - d. by October 31, 1671; Winnisse-
    met, Massachusetts
Mary - m. Aaron Way of Winnissemet,
    Massachusetts
    d. aft November 3, 1696
Ruth - m. Deacon Francis Smith (December
    23, 1658-November 14, 1744; Reading,
    Massachusetts); Reading, Massachu-
    setts
    d. November 27, 1717; Reading,
    Massachusetts
Paul - b. June 10, 1657
    m. Jemima (b. May 29, 1665), dau of
    Lt. John and Mary (Bell) Smith of
    Winnissimet, Massachusetts
    d. aft 1709
Rebecca - b. January 1, 1659/60
    m. George Thomas (d. aft 1696)
    d. aft November 3, 1696
Mary - m. Rev. James Parker of Weymouth,
  Massachusetts; c. 1635
  Children
     John   James   Thomas
     Azricam   Fearnot
Moses - b.c. 1611
  m1 Remember, dau of Isaac and Mary (Norris)
  Allerton of the "Mayflower"; by May 6, 1635
  m2 Eunice, wid of Thomas Roberts
  d. January 28, 1685/6; Marblehead, Massachu
  setts
  Children
    Rebecca - bpt. August 7, 1639
       m. John Hawkes of Lynn, Massachusetts
       d. November 4, 1659; Lynn,
       Massachusetts
    Mary - bpt. February 14, 1640/1
       d. February 20, 1655/6; Boston,
       Massachusetts

d. February 20, 1655/6; Boston,
Massachusetts
Abigail - bpt. January 12, 1644/5
m. Maj. Samuel, son of Samuel Ward of
Hingham and Charlestown, Massachusetts
d. January, 1685/6
Elizabeth - bpt. November or December,
1646
d. young
Samuel - bpt. December 19, 1647
Elizabeth - bpt. September 30, 1649
m1 Nathaniel Grafton (b. 1640; d.
February 11, 1670, Barbadoes) of
Salem, Massachusetts
m2 _____ Skinner
Remember - bpt. September, 1652
m. Edward Woodman (d. by November 29,
1698)
d. by November 29, 1698
Mary - bpt. September 6, 1657
m. Archibald Ferguson of Marblehead,
Massachusetts
d. 1695; Marblehead, Massachusetts
Moses - bpt. March 4, 1659/60; Boston,
Massachusetts
Aaron - bpt. March 20, 1662/3
d. young
Sarah - m. John Norman; November 10, 1683;
Marblehead, Massachusetts
Aaron - b. by July 2622
d. young
Abigail - m. John Manning of Boston, Massachusetts
d. June 25, 1644
Children
John - b. May 25, 1643
Mary - b. June 3, 1644
Antipas - d. July 2, 1678
Children
Abigail - m. Edward Gilman of Exeter, New
Hampshire
Katherine - m. Stephen Paul of Kittery,
Maine

Samuel Maverick
b.c. 1602, England
m. Amias, dau of William Cole of Plymouth, Devonshire,
England and wid of David Thompson (d.c. 1628; Thompson
Island, Boston Harbour, Massachusetts) of Plymouth,
Devonshire, England; aft 1627
d. betw 1670 and May 15, 1676
Children
Nathaniel - wll dtd August 16, 1670
wll pro February 24, 1673/4; Barbadoes
Children
Moses   John   Mary
Capt. Samuel   Nathaniel
Samuel II - m. Rebecca, dau of Rev. John and Mary
(Hutchinson) Wheelwright of Hampton; December
4, 1660
d. March 10, 1663/4; Boston, Massachusetts

                       Hannah
Mary - m1 John, son of Richard and Ann Palsgrave of
       Boston, Massachusetts; February 8, 1655/6
       m2 Francis (d. January, 1694/5), son of
       Humphrey Hooke of Kittery, Maine

     Several Mavericks who may have been related to the family
of this genealogy appeared in early Devon records. For
example, an Edward Maverick had children baptized in 1590 in
Awliscombe and another Edward Maverick in 1643, 1646, 1651 and
1653 in Honiton, Devonshire, England. In Honiton an Edward
Maverick married Joane Darke on December 24, 1642. Also in
Honiton, an Edward Maverick was buried on May 3, 1598 and
another Edward on April 5, 1676. Henry Maverick of Honiton
married Sara in 1614/5 and had five children baptized between
1615 and 1632. All of these Devon Mavericks were possible
relations to the Robert Maverick family. The connection has
just not yet been found.

     The English Origins of the "Mary and John" Passengers
related that Robert of this genealogy was of yeoman stock.
Upon his death in 1573 he was described in parish records as
a "clerk" which normally meant he was a cleric. Since he was
married, he either was of a minor order which did not require
celibacy, or he was ordained after the break with the Catholic
church. His predecessor in the Awliscombe church was installed
on May 11, 1554.

     Although Robert's son Radford (see Appendix VI) studied
at Exeter College, Oxford as early as 1581; supposedly he did
not receive his B.A. until 1599. He was instituted as vicar of
Islington, Devon, on July 1, 1597, received his M.A. in 1603,
and became the minister for the city of Exeter. However,
parish records at Exeter disclosed his ordination as priest on
June 15, 1583. In 1586 he was admitted to the rectory of the
church of Trisham. Radford resigned his position at Islington
in 1621 and was succeeded by Christopher Warren.

     Ordination records of 1597 Exeter, Devonshire, revealed
"Deacon and Priest: John Maverick literatus 29 July." In 1615.
having received his M.A., John was admitted to the rectory of
Beaworthy. He appeared to have died by the time of his brother
Radford's 1622 will.

     Brother Alexander's wife, Alice Crabbe, may have been the
"Alice Mavericke als. Tucke widow" who was buried in Awliscombe on December 16, 1607.

     In his will Radford referred to Peter as his eldest
brother, so Peter was probably born circa 1550. According to
ordination books, Peter was ordained as deacon in a private
chapel at the Bishops Palace in Exeter on January 15, 1573/4
and became a priest on March 16 of that year. He was admitted
to the "Perpetual Vicarage of Aulscombe" on the resignation of
Richard Bacon, clerk, the last incumbent, and was there in
1580. He was succeeded after his death by John Hassard.

     One of the entries in the ordination books referred to
him as "Peter Bull alias Maverick" and another referred to him
as "Peter Maverick alia (sic) Bull." Institution Books at
Exeter for 1580 read "Peter Maverick alias Bull, clerk." While

no explanation for the two names has been found, there are several possibilities. The most reasonable explanation was that as the eldest brother, in reality Peter was a step-brother. Peter may have been the child of his mother's first marriage. But in that case, Robert would not have been the father of Peter.

In 1577 Peter Maverick married Dorothy Tucke, daughter of tenants of the Mayor of Exeter. Perhaps Dorothy was a relation of the "Alice Mavericke als. Tucke widow" referred to above. Peter and Dorothy produced two sets of twins. Both sets died shortly after birth.

According to English Origins of the "Mary & John" Passengers, Peter met a violent death circa 1616. However, no details were given.

His son John was baptized on December 28, 1578 in Awliscombe.John attended Exeter College at Oxford where he received his B.A. on July 8, 1599 and his M.A. on July 7, 1603. John had been already ordained as priest at Exeter, Devon County, on July 29, 1597. Based on her genealogical research reported in the April, 1915 NEHGR, Elizabeth French believed John may have been curate to his uncle Radford who was vicar at Ilsington. John married Mary Gye there on October 28, 1600.

The Maverick family, in particular Radford Maverick, may have been related to the Gye family. In "The Ancestry of Mary Gye, Wife of Rev. John Maverick", John G. Hunt reported that Mary's great-uncle was Nicholas Radford, a noted judge who was murdered circa 1455 and suggested that Radford Maverick might have been named after Nicholas or some other member of the Radford family.

The Gye family (see Appendix VI) owned land in Ilsington where Radford Maverick became rector, and Robert Gye gave a large sum of money to him to raise Gye's daughter Mary. Hunt reported that Radford Maverick gave Mary in marriage to "his german-cousin" John Maverick.

Hunt claimed that in the 16th and 17th centuries that "cousin-german" meant "first cousin". However, in a codicil to his 1622 will, Radford Maverick referred to "Radford my brother John Mauericke's son" as his cousin. So Radford referred to his nephew as "cousin". In addition, the nephew Radford mentioned in the will was a true "cousin-german" to the John Maverick who married Mary Gye.

On August 30, 1615 John Maverick was inducted to the rectory of St. Albans, Beaworthy in North Devon County. He resigned that post on December 4, 1629 and, according to The English Origins of the "Mary & John" Passengers, the family resided near Honiton until their immigration. On March 24, 1629/30 John was chosen a teacher of the puritan church at Plymouth, England.

John, Mary, and their children (Elias, Mary, Moses, Aaron, Abigail, Antipas, and Margaret) emigrated to New England on board the "Mary & John" on March 20, 1629/30 from Plymouth, England. Their son Samuel had already emigrated to New England.

In his "Some Passengers of the 'Mary and John' in 1630," John Hunt related that the early settlers from Dorchester "included two unlike clerics, John Warham, a nonconformist, and John Maverick, a conformist." While many of the group came from Exeter, Maverick "lived forty miles off" at the time. But along with Warham, he became the religious leader of the group.

According to <u>The Founding of Harvard College</u>, the Mavericks were with the group containing John Warham and other West Countrymen who settled Dorchester, Massachusetts. While at Dorchester; along with Warham, Gaylord, and Rockwell; John signed early orders for distribution of land.

There was evidence that John had been intending to remove to Connecticut when he died suddenly at Dorchester on February 3, 1635/6. Winthrop wrote that John was a "man of very humbel spirit, and faith full in furthering the work of the Lord her, both in the church and civil state."

His wife Mary was found to be living with her son Samuel in 1665. Furthermore, Samuel sent his mother's regards in a 1666 letter to Sir William Morrice.

John's son Elias Maverick and his wife resided first in Chelsea and then in Charlestown, Massachusetts, where he joined the church. John's daughter Mary married Rev. James Parker of Weymouth and moved to Portsmouth, New Hampshire and, and before James' death, to Barbadoes. Abigail married John Manning of Boston and removed to Charlestown, Massachusetts. Antipas was a merchant on the Isles of Shoals and then removed to Kittery, Maine and, finally, to Exeter, New Hampshire.

John's son Moses Maverick first married Remember Allerton who emigrated to New England aboard the "Mayflower" in 1620 (see Appendix X). His second wife was Eunice Roberts, a widow. After leaving Dorchester, Moses removed to Salem where he became a freeman on September 3, 1634. The next year he was at Marblehead, Massachusetts and was there for most of the rest of his life. He served on the Grand Jury in 1645 and 1649. In 1645 Moses Maverick and David Carwethan acted as attorneys for William Walton, John Peck, and other Marblehead residents in a trespassing court case against Phillip Alke, Thomas Dyer, and Christopher Rogers. In 1647, Moses sued John Legg and his wife Elizabeth for defamation of character. And then in 1636, he rented Noodles Island from the General Court and was in charge of it while his brother Samuel was in Virginia. But by 1650 he was back purchasing land in Marblehead.

His informal will (see Appendix VI), with no signature or witness, was presented by his second wife Eunice at Ipswich on March 30, 1686. He remembered his wife and four daughters - Elizabeth Skinner, Remember Woodman, Mary Ferguson, and Sarah Rosman. He also referred to Moses Hawks, the child of his deceased daughter Rebecca; and to Samuel Ward, Abigail Hinds, Mary Dollabar, and Martha Ward, the children of his deceased daughter Abigail. His children objected and it was held over until the next court term. The will was administered on July 15, 1684, docket number 1472. The will may not have been accepted, but Eunice was made administratrix of the estate. Edward Woodman, husband of Remember, petitioned the court three times demanding an accounting of Moses' estate. The final settlement of the estate wasn't made until November 29, 1698.

According to The English Origins of the "Mary & John" Passengers, the motivation of John's probable son Samuel for emigrating to the New World was not religious. He was an Anglica who emigrated long before his parents and in his "Briefe Description of New England" he wrote about his observations upon his arrival in 1624. In 1625 he fortified a house at Winnissimet (Chelsea) "with a Pillizado and fflankers and gunnes." Hart, in Commonwealth History of Massachusetts, reported that in 1627, only blacksmith Thomas Waldorf / Wolford at Charlestown, "prelatist" Samuel Maverick at Noodles Island, recluse clergyman William Blackstone at Boston, and the small group at Cape Ann lived between Plymouth Colony and New Hampshire.

So Anglican Samuel Maverick was already established when Winthrop's Fleet arrived in 1630. On June 17, 1630, Winthrop recorded in his journal his first contact with "Mr. Maverick."

The Puritans had arrived too late in the season to plant enough to survive and Endicott's group had little to spare. So Samuel helped keep many of the new settlers from starving during that first winter. Then, when small pox attacked the Indians in 1633, Samuel cared for them.

Massachusetts Bay: The Crucial Decade, 1640-1650 claimed Samuel became a freeman in May, 1631, before church membership became a qualification. However, French claimed he did not become a freeman until October 2, 1632. He was listed in Volume 1, page 74 of Colonial Records, as the lone person to take the oath on October 2, 1632. On May 18, 1631, a John "Mavericke" had taken the oath. Then in April, 1633, claimed Samuel may have received a grant of Noodles Island. However, Hart had reported Samuel was living on Noodles Island as early as 1627.

He married Amias, the daughter of William Cole, a ship-wright from Plymouth; and the widow of David Thompson, an apothecary. Amias had first married Thompson in St. Andrew's Church, Plymouth, Devon County, England. According to Eliza-beth French, Thomas went to Piscataqua in 1623 and to an island in Boston Harbor later known as Thompson Island in 1626. He died there in 1628.

In the 1674 book An Account of Two Voyages to New England, John Josselyn wrote that on July 10, 1638 he "went a shore upon Noodles island to Mr. Samuel Maverick the only hospitable man in all the Countrey, giving entertainment to all Comer grate's." He stayed with Samuel for several days before starting out towards Maine. Then from September 30 into October, 1639, Josselyn was again entertained by Maverick.

In 1632 a Mr. Pynchon (probably William Pynchon) paid Samuel Maverick a month's wages. In April, 1633, the Court of Assistants recognized Samuel's ownership of "Noddles Island upon payment of a quitrent of 'either a fatt weather a fatt hogg or eleven shillings'." On Noodles Island he operated fishing, trade, and farming businesses. Darrett Rutman described the farm as having a "mansion house, millhouse and mill, bakehouse ... outhouses barnes staples." Then in 1634, a committee was set-up to divide Maverick's Noodles Island grant among the people. Each adult male received two acres and each youth one acre. However, Samuel appeared to have stayed on His Noodles Island farm.

In addition to his land on Noodles Island, Samuel had numerous grants of land from Massachusetts to Maine. In 1635 he spent nearly a year in Virginia.

Samuel Maverick was admittedly, an oddity. In addition to helping the natives, he was an early slave holder and was fined heavily for sheltering suspected adulterers who had escaped from prison. In fact, according to Rutman, one of Maverick's three slaves claimed to be "a Queen in her own Countrey."

As a member of the Church of England and a supporter of the King of England, Samuel was not the most popular settler in Massachusetts and was in constant opposition with the government.

In 1647, Massachusetts was no democracy. Samuel, along with a number of other prominent men sent as petition to the General Court protesting the lack of civil liberties. The petition signers were fined for maligning the government, for slandering the church, and, later, for conspiring against Massachusetts Bay Colony.

Samuel returned to England complaining bitterly. While there, he wrote to the King that he had lost all of his civil and religious liberties and warned the King that there were thousands of his subjects in the same situation.

However, in 1664 Samuel Maverick returned to Massachusetts as one of Charles II's four royal commissioners; along with Nicolls, Cartwright, and Carr; to settle affairs in New England and to rid the New Netherlands of the Dutch. They were to make the citizens accept changes in the charters and to place their militia under authority of the crown. The commissioners were sent because the King had heard the Puritan governments had been trampling on the rights of non-Puritans and had not been properly supportive of the crown. The commissioners were to be champions of the English and Indians. By strengthening the rights of the English in New England, it was hoped the commissioners would strengthen the King's support. In Invasion of America, the commissioners' arrival was called "a new era." Although they were "but four persons without any of the paraphernalia of power except the royal seall ... they spoke and acted with the confidence of men who can summon power at need."

The arrival of the commissioners and their mission was to be a surprise. But Maverick couldn't wait. As soon as he arrived in Portsmouth, New Hampshire, a few days before their arrival in Boston, Samuel Maverick dashed off a note to Captain Breedon in Boston. Maverick instructed Breedon to go to the governor and tell him what was in store for the colonists. Maverick had been in the New World before any of them and; simply because he was different; he had been forced to the governor and tell him what was in store for the colonists. Maverick had been in the New World before any of them and; simply because he was different; he had been forced to move, was fined, and was finally imprisoned. Suddenly he was the man in charge and he felt the need to gloat. So by the time the commissioners arrived in Boston, word had spread, and Endicott and his people were ready for them.

Some colonists quibbled, some evaded, and some pretended to be loyal in an attempt to deceive the commissioners. But few cooperated with the commissioners. When Samuel proposed eight changes in civil and religious law, Massachusetts refused to accept any of them. Eventually the commissioners gave up.

Unsuccessful in Massachusetts, Samuel Maverick finally settled in New York after the French had left. He was accorded a house there as a reward for his fidelity to the King.

Nash Family

James Nash (Lt.)
    m. Alice, poss dau of Robert (d.c. 1626) and Alice Burges
    of Stanton Drew, Somerset County, England; by November
    17, 1626; England
    d.c. 1650, prob Weymouth, Massachusetts
    Children
        Jacob (see below)
        John - m2 Rebecca (bpt. February 28, 1642/ 43), dau
            of Lawrence and Mary Smith
            m3 Mary (d. October 8, 1662); Weymouth,
            Massachusetts
            d. aft 1680
            Children
                Mary - b. November 26, 1667; Boston,
                    Massachusetts
                John - b. March 9, 1671/2; Boston,
                    Massachusetts
        Joseph - m. Elizabeth, dau of Captain John and
            Elizabeth (Stream) Holbrook of Weymouth,
            Massachusetts
            d. Boston, Massachusetts
            Children
                Joseph - b. June, 1674; Weymouth,
                    Massachusetts
                Elizabeth - b. Weymouth, Massachusetts
                James - b. Weymouth, Massachusetts
                ? Simeon - b. Weymouth, Massachusetts
        James Jr. - m. Sarah, dau of Moses and Sarah Simmons
            of Duxbury; by 1669; Weymouth, Massachusetts
            Children
                Sarah - b. April 21, 1669; Weymouth,
                    Massachusetts
                  m. William (b. May 30, 1661; Wey
                    mouth, Massachusetts), son of Thomas
                    and Jane (Holbrook) Drake
        Sarah
        Rebecca

Jacob Nash (Lt.)
    b.c. 1640
    m. Abigail (b. July 9, 1647; Weymouth, Massachusetts),
    dau of Dea. Thomas and Agnes Dyer; c. 1666; Weymouth,
    Massachusetts
    d. March 13, 1718/19; Weymouth, Massachusetts
    Children
        Joseph (see below)
        Jacob - b. December 4, 1667; Weymouth, Massachusetts
            d. aft July 15, 1690
        John - b. October 8, 1671; Weymouth, Massachusetts
            Children

Mary	Jacob	Abigail
John	Margaret	Sarah
David	Miriam	Jonathan

        Abigail - b. August 17, 1673; Weymouth, Massachu-
            setts
            m. Richard Ager of Weymouth, Massachusetts
        Mary - b. March 20, 1675; Weymouth, Massachusetts

                    m. Samuel, son of Sgt. John and Deliverance
                    Porter
          James - b. 1678; Weymouth, Massachusetts
                    d. August 27, 1725
          Thomas - b. January 11, 1681/2; Weymouth,
                    Massachusetts
                    d.c. 1724
                    Children
                          Daniel - m. Ruth Wild
          Benjamin (tw) - b. March 24, 1685
                    Children
                          Benjamin   James
                          Rebecca   Gideon
          Alice (tw) - b. March 24, 1685
          Sarah - b. June 7, 1688; Weymouth, Massachusetts
          Experience - b. Weymouth, Massachusetts

Joseph Nash (Lt.)
     b. October 11, 1669; Weymouth, Massachusetts
     m1 Phebe (b. May 7, 1676; Braintree, Massachusetts d.
     April12, 1728; Weymouth, Massachusetts), dau of Alexander
     and Bashua/ Bathsheba; March or May 17, 1699
     m2 Hannah ( ) Sturges; January 18, 1730
     m3 Hannah, wid of Samuel Vinson of Weymouth, Massachu-
     setts; December 4, 1735; Weymouth, Massachusetts
     Children
          Mary   Joseph   Alexander
          Rachel   Katherine   Job
          Moses

     The Nash name was probably a corruption of "Atten-Ash",
which meant "at the ash tree." A number of Nash families were
prominent in the late 1500's through the early 1600's. A
Thomas Nash was an important Elizabethan writer. Born in
November, 1567 to William Nashe, a minister from Lowestoft,
Suffolk; Thomas went to Cambridge before settling in London.
He accused Puritans of being hypocrites and considered many of
them lunatics for proposing the abolishment of universities
because of their "popish" origins.

     Yet another Thomas Nash was important to the Puritan
movement. That Thomas emigrated to Leyden before finally going
to Connecticut.

     James Nash of this genealogy first appeared in the
November 17, 1626 will of his father-in-law Robert Burges.
Robert's son John Burges settled by 1660 in Weymouth, Massa-
chusetts, near his brother-in-law James Nash

     Stanton Drew, England, where James' wife was born, had a
legend concerning the strange stones in the area. According to
the ancient legend, large fiddlers and dancers at a marriage
celebration were persuaded to continue until after midnight
and were turned to stone as punishment.

     A Samuel Nash in Weymouth as early as 1641, may have been
a relative of James. Samuel was a shoemaker from Burrough-
Greene, Cambridgeshire, England.

     James Nash was also a shoemaker in Weymouth and became a
freeman in May, 1645, at the same time as Peter Aspinwall. He

served as representative from Weymouth in 1655, 1662, and 1667. He died in 1680 and his sons John and Jacob were named administrators of his estate.

Palfrey Family

Peter Palfrey
    m1 Edith
    m2 Elizabeth, wid of John Fairchild
    m3 Alice (d. March 21, 1677)
    wll dtd. October 21, 1662
    d. September 15, 1663
    Children
        Jonathan - bpt. December 25, 1636
            Children
                William - m. Constance Windsor
                    Children
                        William - m. Abigail Briscoe
        Remember - bpt. September 16, 1638
            m. Peter Aspinwall; February 12, 1662; Boston,
            Massachusetts
            d. by April 4, 1701
            Children
                (see Aspinwall)
        Mary - b. December 15, 1639
        Hannah - m. Matthew (bpt. March, 1633), son of Capt.
            Edward (bpt.September 16, 1598; Canterbury) and
            Susan (Munnter / Munter) Johnson of Woburn,
                Massachusetts; November 12, 1656
            d.c. August, 1662
        Jehoiadan - d. young
        dau - m. Samuel Pickman
        dau - m. Benjamin Smith

The Palfrey / Palfry / Palfray / Palfree name probably
stemmed from the Old French "palfrei" which meant "a saddle-
horse." A modification of "palfrei" might have been assigned
to anyone associated with saddlehorses. But it usually
referred to a horse docile enough for a gentlewoman. John
Palfreyman in the 1200's may have been a caretaker for such
horses.

There were a number of English Palfreys who may have been
related to Peter of this genealogy. In 1576, a William Palfrey
married Joan Bowditch in Winsham, Somersetshire. Joan was a
relation of William Bowditch who died in Salem, Massachusetts
over a century later. A Jonas Palfrey married Elizabeth Ingram
on January 17, 1625 at Fordinton St. George, Dorsetshire,
England. Most likely Peter Palfrey was the son of William and
Johan Palfrey who married by 1605. Johan was the daughter of
Agnes Hackham of Membury, England. In Agnes' February 26, 1605
will, she mentioned Johan, William, and her grandson Peter
Palfrey.

Wherever he originated, Peter arrived on the "Zouch
Phenix" along with Thomas Gardner, probably from Dorset
County, and John Balch, probably from Somerset County. They
arrived at Cape Ann in 1624. Peter's wife probably did not
accompany him. He may have remained with the Cape Ann group
until Conant led the survivors to Salem.

Peter Palfrey was at Salem, Massachusetts in 1626;
requested to become a freeman on October 19, 1630; and took
the oath on May 18, 1631. He was a representative to the
General Court in 1635. That year the General Court had granted

a parcel of land to John Humphries on the condition that no Salem inhabitant had already claimed it. In November, 1635, Salem residents asserted their rights. In a history of Harvard University are the May 2, 1636 records concerning land being considered as a sight for the proposed university.

"In the reading of an order for division of Marble head neck; A motion was brought in by Cp. Endicott in behalfe of mr. John Humphries for some Land beyond Forest River, moved by spetiall argument one whereof was, Least that should hinder the building of a Colledge which would be manies [mens] losse.

It was agreed upon this motion that six men should be nominated by the towne to view the Lands, and to consider of the premisses, and for that end was named."

mr. Thomas Scrugs   Cp Trask
mr. Roger Conant   mr Townsen Bishop
John Woodbery   Peter Palfrey

Peter supposedly removed to Reading, Massachusetts circa 1639 and he died there in 1663. While there, a Peter Palfrey was listed as a juror or grand juror on records for Salem's Quarter Court in 1644 and 1647.

He did not mention any sons in his will. But since his estate was small, he may have given his sons their bequests before his death. His widow Alice died on March 21, 1677.

A John Palfrey appeared in the Cambridge town records on a fairly regular basis between 1656 when he was granted permission to "fell a tre or two for his trade" and 1689 when he was among those chosen "to confider about the laying out of rocks." While he did not appear to be a member of the Palfrey family of this genealogy, the possibility was not eliminated.

Payne / Paine Family

John Payne
  m. Jane Couchman; probably Frittenden, Kent County,
  England; by 1539
  Children
      Nicholas (see below)

Nicholas Payne
  b.c. 1539; Frittenden, Kent County, England
  m1 Agnes Crofton (bur August 24, 1591; Frittenden, Kent
  County, England); c. 1564
  m2 Joyce (bur. January 18, 1610; Frittenden, Kent County,
  England)
  m3 Mary Bezbeech; July 9, 1611
  bur January 24, 1617; Frittenden, Kent County, England
  Children
      Moses (see below)
      Katherine - bpt. July 1, 1565; Frittenden, Kent
          County, England
      John - bpt. May 15, 1569; Frittenden, Kent County,
          England
      Grace (tw) - bpt. January 9, 1571/2; Frittenden,
          Kent County, England
          bur. January 10, 1571/2; Frittenden, Kent
          County, England
      Jane (tw) - bpt. January 9, 1571/2; Frittenden, Kent
          County, England
          bur. January 12, 1572; Frittenden, Kent County,
          England
      Thomas bpt. March 24, 1576/6; Frittenden, Kent
          County, England
          bur. March 25, 1576/7; Frittenden, Kent County,
          England
      Jane - bpt. September 26, 1574; Frittenden, Kent
          County, England
          m. Thomas Young; September 9, 1597
          d. aft 1617
          Children
              Nicholas   Anne
              John   Jane
      Thomas - bpt. March 24, 1576/7; Frittenden, Kent
          County, England
          bur. March 25, 1576/7; Frittenden, Kent County,
          England
      William (tw) - bpt. June 22, 1578; Frittenden, Kent
          County, England
          bur. August 22, 1606; Frittenden, Kent County,
          England
      Elizabeth (tw) - bpt. June 22, 1578; Frittenden,
          Kent County, England
          bur. July 20, 1578; Frittenden, Kent County,
          England
      Tabitha (tw of Moses) - bpt. April 23, 1581;
          Frittenden, Kent County, England
          m. Nathan Hubert
          Children
              Henry   Sarah
              John   Elizabeth

90

Moses Payne (tw to Tabitha)
    bpt. April 23, 1581; Frittenden, Kent County, England
    m1 Mary (bur. March 6, 1617/8), dau of John Benison;
    November 2, 1615; St. Mildred's, Tenterden, Kent County,
    England
    m2 Elizabeth (bpt. October 26, 1589; Cranbrook, Kent
    County, England), dau of Richard and Margaret (Roberts)
    Sheafe, wid of Timothy Collier; c. 1619
    m3 Judith (d. March 29, 1654; Boston, Massachusetts), dau
    of ____ Pares, wid of Edmund Quincy; betw 1639-1643
    bur. June 21, 1643; Braintree, Massachusetts
    est inv. September 1, 1643
    wll pr. October 30, 1643
    Children
        Moses Jr.(see below)
        John - bpt. November 3, 1616; Tenterden, Kent
            County, England
            d. 1617
        Elizabeth - bpt. July 23, 1620; Tenterden, Kent
            County, England
            m. Lt. Henry Adams (d. February 21, 1676);
            November 17, 1643
            d. February 21, 1676
        Margaret bpt. November 4, 1621; Tenterden, Kent
            County, England
        Stephen - bpt. May 7, 1626; St. Mildred's, Tenter-
            den, Kent County, England
            m. Hannah, dau of Dea. Samuel Bass; November
            15, 1651; Braintree, Massachusetts
            Children
                Stephen - b. March 8, 1652; Braintree,
                    Massachusetts
                    m. Ellen, dau of William Veazier;
                    February 20, 1682
                    Children
                        Stephen   Ellen
                        2 Samuels
                Samuel - b. June 10, 1654; Braintree,
                    Massachusetts
                Hannah - b. January 28, 1655; Braintree,
                    Massachusetts
                Sarah - b. March, 1657; Braintree,
                    Massachusetts
                    m. Roger Billings; January 22, 1678
                Moses - b. March 26, 1660; Braintree,
                    Massachusetts
                John - September 21, 1666; Braintree,
                    Massachusetts
                    m. Deborah, dau of Henry Neal;
                    January 20, 1689
                    Children
                        John   Joseph
                        James   Seth
                        2 Deborahs   Moses
                        Stephen   Benjamin
                Lydia - b. September 20, 1670; Braintree,
                    Massachusetts
                    m. Benjamin Neal; January 20, 1689

Moses Payne, Jr.
    bpt. November 16, 1623; Frittenden, Kent County,

England
m. Elizabeth, dau of Elder William and Margery Colburn;
c. 1645
d. December 15, 1690, Boston, Massachusetts
Children
        Moses III - b. July 16, 1646; Braintree, Massachu-
            setts
            d. February 2, 1647/8; Braintree, Massachusetts
        Elizabeth - b. August 5, 1648; Braintree,
            Massachusetts
            m. John Cleare
            Children
                William
        Sarah - b. January 3 or 30, 1650/1; Braintree,
            Massachusetts
            d. August 10, 1651; Braintree, Massachusetts
        Moses - b. June 24 or 26, 1652
            d. August, 1657
        Mary - b. March 12, 1655/6; Braintree, Massachusetts
            m. _____ Small
        William - b. April 1, 1657; Braintree, Massachusetts
            m. Sarah Sanford
        John - b. October 12, 1659; Braintree, Massachusetts
            d. April 1, 1660; Braintree, Massachusetts
        Sarah - b. May 2, 1662; Braintree, Massachusetts
        Margaret - b. ? December 20, 1664; Braintree,
            Massachusetts
        ? Rebecca - b. ? June 23, 1664; Braintree,
            Massachusetts
            m. Thomas Walker, Jr.

    Originally the Payne / Paine / Pain / Payn names were
given to the most rustic of English countrymen. According to
"Moses Paine of Braintree, Massachusetts and His Ancestry in
England" in the January, 1945, American Genealogist, Mary
Lovering Holman traced the Paine / Payne family back to John
Payne born circa 1420 in Frittenden, Kent county, England and
his wife Agnes Payne (see Appendix VII). However, Holman
reported that in approximately 1930, J. Gardner Bartlett of
Boston had traced the family back even farther. He used, in
addition to other records; the Patent Rolls, 13 Henry VI,
m.32; which read
        "On June 24, 1435, a pardon was granted to William
    Appelby of Bidynden, co. Kent, for not appearing before
    Robert Hull and his fellows, justices of the Kings
    Bench of his late Majesty Henry IV (reigned 1412-1422)
    to answer Richard Payn, late chamberlain of the Bishop
    of St. Davids and Stephen Payn brother of said Payn,
    executors of the will of John Payn, chamberlain of the
    Bishop of St. Davids, touching a plea that he render
    6 (pounds)-8 (shillings)."

    Nicholas Paine / Payne of Frittenden, Kent County,
England, was born circa 1539, the son of John and Jane
(Coucheman) Payne. His children were all baptized in St.
Mary's, Frittenden, England. He left a very long will. To his
son Moses he left all his "messuages lands tenements and
hereditaments." Nicholas set his "hand and seale the daye and
yere first above Written And in the fifteenth yere of the

Raigne of our sou'aigne lord kinge James that nowe is of England and Scotland.

Holman claimed that Nicholas' son Moses arrived in New England on board the "Castle" in 1638 accompanied by his three surviving children - Elizabeth, Moses, and Stephen - and settled in Braintree.

The 17th Century Colonial Ancestors listed Moses Payne as a landowner in Massachusetts. In fact, he must have started out rather well-off because he began purchasing large amounts of land almost as soon as he arrived in the area. In 1642 Peter Bracket and Moses Payne purchased from the Indians a large tract of land near Mendon which they later deeded to the town. By the time he died in 1643, only five years after his arrival in the New World, Moses Sr. had also purchased land in Cambridge, Concord, and Piscataqua.

He was made a freeman on June 2, 1641 and, despite the fact he was over sixty years old, he was commissioned Ensign in the Braintree military company.

According to his will, one-half of his estate went to his son Moses, one-quarter to daughter Elizabeth, and one-quarter to son Stephen. At the time of the inventory of his estate, he owned a house and land at both Concord and Cambridge; and another house, barn, and land at an unnamed location; probably Boston or Braintree. It was interesting to note that a codicil added three days after the will was originally written bequeathed only twenty shillings to his widow Judith to be paid within ten years of his death.

Moses Payne, Jr. had nine or ten children of his own. Savage claimed that Moses Payne Jr. removed to Boston by the April 20, 1671 birth of his daughter named Hannah and the August 23, 1674 birth of Lydia. Holman did not list Hannah and Lydia as daughters of Moses. He would have been 48 years old and have been married 26 years when Hannah was born. Although Moses and his wife were older at the time of Hannah's birth, they still could have been her parents.

He was made a freeman in 1647, and lieutenant and representative in 1666. There was evidence that Moses Payne served as constable in 1673 and died on December 15, 1690.

Porter Family

The name Porter would have stemmed from the Latin "porta" or the Latin verb "porto." A porter frequently transported produce by two-wheel carts for manor lords or occupation of a twentieth century John Porter might have been messenger or package carrier.

The name was also given to men who were gate watchers or guards, doormen or doorkeepers. Members of a Porter family, who were of the lesser gentry of Mickleton, got their name from an ancestral porter who guarded a gates of a fortress. That family traced their lineage back through Robert Porter of Elrington, Warwickshire whose great-great grandfather was William, Sergent-at-arms to Henry VII.

Francis le Porter appeared in the tax rolls of Henry III (1216-1272). During Edward I's reign (1272-1307) Robert and Richard le Porter appeared in tax records. Robert's descendants, Edymion and Sir William Porter, lived in the early 1400's.

Part I
The John Porter Family

John Porter
    b. betw 1590-95; Felsted or Bromfield, Essex County; England
    m1 Margaret
    m2 ? Anna, dau of Robert White
    m3 ? Mary (d. 1683)
    d. 1676, pos Salem, Massachusetts
    Children
        John - b.c. 1618
            bpt. September 9, 1638; Salem, Massachusetts
            m. - never married
            d. September 16, 1684; Salem, Massachusetts
        Samuel - bpt. September 9, 1638; Salem Massachusetts
            m. Hannah Dodge
            d. 1660
            Children
                Samuel - b. 1660
                    m. Joanna (1664-1713), dau of Capt. Aaron Cook
                    d. 1722
                Nathaniel
        Joseph - b. 1638; Hingham, Massachusetts
            m. Anne Hathorne/Hawthorne
            d. 1714; Salem, Massachusetts
            Children
                Joseph - b. 1665
                    d. young
                Ann - b. 1667
                Samuel - b. 1669
                Nathaniel - b. 1671
                    d. 1758
                Mary - b. 1672
                William - b. 1674
                    d. 1732
                Eliazer - b. 1676
                    d. young

                    Abigail - b. 1676
                    Hepzibab - b. 1678
                        Children
                            Hepzibab II - m. Sarah Wright;
                                August 25, 1719
                                Children
                                    Hepzibab III - b.
                                        September   11,
                                        1720; Hartford,
                                        Connecticut
                                    Sarah - b. March 7,
                                        1724; Hartford,
                                        Connecticut
                    Joseph - b. 1681
                    Ruth - b. 1682
                    Mehitable - b. 1682
        Benjamin - bpt. November, 1639; Salem, Massachusetts
            m. never married
            d. 1723
        Israel - bpt. February 12, 1643/44
            m. Elizabeth Hathorne/Hawthorne (July 5, 1649-
            1706); November 20, 1672
            d. November, 1706
            Children
                    Elizabeth - b. 1673
                        m. Joseph Putnam
                    Sarah - b. 1675
                        m. Abel (b. 1673), son of Samuel and
                        Mary (White) Gardner
                    John - b. 1677
                        d. 1715
                    Ginger - b. 1679
                    Israel - b. 1683
                    Anne - b. 1687
                    William - b. February 12, 1689; Salem,
                        Massachusetts
                        m. Edith Herrick; February 1, 1708/09
                        Children
                            Israel - bpt. August 20, 1710
                                m. Abigail Balch of
                                Beverly; October 16, 1741;
                                Beverly, Massachusetts
                    Benjamin - b. May 17, 1693
                        m. Hannah Endicott (1691-aft January,
                        1727; April 3, 1712
                        d. 1726
                        Children
                            Benjamin - b. 1717
        Mary - bpt. August 12, 1645; Hingham, Massachusetts
            m. Thomas Gardner; April 21, 1669
            bur. 1695
        Jonathan - b. 1648
            d. young
        Sarah - b. June 3, 1649; Salem, Massachusetts
            m. Daniel Andrews
            Children
                    Daniel - b. 1677
                        d. young
                    Thomas - b, 1678
                        d. 1702
                    Samuel - b. 1683

                              95

```
                    d. 1702
              Daniel - bpt. 1686
              Israel - b. 1689
              Sarah
              Mehitable
```

John Porter emigrated from Bromfield or Felsted, Essex
County, England. Bromfield was one of many English towns like
Bromley, Brompton, and West Bromwich whose name derived from
the trees in the area.

According to early Essex County, England records, in 1682
King William I and his wife Matilda gave several manors,
including the one named "Feldestede" to the Abbey of Holy
Trinity at Caen. Originally Felsted may have been given to
Matilda by William.

A John Porter was named in the January 15, 1615 Bromfield, Essex County will of Thomas Brett. He bequeathed to his
"cousin John Porter (his) tenement called Philles, with the
land &c. in Little Baddowe, Essex, which said tenement is
mortgaged to Mr. Thomas Emerye of the same town." Brett named
John Porter and Nathan Lyther as executors. The John who
inherited the "Philles" could have been the John Porter of
this genealogy.

Brett also made bequests to William "Pinchon", his
nephew. A William Pinchon / Pynchon of Springfield, Essex
emigrated to New England with the Winthrop Fleet and founded
first Roxbury and then Springfield, Massachusetts. According
to Essex County, England wills, both William Pynchons had
sisters named Frances, Ann, Jane, Alice, and Susan / Suzanne.
The coincidences were too many. The two William Pynchons were
the same man.

So John Porter of Salem was related, although perhaps
distantly, to William Pynchon who arrived in 1630 and founded
Roxbury. Perhaps they emigrated at about the same time.

John did emigrate to Hingham, but not in 1635 as mentioned in the Porter family genealogy in the December 1937,
National Genealogical Society Quarterly. John, his wife
Margaret, and four children emigrated in 1630 with the
Winthrop Fleet to Salem.   Several other sources,
including Bank's The Winthrop Fleet of 1630, have placed John
as a freeman in Hingham as early as November 5, 1633. However,
a John Porter of Roxbury has frequently been confused with the
John Porter of Hingham.

Depending upon the source, John had up to three wives. He
may have divorced wife Margaret in 1665. Another wife may have
been Anna, the daughter of Robert White. John may have married
her circa 1620. And the third possible wife was Mary who he
possibly married in Hingham in 1636.

Although John Porter purchased 300 acres in Salem in 1643
and moved there from Hingham, he did not sell the house and
land in Hingham until January 15, 1648. His wife joined the
First Church of Salem in 1644. John was listed on Salem's
Grand Jury in 1647. Later John or his son served as deputy of

the General Court from there. He was a substantial landholder when he died at Salem in 1676. John owned 2000 acres.

Of John's eight children, three - John Jr., Benjamin, and Jonathan - never married. Like his brother Samuel, John, Jr. was a mariner. According to J.A. Doyle, John, Jr. "squandered his father's capital in thriftless and vagabond courses in the West Indies." Later he was thrown into an English debtor's prison, but was bailed out by his father. But he did not appear grateful. One researcher reported that John Porter,Jr. was later jailed in Salem, Massachusetts, for abusing his parents. Doyle wrote that his "language to his pareents might have exposed him to the punishment of death, but that they forbore to press the case." Instead he was whipped and fined.

Israel's daughter Anne may have been the "Anna Porter of Salem" whose intentions to marry William Elliot, Jr. of Beverly were published on October 2, 1708.

Part II
Richard Porter Family

Richard Porter
    b.c. 1600; prob Dorsetshire, England
    wll dtd. December 25, 1688
    est inv. March 6, 1688/89; Weymouth, Massachusetts
    Children
        John (see below)
        Ruth - b. October 3, 1639; Weymouth, Massachusetts
            m. Thomas Bayley, Jr.; September 19, 1660;
            Weymouth, Massachusetts
            Children
                Samuel
        Thomas - b.c. 1650; Weymouth, Massachusetts
            m. Sarah, sis of John Vining of Weymouth;
            Massachusetts; c. 1669
            est inv December 17, 1672
            Children
                Thomas - b. February 3, 1672/73
        Mary - m. John Bicknell of Weymouth, Massachusetts;
            December 2, 1658

John Porter (Sgt.)
    b. Weymouth, Massachusetts
    m. Deliverance (d. September 30, 1720; Weymouth,
    Massachusetts), dau of Dr. Nicholas and Martha (Shaw)
    Byram; april 9, 1660
    d. August 25, 1717
    wll dtd. February 8, 1715/16
    Children
        Mary - b. October 22, 1662; Weymouth, Massachusetts
            m. William Pettee of Weymouth, Massachusetts
        Susannah - b. June 2, 1665; Weymouth, Massachusetts
            m. Matthew Pratt of Weymouth, Massachusetts
        John (Sgt) - b. July 2, 1667; Weymouth, Massachu-
            setts
            m1 Mary or Mercy (d. March 8, 1708/9) c. 1693
            m2 Margaret (d. June 11, 1734) dau of Dea.
            William and Sarah (Dingley) Ford; June 16,
            1709; Marshfield
            Children
                2 Mercy   Richard
                2 John   Deliverance
                Joseph   Peter
        Samuel - b. Weymouth, Massachusetts
            m. Mary, dau of Jacob and Abigail Nash
        Nicholas - b. April 11, 1672; Weymouth, Massachu
            setts
        Ruth - b. September 18, 1676; Weymouth, Massachu-
            setts
            m. Nathaniel Willes
        Thomas - b. Weymouth, Massachusetts
            m. Susannah Pratt
        Ebenezer - b. Weymouth, Massachusetts
            m. Sarah Humphrey; December 3, 1707
        Sarah - b. Weymouth, Massachusetts
            m. John Dingley

    Since Richard Porter arrived with Rev. Joseph Hull's
Company, he may have emigrated from Somersetshire, England.

However, when he left England on March 20, 1635; the register
of passengers on board the "Waimouth" ("Weymouth") listed
Richard as being from Dorsetshire and no wife was listed as
accompanying him. According to Chamberlain's Genealogies of
the Early Families of Weymouth, his family was one of twenty-
one families that were founding settlers of Wessaguscus. In
1652 he was granted a large lot and in 1663 Richard received
another 40 acres land.

In 1653 he became a freeman. For some reason, the May 23,
1653 and the May 23, 1655 lists of freemen were virtually the
same. So it could have been either date. However, the 1653
date was the more likely.

Richard gave his grandson Thomas, Jr.; only son of
Thomas, Sr.; his home, barn, orchard, adjoining land, and
other land at age 21. If Thomas, Jr. died before reaching age
21, Richard's granddaughter Ruth, and his son John inherited.
The rest of Richard's estate went to John Porter whose will
was written on February 8, 1715. He described himself in it as
"being aged."

                              Preston Family

William Preston
     b.c. 1591; Giggleswick, York County, England
     m. Mary (b.c. 1601)
     Children
          Edward (see below)
          William - bpt. October 5, 1614
               bur. June 4, 1633; Chesham
          John - b.c. 1617
               bur. November 18, 1623; Chesham
          Daniel - bpt. March 3, 1621; Chesham
               m. Mary
               d. November 10, 1707; Dorchester, Massachusetts
          Elizabeth - bpt. January 18, 1623
               m. Joseph Alsop
               d. August 29, 1693
          Sarah - bpt. July 18, 1626
               m. William Meeker
          Mary - bpt. December 13, 1629
               m. Peter Mallory
          John - bpt. March 4, 1632
          Jehiel - bpt. June 14, 1640
               m1 Sarah (b. 1641), dau of Thomas and _____
               (Seabrook) Fairchild
               m2 Temperance (b. 1662), dau of Isaac and
               Margery Nicholls
               d. 1684
               Children
                    Samuel - b. July 1, 1663
                    Joseph - b. July 10, 1666
                         d. young
                    Mary - m. Daniel Jackson
                         d. August, 1734
          Heckaliah - bpt. April 9, 1643
               m. dau of Thomas and ____ (Seabrook)
               Fairchild
               d. November 20, 1692
          Eliasaph - bpt. April 9, 1643
               m1 Mary
               m2 Elizabeth (b. 1652), dau of John and Mary
               Beach; c. 1675
               m3 Martha, dau of William and Alice (Pritchard)
               Bradley, wid of Samuel Munson
               d. 1707

Edward Preston
     bpt. November 14, 1619
     m. Margaret Hurst
     d. December 28, 1690
     Children
          William - b. November, 1651; Boston, Massachusetts
          Mary - b. January 1, 1653; Boston, Massachusetts
          Hannah - b. September 14, 1653
          Elizabeth - b. September 29, 1655
               m1 John (April 27, 1640-October 26, 1696), son
               of John and Rachel Levins; november 23, 1674
               m2 Peter, son of Thomas Aspinwall; March 24,
               1699
               Children
                    Benjamin - b. April 15, 1692; Roxbury,

                                  100

                    Massachusetts
          Joseph - b. November 15, 1683; Roxbury,
                    Massachusetts
          James - b. October 14, 1679;
          Peter - November 15, 1677; Stratford,
                    Massachusetts
          Rachel - b. December 15, 1685; Roxbury,
                    Massachusetts
     Abigail - b. January, 1664
          m. Joseph Thomas; March 21, 1687/88
     Samuel - b. June, 1668
          m. Abigail
          d.c. 1693

     The name Preston may have stemmed from "priest". More
likely though, Preston was one of the thousands of English
surnames derived from villages or obscure towns.

     A John Preston, son of Alice and Thomas Preston of Upper
Heyford, Northamptonshire, attended Kings College, and later
Queens College, Cambridge. As a Puritan Leader, Preston became
an important teacher and preacher at Cambridge before even-
tually being appointed to the household of Prince Charles mof
England.

     However, the William Preston family of this genealogy
originated in York, England. Circa William's birth, another
Preston was becoming notorious in York. Jennet Preston of
Gisburn, Craven, Yorkshire, England was charged with witchcraft and tried at York on July 27, 1612. Jennet was a poor
woman who was among the group known as the Samlesbury or
Lancashire Witches. Since she was the only one of the accused
who was from Yorkshire rather than Lancashire, Jennet was
tried separately.

     By early 1612 Jennet Preston had been acquitted of the
murder of a child. But within a week she was seen at a meeting
at another accused witch's home. Then it was suspected that
Jennet's witchcraft had been aimed toward the Lister family
who resided about half a mile from Gisburn. Finally, years
after the event, she was accused of the murder of Thomas
Lister who had died February 8, 1607. After his death, various
goods and cattle of the Lister's had disappeared.

     An accused witch testified against her. But the primary
evidence against her was that after Lister's death
          "Iennet Preston, the Prisoner at the Barre, being
          brought to M. Lister, after hee was dead & layd out
          to be wound vp in his winding-sheet, the said Iennet
          Preston, coming to touch the dead corpes, (it) bled
          fresh bloud presently, in the presence of all that
          were there present."
Jennet was found guilty and hanged on July 29, 1612, still
proclaiming her innocence.

     There was no proof that Jennet was related to the William
Preston of Giggleswick who emigrated to the New World.
However, the William Preston who witnessed the September 4,
1550 (proven December 22, 1550) will of Peter Currer of
Giggleswick, Yorkshire; was probably a relative of, possibly
even the father or grandfather of, the emigrant William.

According to _Planters of the Commonwealth_, William Preston, his 34 year old wife Mary, and four of their children - Elizabeth age 11, Sarah age 8, Mary age 6, and John age 3 - emigrated from Yorkshire to New England. They left aboard the "Truelove" in September and arrived in Boston in November, 1635.

For some reason their son Edward had gone ahead to the New World. In a large Rolls Office volume in London was the notation for "16 Marcij 1634. Theis vnder written names are to be transported to new England imbargued in ye 'Christian' ... the men have taken ye oath Allegeance & Supremacie." Edward Preston was listed as age 13.

Edward Preston's daughter Elizabeth married John Levins/ Leavens on November 23, 1674 as his second wife. They moved to Stratford; then to Roxbury, Massachusetts; and finally to Woodstock, Connecticut. Two years after John's death Elizabeth married Peter Aspinwall. Peter's March 24, 1689/90 marriage to widow Elizabeth (Preston) Leavens was not a typical marriage. _Genealogies of Connecticut Families from NEHGR_ referred to Peter as "a bachelor some years younger then herself (Elizabeth)." She was nine years older than Peter, Jr. The Aspinwall records did

> "not speak kindly of this alliance, but she seems
> to have been a faithful wife and he was a man of
> versatile power and eminent usefulness."

Dr. William Aspinwall wrote that "she always kept him low," and was "not so meek as her husband," and was even fined for libel during her first marriage.

Russell Family

In old records, the Russell name was occasionally written as Rushall. According to "British Russell: The Famous and Infamous" in the Russell Register, variations of the Old French word "Rous" meaning "red" was used in English, French, Irish, and Scottish nicknames. A person with red hair or a red face might have been called Ross, Rowse, Ruse, or Russ. The "et" and "el" endings, meaning "little" or "son of," were added to make Russet and Russel.

Other Russells originated in France. In Normandy, the early Barony of Briquebec was a castle named Le Rozel. Hugh du Rozel was born in the area circa 1021. Members of the family crossed to England shortly after William the Conquerer. Robert de Russell who was in the Battle of Lincoln in 1141 may have been from that family. Another French form of the name was Rossell.

In England there was a Ralph Russel in Huntingtonshire and a Robert Russe in Somersetshire in the 1100's. In Scotland a Walter Russell was in Paisley as early as 1165. In Ireland, Russells were in Down-Patrick in 1200.

By the 1790 U.S. census there were 202 families in Massachusetts with the surname Russell. The 1120 persons named Russell made up .3% of the Massachusetts population.

Part I
John Russell Family

John Russell
    m1 Elizabeth (d. December 16, 1644)
    m2 Elizabeth Baker (d. January 17, 1689); May 13, 1645
    d. June 1, 1676
    bur. Kings Chapel Burying Ground, Boston, Massachusetts
    Children
        John (see below)
        Mary - m. Timothy Brooks; December 21, 1659

John II Russell (Rev.)
    b.c. 1640
    m. Sarah (d. April 25, 1696); dau of John and Joan
    Champney of Cambridge, Massachusetts; October 31, 1661
    d. December 21 or 24, 1680; Boston, Massachusetts
    bur. Kings Chapel Burying Ground; Boston, Massachusetts
    Children
        John III - b. August 1, 1662
            m. Elizabeth Palmer (1662-1723); December 21,
            1682
            d. July 26, 1717; Woburn, Massachusetts
            Children
                Ruth - b. 1699
                    eng. Samuel Eaton (1702-1728);
                    November 15, 1722
                Jonathan - b. November 7, 1700
                    m. Mary Cooledge
                Stephen   Elizabeth
                Samuel   Sarah
                John IV   Mary
                Thomas   Joseph

103

Joseph - b. January 15, 1663/64; Woburn, Massachu-
        setts
        m. Mary
        d. March 13, 1713/14
        Children
                Benjamin
Samuel - b. February 3, 1667; Woburn, Massachusetts
        d. by May 7, 1708
Sarah - b. February 10, 1670/71; Woburn, Massachu-
        setts
Elizabeth - b. February 19, 1672/73; Woburn,
        Massachusetts
        m. Pierce/Peirce
        d. June 20, 1708; Woburn, Massachusetts
Jonathan - b. August 6, 1675; Woburn, Massachusetts
        d. June 20, 1708; Woburn, Massachusetts
Thomas - b. January 5, 1677/78; Woburn, Massachu-
        setts
Ruth

The first John Russell of this genealogy was possibly a
proprietor in Cambridge, Massachusetts in 1635. His parentage
and English home have remained undetected. If he was the John
of Cambridge, he became a freeman on March 3, 1635/36 and
served as the clerk of writs. In 1639, John "Ruffe" was
appointed to return all found goods to the original owner.
John was to receive from the owners of the lost goods, one
pence for every shillings worth of goods returned. He was also
given permission that year to help move a herd of cattle
across the river. He was chosen as Selectman in 1642 and 1643;
fenceviewer in 1638 and 1649; surveyor in 1641, 1645, and
1646; and constable in 1648. He was appointed to layout a
highway in 1649 and to report citizens lacking a ladder in
1650.

According to Pope, the family removed to Woburn and John
was a proprietor there in 1640. However, records showed John
Russell holding office and receiving land grants in Cambridge
up until 1652, when he owned eighty acres. Since so many
Russells lived in the Bay area at the time, they were frequently confused with each other.

Graves, in her genealogy, referred to John Russell as
"Baptist Elder." Records quoted by Pope referred to him as
"the Anabaptist."

He died in 1676 and was buried in Kings Chapel Burying
Ground in Boston. John I made bequests to his wife Elizabeth,
son John II, and daughter Mary Brooks. His widow died on
January 17, 1689/90. Their grandson John III settled the
estate.

His son, Rev. John Russell, became pastor of First
Baptist Church of Boston on July 28, 1679. John II died in
Boston on December 21, 1680 and, according to Murray, he also
was buried in the Kings Chapel Burying Ground.

Unknown Russell
    Richard (see below)
    dau - m.. _____ Corbet of Bristol, England
    son - m. Sarah of Bristol, England

Richard Russell
    b.c. 1611, pos Hereford
    m1 Maud (d. 1652), dau of William and Mary Pitt of
    Bristol, England
    m2 Mary (Sharp) (Wade) (Chester) Davison (d. 1688); c.
    1655
    d. May 14, 1676
    bur. May 16, 1676
    Children
        James (see below)
        Katherine - b.c. 1633
            m. William Roswell, 1654
        Elizabeth - b. October 12, 1644; Charlestown,
            Massachusetts
            m. Nathaniel Graves
        Daniel (Rev.) - b. October 4, 1642 or 1646;
            Charlestown, Massachusetts
            m1 Margaret Springer; January 20, 1675; New
            London, Connecticut
            eng. Mehitable Willis/Wyllys; January 27, 1679
            wll dtd. - December 26, 1678
            d. January 4, 1678/79; Charlestown, Massachu
            setts
            Children
                Mabel - b. October 6, 1677; New London,
                    Connecticut
        ? Thomas (Capt.) - b.c. 1646
            m. Prudence Chester, step-daughter of husband's
            father
            d. October 20, 1676; Charlestown, Massachusetts

James Russell
    b. October 1, 1640; Charlestown, Massachusetts
    bpt. May 30, 1641
    m1 ? Mabel Haynes; August 28, 1644; Hartford, Connecticut
    m2 Mary "Holioke"; February 5, 1676/77
    m3 Mary Wolcott; January, 1679
    m4 Abigail Curwin Hathorne; August 28, 1684
    d. April 28, 1709; Charlestown; Massachusetts
    Children
        Mabel - b. May 1, 1665
        Richard - b. January 12, 1666/67
        James - b. January 7, 1667/68
        Mabel - b. January 21, 1669
            m. Capt. Thomas Jenner
        Richard - b. March 16, 1672
        John - b. June 29, 1673
        Maud - b. April 22, 1676
            m. Daniel Lawrence
        Eleazer - b. January, 1678
        Mary - b. June 22, 1680
            m. Capt. John Miller
        Daniel - b. November 30, 1685

m1 Rebecca Chambers; January 9, 1710/11
m2 Faith Savage, c. 1736
d. December 6, 1763; Charlestown, Massachusetts
Children

Rebecca (2)	Charles	James
Richard	Daniel	George
Abigail		

In his genealogy, George Russell suggested that Richard Russell may have been a member of the Paul Russell family of Hereford, England. Richard was an apprentice in Bristol, England in 1628, and Pope called him a "woolen-draper".

Richard and his first wife Maud arrived in Charlestown in 1640. Circa 1655, he married Mary Sharp Wade Chester Davison, the widow of Leonard Chester among others. On July 11, 1667 her daughter Prudence was recorded to have loaned mortgage money to B. Barnard.

Richard Russell was admitted to the church in Charlestown and became a freeman on June 2, 1641. According to George Russell's genealogy, Richard was a "prominent merchant, agent, official, representative, councillor, speaker, treasurer, assistant ... with extensive business dealing in America." In addition to his home, Richard's holdings included a warehouse, shop, slaves, cattle, and vessels. Pope related that Richard owned property "at Pemaquid and other points along the coast."

In his will, Richard named his wife Mary, his sons James and Daniel, his daughters Katherine Roswell and Elizabeth Graves, two of his sister, and his sister-in-law Mary (Pitt) Newell. His son James was named executor. He made bequests to Harvard College, the church, the town, several minister, and servants. Richard Russell's estate was valued at 3505 pounds.

Interestingly Frederick Weis recorded that Richard's son Daniel edited an almanac in 1671. Daniel Russell received his B.A. and M.A. from Harvard College and was a Fellow at Harvard in 1676. He preached at New London, Connecticut, but settled in Charlestown, Massachusetts between 1676-1678.

A 1668 deed showed that Richard's son James Russell owned a shop joined on the east to Dr. Thomas Starr's home in Charlestown, Massachusetts. When Starr died, his heirs sold the homestead to James for 26 pounds.

According to Commonwealth History of Massachusetts, James was joint owner of some Charlestown land, but his title had not been confirmed by payment of a quit rent. So the Governor gave it to Colonel Lydgate, a council member. When James protested, a Writ of Intrusion was issued to eject him from a farm of which he was sole owner. James petitioned to stop the prosecution.

In another problem. James was told by a surveyor that he would have to pay the Governor if he wanted to keep his island in Cosco Bay. Otherwise, he was warned, the property would go to Mr. Usher, the treasurer.

A Capt. Thomas Russell who died in Charlestown on October 20, 1676 at the age 30 as another possible son of Richard's.

Thomas Russell married Prudence Chester, daughter of Richard's second wife. Thomas was a merchant and constable.

Part III
William Russell Family

William Russell
    b. Abbotts Langley, England
    m. Martha Davyes (d. 1694); May, 1636; St. Albans,
    Herefordshire, England
    wll dtd. February 2, 1661/2
    d. February 14, 1661/2
    Children
        Joseph b.c. 1637, England
            m. Mary Belcher of Ipswich; Cambridge,
            Massachusetts
            d. 1694; Cambridge, Massachusetts
        Benjamin - b.c. 1643
            m. Rebecca; c. 1665; prob Cambridge,
            Massachusetts
            d. aft 1680
            Children
                William - b. June 12, 1667; Cambridge,
                    Massachusetts
                    m. Hannah Adams (b. July 25, 1670;
                    Concord, Massachusetts); April 24,
                    1688
                    Children
                        Tabitha
        John - b. September 11, 1645
            m. by 1669; Elizabeth Fiske
            d. March 6, 1733; Cambridge Farms (Lexington),
            Massachusetts
        Martha - m. Joseph Gleason of Watertown and Sudbury,
            Massachusetts; by 1671
        Philip - b.c. 1650
            m1 Joanna Cuttler; June 19, 1680; Cambridge,
            Massachusetts
            m2 Sarah Brooks; October 18, 1705; Cambridge,
            Massachusetts
            d. February 7, 1730/1; Lexington, Massachusetts
        Thomas - d. August 21, 1653; Cambridge, Massachu
            setts
        William, Jr. - b. April 28, 1655
            m. Abigail Winship; March 18, 1682/3; Cam-
            bridge, Massachusetts
            d. May 17, 1744; Menotomy (Arlington),
            Massachusetts
        Jason - b. November 14, 1658
            m. Mary Hubbard; May 27, 1684; Cambridge,
            Massachusetts
            d. aft 1704
        Joyce - b. March 31, 1660
            m. Edmund Rice of Sudbury, Massachusetts;
            October 13, 1680; Cambridge, Massachusetts

    The William Russell of this genealogy was probably the
William Russell, a carpenter from Abbotts Langley, who married
Martha "Davyes" at St. Stephen's Church, St. Albans, Hertford-
shire, England on May 26, 1636.

    William and Martha Russell emigrated shortly after their
marriage, settling in Cambridge, Massachusetts. While there,
wife Martha and son Joseph joined the First Church of Cam-

bridge and, in 1643, William Russell was a carpenter, proprietor, and landowner.

A John Russell appeared in Cambridge records from the late 1630's through 1652, who may have been related to William (see John Russell Family genealogy). However, no connection was found.

William appeared in a number of early Cambridge records. In 1648 William Russell, Sr. was given permission to "fell fome" timber for a barn; in 1649 for fencing; and then in 1650, 1656, and 1657 for repairing fencing and other buildings. In 1652, William Russell had lot number 86 and owned 60 acres. In 1656 and 1657, William was appointed a fence viewer.

The next year he was fined 2 shillings 6 pence for not "ringing his swine," but did not have to pay the fine since he had lost land when the town built a highway. However, later that year he was fined 1 shilling for the same offence.

William's will was signed February 2, 1661/2 in the Menotomy section of Charlestown, Massachusetts, He died twelve days later, leaving his wife as executrix of his estate. When William died, his children ranged from 24 years down to 1 year of age. In 1661 and 1665, "widdow Russell" was given permission to cut timber for fencing and building. In 1662, her name was turned in for not "yoaking and ringing" her swine.

Martha Russell married Humphrey Bradshaw after William's death. In December 13, 1681 Cambridge records, Humphrey and Martha Bradshaw signified "by a note vnder theare hand that they ded give to theare fones (sons) William and Jafon Rufsell the priuilgd that belong to theare houfe." Martha married Thomas Hall third.

William and Martha's son Joseph was allowed to cut timber on a fairly regular basis from 1663 through 1683, according to Cambridbe records. He held a number of offices, including constable, viewer of fences, selectman, surveyor, tethingman, and driver of the Common fields. In 1680 Joseph Russell was a member of the committee to hire a shepard to care for the sheep. And in 1665 and 1668 Joseph was selected to "execute the orders concrning Swine on the north fide the river."

His brother Benjamin Russell was living on a farm near Concord, Massachusetts on January 10, 1680/81, while brother John continued to live in Cambridge. John appeared in Cambridge town records as early as 1678, afterwhich he served as constable, surveyor for highwas in the "farms" (outside of town) area, viewer of fences, and tethingman for the "farms" area.

William and Martha's son Phillip was a member of a committee building a gallary onto the Cambridge meeting house in July, 1673. He was chosen constable for the "farms" area in November, 1686, tithingman for "ye ffarmes" in 1699. He continued to appear in Cambridge records until March 31, 1702, when a notation in the records read "Phillip Rufsel & Wm Munroe Jur. should Joine with Woburn Perambulators."

Another of William and Martha's son was probably the William Russell who was credited with military service under Capt. Richard Beeres. On November 20, 1675, he was paid 4 pounds 16 shillings for a portion of that service. He also served as surveyor and viewer of fences, surveyor for the highways, and selectman for Cambridge. In 1702, "William Rufsel, Edmund Goffe, and Abraham Watson" were appointed to provide a shepard for a "flock of Sheep for the Ensuing year, and to give sd: Shepard Directions concerning ye: Management of sd: flock ..."

Jason and William Russell, Jr. first appeared together in records when they were assigned to lengthen the south gallary of the meeting house. Then in December, 1681 they were given permission to cut enough timber to build a 26-foot long house with a leanto. The two brothers united at a meeting of proprietors "of the rocks" at Cambridge to consider laying out the area. Jason and William voted against it, but it still passed.

Jason Russell held a number of offices through the years. He was a fence viewer in 1690, 1691, and 1697; constable in 1692 and 1693; highway for "notomy" surveyor in 1690; tything-man for "Minottomie in 1696, 1698, and 1701; perambulator of Charlestown in 1702; driver of "Minottomy" fields in 1686 and 1694; and a shepard for the sheep on the commons in 1702. In 1697 and 1700, Jason was on the committee to decide the minister's rate of pay. Then in December, 1700, he was appointed to survey undivided parcels of land on the common.

All of Jason Russell's appearances in the town records were not concerning offices Jason held. In January, 1692, Cambridge gave Menotomy 1/4 acre of land on the common near Jason Russell's house for a schoolhouse. Then, Jason got into a conflict with a "Mr. Andrews" over a property line. And finally, in 1704, the town paid Jason Russell to keep William Chamberlain's child.

David Russell who was assigned in March, 1702 to "Inspect ye: yoaking & Ringing of Swine and Walter Russell who appeared in Cambridge records a number of times between 1697 and 1702 may also have been descendents of William and Martha Russell, Sr.

                              Sharp Family

Unknown Sharp
     Children
          Robert (see below)
          Alice - m. Peter Aspinwall
               d. 1654
               Children (see Aspinwall)

Robert   Sharp I
     b.c. 1615; poss Islington, England
     m. Abigail (d. by 1676)
     d. July, 1654
     Children
          John (see below)
          Abigail - b.c. 1639
          Mary - bpt. December 5, 1652; pos Roxbury,
               Massachusetts

John Sharp (Lt.)
     b.c. 1643
     m. by 1665
     d. April 18. 1676; Sudbury, Massachusetts
     Children
          Robert II (see below)
          Martha - bpt. 1667
               m. Joseph, son of Joseph and grandson of Thomas
               Buckminister of Muddy River, Massachusetts
               Children
                    Joseph
                         Children
                              William
          John - bpt. 1669; Roxbury, Massachusetts
          Elizabeth - bpt. August 20, 1671; Roxbury,
               Massachusetts
               m. Samuel Craft; December 25, 1693; Roxbury,
               Massachusetts
          William - b.c. 1674; Roxbury, Massachusetts
               m. Abigail (b.c. 1679; d. February 14, 1753)
               r. 1704; Pomfret, Connecticut
               d. November 19, 1751; Pomfret, Connecticut
               bur. Wappaquians Burial Ground, Pomfret,
               Connecticut

Robert Sharp II
     bpt. 1666; Roxbury, Massachusetts
     m. Sarah, dau of Steven Williams of Roxbury, Massachu-
     setts
     d. 1690, Canada
     Children
          Robert III (Capt.) - b.c. 1688
               m. Susannah
               d. 1765
               Children
                    Robert IV - m. Sarah Payson of Roxbury,
                         Massachusetts
                         Children
                              Robert   Jacobs
                              Stephen
                    4 daughters
          Sarah - b. August 12, 1689; Roxbury, Massachusetts

                                 111

A number of Sharps could have been related to Robert
Sharp and his sister Alice. For instance, they might have been
descendants of the Robert Sharpe who married Elizabeth Breedon
in "Bramcote", Nottinghamshire, England, on May 1, 1586. And
there was a Thomas Sharpe who attended an August 26, 1629
conference at Cambridge, England; with John Winthrop, William
Pynchon, and William Colborne to plan their emigration and the
establishment of a plantation in New England. He was probably
the same Thomas Sharpe who with his wife, son, and daughter
emigrated from London to the Massachusetts Bay Company with
Winthrop. According to <u>Builders of the Bay Colony</u>, Thomas
Sharp was a member of the first political assembly. Winthrop,
in his journal, noted on March 16, 1631 that at

"about noon the chimney of Mr. Sharp's house in Boston
took fire, (the splinters being not clayed at the top,)
and taking the thatch burnt it down, and the wind being
N.W., drove the fire to Mr. Colburn's house, being ____
rods off, and burnt that down also, yet they saved most
of their goods."

Another settler who could have been Robert Sharp's
relation was Samuel Sharp, a master gunner who was appointed
as a member of Endicott's council on March 3, 1628. After a
move to Salem, Samuel Sharp became a freeman in 1632. His wife
Alice had become a member of the church in Salem by 1636. His
will was proven in 1666.

Woods claimed the family could be traced back to Robert
Sharp of Islington, England in 1534. Interestingly enough,
Islington was also the home of a number of members of the
Maverick family.

However, Banks reported that Robert was probably from
Roxwell, Essex County in England, and settled near the "neck"
of Boston. But Banks also mistakenly wrote that Robert Sharp
probably died young or returned to England when, in reality,
Robert lived in Dorchester, Massachusetts for a time before
removing to Muddy River (Brookline) circa 1650.

Whatever Robert and Alice's English backgrounds were,
Harriet Woods wrote in <u>Historical Sketches of Brookline,
Massachusetts</u> that Robert Sharp emigrated from London on the
"Abigail" in 1635 at the age of 20. There were 220 passengers
on board. And when it arrived in Boston circa October 8th the
ship was infected with smallpox.

While residing in Brookline, Robert Sharp and his
brother-in-law Peter Aspinwall purchased 150 acres of land.
Peter had married Alice Sharp, "Mr. William Tyng's maid
servant." Alice had possibly earned her way to New England as
Tyng's bonded servant.

Robert Sharp I died in 1654 and his estate was inventoried at 172 pounds 7 shilling 6 pence (see Appendix VIII). By
1656 his widow had remarried and was petitioning that Peter
Aspinwall and Thomas Meekings be appointed guardians of her
minor children - John, Abigail, and Mary. Thomas Meekins took
Robert to "bringe up to his trade." Peter Aspinwall took the
two daughters to

"finde them meate, drink and apparell, learned them
to read, to knitt, to spine and such Housewifery...

until ye age of eighteene; for which said 'Peter'
is to have ye vse and profitt of ye house and land,
yt was said Sharps, only ye said Peeter besides
bringing up ye said daughters, in consideration of
ye benefit of said house and land, alow ye sonne 5
(pounds) per annum."
Nine years later, having "fulfilled their trust," the guardians were discharged of their duties.

John Sharp was twenty-two years old and married when his
legal guardian Thomas Meekins was released of his respon-
sibility. On April 25, 1665, John agreed to pay his sisters
Abigail and Mary 28 pounds each when they reached adulthood
and 50 shillings a year to their guardians as long as the
girls were minors.

On March 10, 1672/3 John appeared in records as surveyor
for the town of Muddy River. Then on April 7, 1675 John Parker
and John Sharp were "injoyned to order & oversee the makinge
of ye fence of the comon ffield there..."

In a letter written in 1676 to his old guardian, Thomas
Meekins, John wrote "my mother bose is ded and my sister
Swift." So John's mother or mother-in-law was married to a man
named "Bose" and one of his sisters had married a man named
"Swift".

When he was writing the letter John was in the middle of
fighting in King Philip's War and wrote -
"I have been out 7 weeks myself and if provisions had
not grown short we had folood the enimi into your
borders, and then I would have given you a visit if
it had been possibel, for I went out a volintere under
Captain Wadsworth of Milton, but he is coled hom to
recrout about their owne town...There is many of our
friends taken from us. Cap Jonson (Johnson) of Roxberi
was slaine at Naraganset, and Will lincoln died before
his wound was cured; filip Curtis was slane at a wigwame
about Mendham."
Just over a month later, Lt. John Sharp was also dead, killed
along with Capt. Wadsworth at the battle at Sudbury. He left
four children.

His daughter Martha Sharp married Joseph Buckminster who
according to Wood's Historical Sketches of Brookline, Massachusetts, was the great grandson of Thomas Buckminster, the
author of an almanac printed in London in 1599. Joseph's
father emigrated circa 1640 and died in Brookline in 1656.
Joseph and Martha Buckminister removed from Brookline to
Framingham.

John's son William Sharp was active in the community
beginning in 1704 when he signed the petition requesting that
Muddy River be "invested with such powers ... to manage the
general affairs of the said place" and establish at "said
place a separate village." Between 1702-1712 he was frequently
chosen as surveyor of highways. In 1713 he was chosen constable. However, at a March 26, 1716 town meeting Caleb
Gardner and William Sharp were discharged for "negglect of
making up their accompts...with the Town Treas'r." But at the
same meeting, William was granted a forty shillings gratuity

for his service as constable during "a year of extra ordinary charges in ye town." And finally, on May 1, 1718, William Sharp was assigned "that spott or room between the stairs leading up into the women's Gallery & the Easterly Door" of the meeting house.

John's other son Robert Sharp took part in a 1690 operation against the Indians in Canada. On April 16, 1690 he assigned his father-in-law Steven Williams as his "lawful attorny for and in behalf of...all things." And like his father, Robert never returned. He died during that expedition against the Indians.

His widow Sarah married secondly Thomas Nowell who died in 1694 during another Indian conflict. Prior to her third marriage to Solomon Phipps of Cambridge, Massachusetts, she willed her house and lands to her son Robert Sharp, and sixty pounds and various houehold goods to her daughter Sarah. Robert Sharp II was required to pay his sister two additional payments of twenty pounds each. Although there was a bill of sale for a slave named Rose, there was no mention of her in Sarah's will.

Robert II's son Robert was also active in town affairs. Through the years he served as surveyor in 1711, fence viewer in 1717, leather sealer in 1719, trustee in 1721, assessor (1727), and a member of a variety of committees. Woods called him a "shrewd, successful man in business." He owned a great deal of land and boarded cattle, sheep, and horses on it for people residing in Boston. According to early documents, Robert Sharp III had an indentured servant named Dunkan (Duncan) Mackeever from Londonderry, Ireland and two Black slaves named Luce (Lucy?) and Jane.

Stone Family

Unknown Stone
    Children
        Gregory
        Simon
        Samuel
        ?John

Men with the Stone name may have been masons - journeymen or apprentices - when they acquired their names. Actually the name came from the Anglo-Saxon "stan" which meant "stone". The surname might also have referred to someone who resided near a Druid stone or some other curious stone. In addition to being a frequently found surname, Stone also became the name of numerous English towns and parishes.

A number of other Stones in New England may have been related to Gregory and Simon Stone. In 1634, for instance, a Capt. John Stone, a trader on the Connecticut River was murdered by Indians. According to The Invasion of America, Stone was actually a "West Indian trader-cum-pirate who had tried to hijack a Plymouth vessel before coming to the Bay Colony." Then, in Boston, he was caught "rolling in bed with another man's wife." After threatening magistrates, he was banished. On leaving the colony John Stone kidnapped some Indians for ransom. After the Indians murdered him, authorities demanded the Indians surrender the guilty parties. But the Indians explained they had been rescuing other Indians who had been shackled by Stone and treated like prisoners.

A different John Stone was a fisherman and mariner who was in Hull by 1644. He died in 1659, leaving a wife named Joan and no children. He bequeathed sixty pounds to his "brother Symon Stone's children which sometime lived in Cousingtone in Somersetshire in Old England..."

Part I
Simon Stone Family

Simon Stone (Rev.)
    b.c. 1585; pos Great Bromley or Boxstead, Essex County, England
    m1 Joan (b. 1597); dau of William Clark
    m2 Sarah (d. 1663; Watertown, Massachusetts), wid of Richard Lumpkin of Ipswich, Massachusetts;1654
    d. 1665; Cambridge, Massachusetts
    Children
        Francis - b.c. 1619, England
        Ann - b.c. 1624, England
        Simon - b. 1630/1
            m. Mary Whipple (d. June, 1720)
            d. February 27, 1707
        Marie - b.c. 1632, England
        "Jo" - b.c. 1635, England

A John Stone emigrated to Watertown on board the "Increase" along "with his brother, Rev. Simon..." According to Virkus, that John Stone finally settled in Guilford, Connecticut.

Whether he was John's brother or not, Symon/Simon Stone did emigrate on board the "Increase" in 1635, when Simon was 50 years old. His wife Joan was 38. Accompanying them were five children - Francis (16), Ann (11), Simon Jr. (4), Marie (3) and Jo. (5 weeks). The family settled in Watertown where Simon became a freeman on May 25, 1636. Simon's second wife was Sarah Lumpkin, a widow from Boxstead, Essex County, England. Some researchers have suggested that because of his marriage in New England to someone from Essex County, England, that Simon and his brother were also from Essex. Obviously, while it was a possibility, it was not necessarily the case.

Part II
Gregory Stone Family

Gregory Stone
    b. 1590, England
    m1 Margaret Farrard / Garrad
    m2 Lydia (d. June 24, 1674), wid of ____ Cooper
    d. November 30, 1672; Cambridge, Massachusetts
    Children
        John - b.c. 1619
            m. Ann (d. 1639), dau of Elder Edward Howe of
            Watertown, Massachusetts
            d. 1683
            Children
                Nathaniel - b. 1660
                    m. Sarah Waite, 1684
                    d. 1732
                John
                David
                Daniel
                Hannah - m. ____ Bent
                Mary - m. ____ Fox
                Elizabeth - m. ____ Stowe
                Margaret - m. ____ Brown
                Tabitha - m. ____ Rice
                Sarah - m. ____ Hill
        Samuel - b.c. 1635
            d. September, 1715
        Elizabeth - m. ____ Potter of Ipswich, Massachusetts
        Sarah - m. Joseph Miriam (c. 1630-1677) of concord,
            Massachusetts
        David - m1 Elizabeth
            m2 Dorcas
            Children
                David - b. April 16, 1650
                    m. Mindwell Priest of Watertown,
                    Massachusetts
                Daniel - b.c. 1651
                    m. Joanna
                Dorcas - b. December 18, 1652
                Jonathan - b.c. 1654
                Samuel - b. June 19, 1656
                Nathaniel - b.c. 1658
        Daniel

    Simon's brother Gregory Stone, along with Gregory's wife
and six children, emigrated circa 1635 from England. A
contributor to Virkus suggested that Gregory was born in
Essex, England. Gregory was admitted as a freeman along with
his brother at Watertown on May 25, 1636. But the family
probably settled in Cambridge, Massachusetts. Before that,
Gregory Stone appeared in Cambridge records as early as
February 6, 1636. After that he appeared off and on as he was
granted permission to cut timber in 1651, 1659, and 1662; and
voted at numerous public meetings. In 1652, he was on the
committee that drew up the job descriptions for town offi-
cials. Gregory Stone was active as a deacon of the church and
deputy of the General Court.

Virkus wrote that Lydia Stone was the wife of John, Gregory's possible brother. However, in his 1672 will, Gregory Stone, not John, left his dwelling house and lands to his "dearly beloved wife Lidea."

As for Gregory's sons, John settled in the wilderness among the Indians at the "Great Falls" on the borders of the Sudbury Plantation. He was probably the John Stone whose 1683 will was quoted in the April, 1854 NEHGR. W.F. Stone who was the contributor of the will related that John had settled "upon the banks of Sudbury river where it received the waters of Cochitua brook." He also said that John Stone was "probably the first white man among the red men of Cochitua Dale."

Gregory's son Daniel was a "chirurgeon" (surgeon) of Cambridge and then Boston. Coupled with Gregory's 1672 will in the January, 1854 NEHGR was the notation that at one point Daniel had to sue a patient in Charlestown who would not pay the doctor's bill for amputating his leg. Included in the bill was thirty pounds "for going over the ferry 65 times to heal the wound."

David and Samuel Stone settled in the Lexington area where Samuel became one of the first deacons of the church.

Stubbs Family

Richard Stubbs I
     b.c. 1619
     m. Margaret (b.c. 1636; Weymouth, Massachusetts), dau of
     William and Susannah (Hayme) Read of Boston, Massachu
     setts;
     March 3, 1658/9
     wll dtd. may 22, 1677; Hull, Massachusetts
     wll pr. June 2, 1677; Hull, Massachusetts
     Children
          Richard (see below)
          ?Mercy - b.c. 1660
               m. John Beney
          William - b. betw 1662-1670
               d. by February 9, 1696
          Margaret - b. betw 1662-1670
               m. pos Luke Squire; Hull, Massachusetts
               d. February 25, 1709/10; Hull, Massachusetts

Richard Stubbs II
     b.c. 1660
     m. Rebecca (b.c. 1670; Hull, Massachusetts d.August 6,
     1743; Hull, Massachusetts), dau of Isaac and Martha
     (Ward) Lobdell; c. 1690
     d. March 5, 1711; Hull, Massachusetts
     Children
          Richard III - b.January 10, 1692; Hull, Massachu-
               setts
          m1 Jael, dau of Benjamin and Deborah Tower of
          Hingham, Massachusetts; February 16, 1715/16;
          Hingham, Massachusetts
          m2 Mary, wid of Joseph Speare, dau of Gersho-
          mand Elizabeth (Poole) Collier
          m3 Rhoda Russell, dau of Capt. Joseph and Sarah
          (Abbott) Chandler
          d. betw March 7 - August 29, 1750; North
          Yarmouth, Maine
          Children
               Hannah - m. Philip Greeley
                    Children
                         Eliphalet - m. Sarah Prince
               Richard - b. July 19, 1717; Hull,
                    Massachusetts
                    m. Mary (b. 1718), dau of Abner and
                    Mary (Morse) Brown; October 13, 1739;
                    Hull, Massachusetts
                    d. July 5, 1785
                    Children
                         William - bpt. October 11, 1741
                         Susannah - bpt. January 23, 1743
                              m1 _____ Bradley
                              m2 _____ True
                         Richard V - bpt. October 21,
                              1744
                              m1 Nabby Kought
                              m2 Ruth Allen
                         Samuel - bpt. April 15, 1750
                              m. _____ True
                         John - bpt. July 18, 1756
                         Moses - bpt. May 28, 1758

```
                         m. Betsy Noyes
                    Mercy - bpt. August 3, 1760
                    Ann - bpt. November 7, 1762
                         m. William Goff
                    Benjamin - m. Rebecca, dau of
                         Peter and Rebecca (Stubbs)
                         Durbar of Falmouth, Maine
                    Jeremiah - m. Jane Bradley True
                    Jonathan - m. Joanna Merrill
                    Jedidiah - m. ____ True
                    Jael - m. Thomas Prince
                    Abigail
                    Abner
            Jael - b. 1724
            Rebecca - b. October 17, 1727
            Sarah - bpt. April 5, 1730; Hull,
                 Massachusetts
            Jonathan - b. March 12, 1731; Falmouth,
                 Maine
    William - b. March 30, 1694
         m1 Dinah Manning`
         m2 Hannah Gorham Manning
         d. by June 3, 1786; Boston, Massachusetts
         Children
              Benjamin         Ann
              Rebecca          2 other children
    Luke - b. July 5, 1696
         m. Mary Newcomb; April 11, 1723; Eastham,
         Massachusetts
         Children
              Samuel           Susannah        Rebecca
              Mary             James           Elizabeth
              Thomas           John
    Experience - b. April 6, 1698
         m. John Barlett; May 26, 1716
    Margaret - b. January 22, 1700/01
         d. aft February 20, 1743
    Benjamin (tw) - b. March 21, 1701/2
         d. September 3, 1721; Hull, Massachusetts
    James (tw) - b. March 21, 1701/2
         m. Hannah (Foster) Bradford
         d. January 20, 1731/2; Kingston, Massachusetts
    Samuel - b. November 22, 1704
         d. betw August 13, 1722 - November 18, 1727
    Rebecca - b. November 18, 1707
         m. Dr. Ralph Pope; November 27, 1729; Hull,
         Massachusetts
         d. July 1, 1791; Stoughton, Massachusetts
    John - b. May 12, 1710
         d. August 23, 1711; Hull, Massachusetts
```

Stubbs, like the name Stebbing, may have been derived from the baptismal name of Stephen. But it also was a surname which could have been given to someone who lived near a conspicuous tree stump; or who was a short, stumpy man.

The English origin of this Stubbs family remained unclear. However, the May 12, 1600 will of John Rowninge of Hunden, Suffolk County was proven by Richard Stubbs, a notary. John Hunt discussed another Stubbe family from Norfolk County in his NEHGR article titled "Mary Stubbe -a Connection of

Elder William Brewster?". Hunt primarily discussed a Stubbe family of Buxton and Strumpshawe in Norfolk and Lincoln's Inn in Middlesex.

In 1642, the General Court named the first Richard Stubbs of this genealogy to be a planter of Nantasket (Hull). Although Richard was employed in the fishing trade when he first arrived in Hull, in later years he was referred to as a "husbandman" and owned a large herd of cattle and a good amount of land, including a number of hills and islands. One grant was on Further Hill and another on Town Hill.

According to <u>Seventeenth Century Hull, Mass, and Her People</u> Richard Stubb's wife Margaret Read may have been his second wife. They were married by Major Humphrey Atherton when Richard was approximately 39 years old. Richard's children were all born after the 1658 marriage. Was he childless in his first marriage or a bachelor until near middle age?

Or could there have been two Richards, father and son? One, born by 1619, would have become a planter in 1642 at age 23 or older. The second might have been born circa 1639, when his father was age 20 or older. That second might have been the one who married Margaret in 1658 (at age 19) and had four children born between 1660 (at age 21) and 1670 (at age 31).

Ethel Farrington Smith discovered a controversy in Hull Town Records between Richard Stubbs and Samuel Baker, his 1671 neighbor on Further Hill. Inevitably, Stubbs was given permission to cross Baker's land "at any time to mend his barn if it be defective, provided Richard acquaint Samuel Baker with it by asking him lieve."

When he died in 1677, all of Richard's children were minors. He left his eldest son Richard one-half his estate and the rest to be divided equally among his remaining children. His wife was not mentioned by name. In the inventory, his wife was referred to as E____. It would be difficult to know from that if the clerk was mistaken or if Richard had taken another wife before his death.

Richard Stubbs II was born circa 1660 and died at about the age of 51. During his life he lived in the Town Hill home he inherited from his father. Among the many civic offices Richard held between 1697 and 1710 were town constable, field driver, surveyor, and fence viewer.

He made Rebecca executrix and bequeathed his entire estate to her "during her widowhood until the youngest child become twenty." Then his estate was to be divided evenly among his living children. Rebecca was to receive one-third of the estate and part of the house for life. According to Smith, when the estate was divided in 1727, it was divided in sevenths since three of his ten children - John, Samuel, and Benjamin - had died.

According to Smith, Richard Stubbs III married secondly Mary Collier Speare, whose first husband Joseph Speare had died of smallpox in May, 1738 while quarantined on Rainsford Island in Boston Harbor. Richard III had been left with six children when his first wife died. When Richard married Mary, four of his children were still under 20 years of age. Mary had been left with eight small children, making for a full house.

Richard Stubbs III's brother William removed to Nantucket for most of his adult life, but returned to Hull after the death of his second wife. He was both a mariner and carpenter. His brother Luke was a "housewright" and brother James was a shipwright.

Talmadge Family

Unknown Talmadge
    Children
        Thomas I (see below)
        John of Newton Stacey, Southampton County, England

Thomas Talmadge I
    b. prob. Newton Stacey, Southampton County, England
    d. 1653
    Children
        Robert (see below)
        Jane - m. Richard Walker
        Thomas II (Capt.) - d. 1691, Easthampton, Long
            Island, New York
            Children
                Sarah - m1 Thomas Bee
                    m2 Thomas Barnes; by Marcy 3, 1691/2
                    d. January 26, 1701/2
                    Children
                        John - b. by 1677
                Nathaniel - b. 1643
                    d. 1716
        William - b. Newton Stacey England
            d. Lynn, Massachusetts

Robert Talmadge
    b.c. 1623
    m. Sarah, dau of Thomas and Margery (Baker) Nash
    d. 1662
    Children
        Abigail - bpt. May 13, 1649
        Thomas (Sgt.) b. October 17, 1650
            bpt. October 20, 1650
            m. Elizabeth (b. June 22, 1650; d. October 12,
            1719), dau of Joseph and Elizabeth (Preston)
            Alsop; c. 1675
            d. 1733
            Children
                Joseph - b. December 2, 1677
                    bpt. January 9, 1686/7
                    m. Elizabeth
                Enos - b. April 13, 1679
                    bpt. January 9, 1686/7
                    d. May 9, 1712
                Elizabeth - b. February 12, 1682
                    bpt. January 9, 1686/7
                    m. Daniel Stone; January 21, 1707/8
                Robert - b. October 5, 1684
                    bpt. January 9, 1686/7
                    m. Abigail (b. May 2, 1686), dau of
                    Joseph and Sarah (Alling) Peck; 1709
                    d. February 20, 1755
                Jemima - b. February 11, 1686
                    bpt. February 12, 1886/7
                    m. Benjamin Beach
                Kezia - b. April 27, 1688
                    bpt. April, 1688
                    m. Zechariah Bostwick
                    d. aft 1737
                John - b. April 11, 1692

                              bpt. April 18, 1692
                              m1 Esther, dau of Theophilus and
                              Esther (Mix) Munson; July 21, 1721
                              m2 Deborah (1700-1751), dau of Isaac
                              and Deborah (Clark) Jones, wid of
                              Nathaniel Maltbie
          Sarah - b./bpt. September 19, 1652
               m. Samuel, son of Samuel and Elizabeth (Clever-
               ly) Hotchkiss; March 18, 1678/79
               Children
                    Mary - b. January 1, 1679/80
                         m. Caleb, son of Thomas and Hannah
                         (Powell) Tuttle
                    Sarah - b. April 7, 1681
                    Samuel - b. March 6, 1682/3
                         m. Mary Hull or Russell
                    James - b. December 8, 1684
                         d. young
                    Abigail - b. February 12, 1686
                         d. aft 1740
                    Ebenezer - bpt. December 16, 1688
                         m. Hannah Peck
                    Robert (triplet) - b. September 8, 1690
                         d. young
                    James (triplet) - b. September 8, 1690
                         d. young
                    Enos (triplet) - b. September 8, 1690
                         d. young
          John - b./bpt. September 11, 1654
               m. Abigail (1659-1710), dau of James and Mary
               (Lewen) Bishop
               d. 1690
               Children
                    Ann - b./bpt. August 15, 1687
                         d. May 23, 1688
                    James - b. June 11, 1689
                         bpt. July 22, 1689
                         m1 Hannah (1690-1743/4), dau of
                         Hannah (Frisbie) Harrison; July 1,
                         1713
                         m2 Mercy, dau of John and Elizabeth
                         (Wilmont) Mix, wid of Ebenezer Alling
          Enos - b./bpt. October 4, 1656
               m. Hannah, dau of Thomas and Mary (Turner)
               Vale; May 9, 1682
               d. 1690

     Talmadge / Talmage / Tallmadge meant "one who carried a
knapsack." Virkus reported that Thomas Talmadge who died circa
1690/1 in Easthampton, Long Island was the son of "Sir Lionel
Tolleemach, high sheriff" who married Lady Catherine Cromwell,
the daughter of Lord Cromwell. However, according to Antonia
Fraser's Cromwell, The Lord Protector, Oliver Cromwell did not
have a daughter named Catherine, but he did have a sister with
that name. However, Fraser also stated that Sir Lionel
Tollemache of Hilmingham Hall, Suffolk County, actually
married Elizabeth, the daughter of Charles I"s attendant
William Murry, the Earl of Dysart; and had eleven children.
One of those eleven children was a Thomas Tollemach who was
born in 1651. Fraser reported that although rumors were
circulated, the Thomas was Cromwell's illegitimate son,

Cromwell was abroad when Thomas was conceived. Fraser said
that Thomas Tollemache died in 1694 during a military expedition to Brest.

So the Thomas who was born in 1651 was not the Massachusetts Bay Colony Thomas in this genealogy. Since Thomas'
father and uncle were uncovered, Lionel could not have been
his father. But there may have been more than one Lionel.

In Calendar of Patent Rolls for May 28, 1572 appeared
"the Lionel Talemache, son & heir of Lionel Talemache ..." So
a Lionel Tolemache may have been the father of a Thomas,
however it would have been a Thomas one generation earlier
than the Thomas of this genealogy.

Burkes reported that Thomas was the brother of John
Talmadge of Newton Stacey, Hants. The July, 1886 NEHGR "New
England Gleanings" also reported that Thomas I was the
"brother of John Talmage of newton Stacey." However, that
article placed Newton Stacey in "Co. Southampton."

Thomas Talmadge went to Charlestown, Massachusetts aboard
the "Plough" in 1631. Through the years he also lived in
Boston and Lynn, Massachusetts. Thomas I became a freeman on
May 14, 1634 and was granted 200 acres in 1638. He removed to
Southampton, Long Island, New York where he received a home
lot in 1642. He became a freeman in 1649, and was fined for
missing a town meeting in Easthampton, Long Island in 1651.

Thomas II was the person Virkus claimed was the son of
Lionel "Tolleemach". Instead, he was one of at least three
sons of Thomas Talmadge I who arrived in the New World in the
1630's. Since Thomas I and II lived in the same areas and had
the same names, it was difficult to determine which Thomas did
what.

After living in Lynn for awhile, Thomas II, like his
father, was granted a town lot in the second ward at Southampton, Long Island in 1642. He later served in a number of
official capacities for Easthampton, Long Island; including
recorder in 1650, lieutenant and captain of the training band
beginning in 1665, and deputy to the General Court.

His daughter Sarah married Thomas Bee. Their son John Bee
was a weaver who sold land in 1698 and witnessed a deed in
June, 1703. Then, according to Easthampton, Long Island
records, in 1704 the town took control of his estate and put
him into the "Town House" where he died having "pinned away."

Thomas I's son Robert Talmadge ended up residing in New
Haven, Connecticut. Heirs of his listed as 1685 proprietors of
New Haven included Thomas, Enos, and John.

In Immigrants to America Appearing in English Records,
Thomas I's son William Talmadge was referred to as "an
original colonist on 'The Phenix'...probably a parishioner of
Stephen Bachiler" who settled in Roxbury and Lynn, Massachusetts. However, in New England Gleanings he was referred to as
"William Talmadge of Boston." In reality, he did go originally
to Boston where he became a freeman on May 14, 1634, and

joined the Boston church as its 59th member before moving to Lynn.

A William Talmadge came to the New World as the indentured servant of Thomas Breedon. According to Winthrop's Boston, that William Talmadge's servitude did not end until 1636, at which time he was given fifteen acres in Muddy River. Because of that, he probably was not the same William Talmadge. He later discovered he had only been given ten of the promised fifteen acres. Ironically, according to Winthrop's Boston, the William who was an indentured servant was considered one of the richer inhabitants, although not one of the gentry. He donated a small amount of money to the school.

Ward Family

Henry Ward
    b. by 1573; England
    bur. May 15, 1642; Hingham, Massachusetts
    Children
        Samuel (see below)
        ? Henry

Samuel Ward I
    b. 1593, England
    m1 (d. November 28, 1638; Hingham, Massachusetts);
    England
    m2 Frances Pitcher Reycroft (b.c. 1607 d. June 10, 1690;
    Boston, Massachusetts)
    d. August, 1682; Charlestown, Massachusetts
    wll dtd. March 6, 1681
    wll pro. October 3, 1682
    Children
        Samuel II (see below)
        Henry - b.c. 1635
            bpt. August, 1642
            m. Remember (1642-1715), dau of John and
            Frances
            Farrow; February 3, 1659/60; Hingham,
            Massachusetts
            d. April 4, 1715; Hingham, Massachusetts
            Children
                Elizabeth - b. August 26, 1663; Hingham,
                    Massachusetts
                    m. James Garnet; June 18, 1685
                Deborah - b. November 6, 1664
                Henry - b. September 20, 1666
                    m. Ruth Bailey, 1694
                    Children
                        Ruth   Mary
                        Lydia   Remember
                        Rachel   Henry
                        Elizabeth
                John - b. November 14 or 15, 1668 or 1669
                    m. Hannah Beal; May, 1698
                    Children
                        Hannah
                Francis or Frances - b. February 17 or 18,
                  1670/1
                  bpt. February 26, 1671
                Edward - b. July 24, 1672
                Nathan - b. October 23, 1675
                  bpt. October 24, 1675
                Samuel III - b. November 15, 1678
                    m. Jael (b. November 21, 1683;
                    Hingham, Massachusetts d. November
                    15, 1764; Weymouth, Massachusetts),
                    dau of Jeremiah and Hannah (Lane)
                    Beal; 1710; prob Hingham, Massachu-
                    setts
                    d. October 3, 1727; Weymouth,
                    Massachusetts
                    Children
                        2 Jael   Elizabeth
                        Hannah   Ruth

2 Samuel

Mary - b.c. 1632
    m1 Ambrose (c. 1631-1708), son of Edmund Gould/
    Gale / Gall; c. 1662
    m2 Deborah, wid of Francis Firdler; August 29,
    1695; Marblehead, Massachusetts
    d. February 5, 1694/5; Marblehead, Massachu-
    setts
Martha - b. 1636/7
    m. Isaac Lobdell (b.c. 1637; Hingham,
    Massachusetts d. May 5, 1710 or by 1718); circa
    1656; Dedham, Massachusetts
    d. May 4, 1708
    Children
        (see Lobdell)

Samuel (Maj.) Ward II
    bpt. November 18, 1638; Hingham, Massachusetts
    m1 Abigail (b. January 12, 1644 d. by 1682), dau of Moses
    and Remember (Allerton) Maverick of Marblehead,
    Massachusetts and gr. dau of Isaac Allerton of the
    "Mayflower"
    m2 Sarah, dau of Gov. Simon and Anne (Dudley) Bradstreet,
    wid of Richard Hubbard of Ipswich, Massachusetts
    d. 1690
    Children
        Martha - b. September 16, 1672; Salem, Massachusetts
            m. John Tuttle (1666-1715/6); December 3, 1689
            d. August 17, 1723; Ipswich, Massachusetts
        Samuel - m. Sarah, dau of Simon Tuttle; November 13,
            1699; Essex, Massachusetts
        Remember - m. William Wilson or Walters
        Mercy - m. Cane
        Mary - m. Peter Doliver/Doliber/Dollabor
        Elizabeth - m. John Kettell
        ? Abigail - m. William, son of William and Sarah
            (Ingersoll) Hines/ Hinds; c. 1681
            Children
                John - m. Hannah Shaw; August 11, 1709
                    Children
                        Hannah   John
                        Elizabeth   Ebenezer
                        Abigail   Susannah

The name Ward came from the Old English "weard" which
meant "one who watches or guards something." Usually a person
given the name Ward / Warde / Warden was a guard, keeper, or
watch-man. Occasionally the name was given to someone who
dwelled in a marsh.

A number of Wards appeared in early records (see Appendix
IX). William de la Ward was in Chester, England, appeared as
early as 1175. Simon le Warde appeared in English records in
1194. John Ward resided at the manor of Kirby-Bedon, Norfolk
County, England in 1363. His descendants were esquires and
knights from Bexley, England and their arms was described as
"cheque, or and azure, a bend, ermine." Margaret Gascoigne
married Sir Christopher Ward who died in 1521 in Givendale,
York County.

Samuel Ward of Ipswich, England married Deborah Bolton, a widow from Islaeham, Cambridgeshire in 1604. Although they went to Holland circa 1635, Samuel died in Ipswich, England in March, 1639/40. He may have been related to the Wards of this genealogy.

The first Henry Ward of this genealogy was born in England. He was probably the father or possibly the brother of Samuel Ward of the Massachusetts Bay Colony. As Samuel's father, he was too old to be the Henry, age 19, "of Worttwell in Norff" who requested to go to the New World in 1637. Of course, Samuel's brother could have been 19 years old in 1637. According to the Hobart Journal, Henry died in Hingham, Massachusetts on May 15, 1642.

Samuel Ward was born circa 1593 in England. A clothier named John Ward of Stratford, Suffolk County, England made bequests to his son Samuel in his will which was proven in May, 1631. There were two Stratford's in Suffolk. Stratford St. Andrew was three miles southwest of Saxmundham and Stratford St. Marey was six miles northeast of Colchester. But, Samuel Ward of this genealogy probably was Henry, not John Ward's son.

Samuel's first wife died on November 28, 1638 in Hingham, Massachusetts. His second wife Frances (Pitcher) Reycroft / Recroft had been born in England in 1607.

According to Hull, Massachusetts genealogies in the October, 1898 NEHGR, in 1636 Samuel Ward I received "a land grant on the lower plain in Hingham." He purchased a good deal land, including land "in the plain neck, Hingham" in 1637, which he transferred to Thomas Jones in 1638. In 1640 he was involved in a lawsuit concerning land he had received as payment for some cloth he had sold.

The Dictionary of Ancestral Heads of New England Families related that Samuel was a cooper and proprietor from Hingham in 1636. He became a freeman on March 9, 1636/7 and a deputy to the General Court that same year. In 1646 he became Hingham's second town clerk. Then, on June 12, 1643, Bozoan Allen, Anthony Eames, and Samuel received permission to establish a common corn mill for the town.

By 1649, when he sold his share of a ship, Samuel had removed to Hull. Aspinwall Records included Samuel's sale.
"Know all men whom these pntes shall concerning
that I Samuel Ward of Hull have bargained & sould
unto Jeremiah Clark of Rhode Island one eigth pt.
of the barke called sea flowre with all the
appurtenances there to belonging for full in hand
received witness my had and seale this 23rd day of
August Anno Dni 1649."
In 1650 he was listed as living on Further Hill in Hull, next to the home lot of George Vickars / Vickery / Vickary. But he only resided in Hull for 10 years.

After moving to Charlestown, Samuel Ward purchased a great deal more land. His wife Frances was admitted to the church in Charlestown on June 9, 1656. That same year, William "Replye" left his son a meadow "lyeing next vnto Samuel Ward,

Eastward, and ye Riuer Southward." On March 31, 1665 Samuel and Frances sold several pieces of land in Hingham.

Samuel appeared in a variety of records during his life in Charlestown. In Bozoan Allen's 1652 Suffolk County will, Samuel Ward appeared as one of Allen's debtors. In 1674 Sarah Metcalf was listed as a servant of Samuel Ward.

Samuel Ward II was Samuel I's youngest son. He became a freeman in Marblehead, Massachusetts in 1665. Both of his wives were of notable backgrounds. Sarah was the daughter of Gov. Simon Bradstreet. Abigail was the daughter of Remember Allerton, who arrived in the New World on board of the "Mayflower", and Moses Maverick (see Appendix X). Samuel II and Abigail's children - Samuel, Abigail, Mary and Martha - appeared in Moses Maverick's unsigned, 1684 will.

Samuel Ward II became a sergeant in 1666, lieutenant in 1670, and captain in 1679. He had earned the rank of major before making his will as he was leaving on an expedition to Quebec, Canada on February 29, 1689/90. He died serving under Sir William Phipps in a battle against Frontenac in Quebec. The will was proven at Ipswich that same year. After the death of the executrix (Samuel II's widow?) in 1719, Samuel Ward's estate was administered by his widowed daughters Mary Walters and Martha Tuttle. In addition to Martha and Mary, heirs included John and Margaret Curtis, Joseph and Mary Doliber / Doliver, Miss Hannah Waters, William and Rebecca Groose, Mark and Martha Haskel, Nathaniel and Mary Warner, William and Abigail Haskel, his grandchildren, and others.

Weston Family

John Weston
    m. Alice
    d. Rugeley, Staffordshire, England
    Children
        Richard (see below)
        John
            Children
                Robert
                    d. 1632
                    Children
                        Rev. John - m. ____ Piers
                        Anne - m. William Piers
                        Elizabeth - Thomas Isles (Dr.)
                        Dorothy

Richard Weston I
    m. Catherine
    d. Rugeley, Staffordshire, England
    Children
        John (see below)
        Alice - m. ____ Barbour
            d. 1571

John Weston
    m. Cecilia Ford (d. 1577)
    d. 1566; Rugeley, Staffordshire, England
    Children
        Richard (see below)
        John

Richard Weston II
    m. Barbara Kniveton (d. 1592)
    d. 1613; Rugeley, Staffordshire, England
    Children
        Ralph (see below)
        Jane - m. Thomas Broughton (alias Smith)
        Anne - m. Thomas Wolseley

Ralph Weston
    m. Anne (d. 1624), dau of George Smythe
    d. 1605; Rugeley, Staffordshire, England
    Children
        Thomas (see below)
        Richard III (Sir) - b. 1575; Rugeley, Staffordshire,
            England
            m. Anne (d. 1626), dau of Richard Barbour of
            Helderston, Staffordshire, England
            wll dtd. 1655
            Children
                Ralph
                    Children
                      Phillip
                      John
        Simon - m. Sarah (d. 1664)
        Andrew - bpt. December 2m 1599; Rugeley,
            Staffordshire, England
            m. Mary and/or Dorothy
            d. 1636; St. Botolph, Aldgate, England
            Children

                    Jane - b. 1633; St. Botolph, Aldgate,
                    England
          Jane - m. John Brandreth

Thomas Weston
     bpt. December 21, 1584; Rugeley, Staffordshire,
     England
     m. Elizabeth, dau of Christopher and Alice (Green)
     Weaver
     d. by November 9, 1647
     Children
          Elizabeth - m. Roger, son of Roger Conant

     English towns around a central town were frequently named
for their position; such as Norton, Sutton, Easton, and
Weston. So Weston was probably one of many surnames derived
from a place.

     One of the better known persons named Weston was Father
William Weston who was born in 1550 at Maidstone, Kent. Father
Weston was a courageous and popular priest during the years
when Catholicism was expressly frowned upon in England.

     According to "Thomas Weston, Ironmonger of London and
America, 1609-1647", the family originated in Rugeley,
Staffordshire, England. Coldham reported that Robert, son of
John II and grandson of John I of this genealogy, was Chancel-
lor of Ireland. He also claimed that Elizabeth Conant,
daughter of Thomas Weston was a member of the "Irish Church".
But no source was given for the information and no other
connection with Ireland has been ascertained as of yet.

     Ralph and Anne (Smyth) Weston had five children. Their
son Richard was knighted and became the Baron of Exchequer.
Ralph and Anne's son Simon was a gentleman who became a draper
at St. Chad's Shrewsbury. Their son Andrew became an ironmonger at St. Botolph Adgate. He took his oath on December 21,
1620 and became a freeman in 1625. In 1609, Ralph and Anne's
son Thomas, after serving an apprenticeship with Rowland
Heylyn, was admitted as an ironmonger. Coldham called Thomas
Weston "an enterprising and colorful rogue." Actually that was
more virtuous a description than Thomas probably deserved.

     In 1615, Thomas Weston arranged for an agent, Edward
Pickering, to represent him in Holland. It seemed innocent
enough. In exchange, Weston agreed to support Pickering who,
as an English Puritan, desperately wanted to leave England.
However, by 1619 Weston and Pickering were bickering over
money. According to Coldham, "Weston accused Pickering of
having enriched himself at his expense,... Pickering alledged
that Weston was frequently behind in his payments to him and
was heavily in his debt." Weston had Pickering arrested for
debt.

     In 1619 an employee of Thomas secretly dumped thirty tons
of alum in order to evade tariffs. More illegal alum was
impounded from Henry Rowland and Edward Rudge who had purchased it from Thomas Weston. Rowland and Rudge sued Weston.
However on October 3, 1620, Andrew Weston; Thomas' brother,
apprentice, and bookkeeper; swore that Thomas was "beyond the
seas."

On March 1, 1622, Thomas Weston and Philemon Powell promised to ship military supplies to New England on board Weston's ship, the "Charity". Andrew Weston did take the supplies abroad for his brother, but he sold them to pirates for an immense monetary gain. On July 28, 1622, at an inquisition at the Guildhall, Andrew Weston swore that he had acted upon his brother's orders and all charges were dropped against Andrew. Their brother Richard Weston acted as counsel for the defendants.

During the same month, Thomas Weston was in England borrowing 486 pounds for John Bewchamp / Beauchamp. He fled without ever repaying the money.

In November, 1623, authorities tried to serve legal papers to Thomas through his wife who was living in Stamford, Lincolnshire, at the time. May, 1624 Exchequer Court records revealed that Thomas had become a fugitive both from justice and from the hands of his creditors."

Gilbert Nash, in his _Historical Sketch of Town of Weymouth, Massachusetts from 1622 to 1884_, mentioned that Thomas aided the Pilgrims in negotiating with the Plymouth Company. So it was natural for Thomas to look to the New World when his problems got out of control in his Old World. But Nash incorrectly claimed that Thomas never accompanied the group to New England.

Weston took his motely crew of men directly from the streets of London established the settlement of Wessagusset on Massachusetts Bay. Before putting together his company Weston had analysed the problems faced by earlier failed groups of settlers. He concluded that religious enthusiasm and accompanying families had had a negative impact on the success of other settlements. However, the lack of religious faith and families depending upon them was exactly what defeated the Weston group.

The first of Weston's group arrived in the New World aboard the "Sparrow" in May, 1622. They chose a well-protected, wooded area at which to build their trading post. They were joined by about sixty more members of the company who arrived along with Weston on board the "Charity" in July, 1622.

Concerning their contacts with Plymouth Plantation, Nash related that Weston's group "certainly showed a disposition to act fairly. In an expedition ... with the Indians ..., Mr. Weston's people took their full share of the labor and privation, acting with energy and honorably discharging all their obligations."

However, in _English Colonists in America_, Nash disagreed and revealed that Weston wrote a letter rebuking Bradford in hopes of "making mischief" between the Plymouth Colony and the London partners backing them and "thus securing for himself any profit that could be got out of the settlement." In addition, Plymouth colonists saw Wessagusset as a commercial rival that could "entangle them in difficulties with the natives or... drain on resources of the colony."

But even if Plymouth Colony was concerned, they still let Weston's group stay at Plymouth until their leaders found a piece to settle on. Doyle wrote that Weston's group showed their "folly and dishonesty" while in Plymouth by stealing corn at night from their hosts.

John Sanders was named the plantation's overseer while Weston went on to Virginia aboard the "Charity". When Weston met with Gorges in Plymouth in late 1623, he blamed Sanders for not being prepared for the severe winter of 1622-23 and failure for the trading post. In fact, Doyle claimed that the Plymouth government had to step in to keep Sanders from robbing the Indians of their grain and that John Sanders left to become a trustee of Gorges Patent in Maine. However, since Gorges did not get his patent until much later, Sanders could not have gone directly from the one colony to the other.

Gradually the plantation fell apart. "Phinehas" Pratt fled to Plymouth. Several survivors of the winter of 1622-23 escaped to Christopher Leavett's plantation. Then, when the remaining group applied to Plymouth Colony for help with the natives, Captain Miles Standish responded by killing off a number of Indians. Of those left from Weston's Company, ten starved to death, two were killed by savages, and then, after Standish's "help", three more of the company were tortured to death by Indians.

By the time Gorges Company arrived in Wesgusset in the middle of September of 1623, the Weston trading post was gone. Rev. William Morrell, an Episcopalian minister reported that Gorges group "pitched upon the place Mr. Weston's people had forsaken."

Coldham reported that when Thomas Weston arrived in New England in 1622, he was "penniless and wearing borrowed clothes" and was "soon expelled." However, Doyle reported that Weston's condition was due to a shipwreck he had experienced. But even if Weston had spent everything he could beg, borrow, and steal to finance his trading post; he was not expelled like Coldham reported.

Afterwards, Weston did go to Virginia. In fact, Hotten listed Thomas Weston, who arrived on the 'George' in 1623, as being among the "dead of West & Sherley and a Sherley Hundred" in 1624 Virginia. Then in 1641, John Beauchamp who Thomas had owed 485 pounds since 1622, sent his power of attorney to an agent in Virginia in an attempt to recover his money from Thomas Weston. Beauchamp's agent was unsuccessful, but the reason for his failure was not determined.

Despite what Hotten had recorded, Thomas was not dead: he had just moved. In the early 1640's, Thomas Weston was Master of the "John" out of Maryland. Coldham reported that a sailor from the "John" described Thomas as, understandably, fearful about returning to England because of the troubles that awaited him should he return.

Weston lived out his life on a 1250-acre manor in St. Mary's County, Maryland. He had died by November 9, 1647 when John Hansford and William Marshall were named administrators of his estate. An inventory of the estate was presented on July 18, 1648 in St. Mary's County Court.

Thomas' only child, a daughter named Elizabeth, eventually met and married Roger Conant, Jr. They resided at Marblehead, Massachusetts.

    After living for a time in the Massachusetts Bay Colony,
William Wood returned to London and published a book in 1635
titled New Englands Prospect and subtitled A true, lively, and
experimentall description of that part of america, commonly
called New England: discovering the state of that Countrie,
both as it stands to out new-come English Planters; and to the
old Native Inhabitants. Laying downe that which may both
enrich the knowledge of the mind-travelling Reader, or benefit
the future Voyager. The results were a detailed account of
the towns in the area immediately surrounding Massachusetts
Bay. The following are excerpts from Wood's account.

    "Boston is two miles North-east from Roxberry: His situa-
tion is very pleasant, being a Peninsula, hem'd in on the
South-side with the Bay of Roxberry, on the North-side with
Charles-river, the marshes on the backe-side, being not half
a quarter of a mile over; so that a little fencing will secure
their Cattle from Woolves. Their greatest wants be wood, and
medow-ground, which ever were in that place; being constrained
to fetch their building-timber, and fire-wood from the Ilands
in Boates; and their Hay in Loyters: It being a necke and
barte of wood; they are not troubled with three great annoy-
ances, of Woolves, Rattlesnakes, and Musketos.   These that
live here upon their cattle, must be constrained to take
Farmes in the Countrey, or else they cannot subsist; the place
being too small to containe many and fittest for such as can
Trade into England, for such commodities as the Countrey
wants, being the chiefe place for shipping and Merchandize.
    "This necke of land is not above foure miles in compasse,
in forme almost square, having on the South-side at one
corner, a great broad hill, whereas shee sayles into any
Harbor within the hill Bay. On the North-side is another Hill
equall in bignesse, whereon stands a Windemill. To the Northwest is a high Mountaine with three little rising hills on the
top of it, wherefore it is called the Tramount. From the top
of this Mountaine a man may over-look all the Ilands which lie
before the Bay, and discry such ships as are upon the Sea-
coast. This Towne although it be neither the greatest nor the
richest, yet it is the most noted and frequented, being the
Center of the Plantations where the monthly Courts are kept
... Here likewise dwells the Governour: This place hath very
good land, affording rich Corne-fields, and fruitfull Gardens:
having likewise sweet and pleasant Springs."

    "Three miles to the North (of Weymouth) is Mount Wolles-
ton (Braintree), a very fertile soyle, and a place very
convenient for Farmers houses, there being great store of
plaine ground, with out trees. Neer this place is Massachusetts fields where the greatest Sagamore in the countrey
lived, before the
Plague, who caused it to be cleared for himselfe. The greatest inconvenience is, that there is not very many Springs, as
in other places of the countrey, yet water may be had for
digging: A second inconvenience is, that Boates cannot come in
at a low water, nor shippes ride neare the shore."

    "The inhabitants...(of Boston), for their enlargement,
have taken to themselves Farme-houses, in a place called
Muddy-river (Brookline), two miles from their Towne; where is

good ground, large timber, and store of Marsh-land and Medow. Cattle in the Summer, whilst the Corne is on the ground at Boston, and bring them to the Towne in Winter."

"By the side of this (Charles) River is built New-towne (Cambridge), which is three miles by land from Charles Towne, and a league and a halfe by water. This place was first intended for a City, but upon more serious considerations it was not thought so fit, being too farre from the Sea; being the greatest inconvenience it hath. This is one of the neat-est and best compacted Towns in New England, having many faire structures, with many handsome contrived streets. The inhabitants most of them are very rich, and well stored with Cattell of all sorts; having many hundred Acres of ground paled in with one generall fence, which is about a mile and a halfe long, which secures all their weaker Cattle from the wild beasts. On the other side of the River lieth all their Medow and Marsh-ground for Hay."

"Six mile...North (of Braintree), lieth Dorchester; which is the greatest towne in New England; well wooded and watered; very good arable grounds, and Hayground, faire Corne-fields, and pleasant Gardens, with Kitchen-gardens: In this Plantation is a great many Cattle, as Kine, Goats, and Swine. This Plantation hath a reasonable Harbor for ships: Here is no Alewife-river, which is a great inconvenience. The inhabitants of this towne were the first that set upon the trade of fishing in the Bay, who received so much friute of their labours, that they encouraged others to the same under takings."

"A mile from this Towne (Dorchester) lieth Roxberry (Roxbury), which is a faire and handsome Countrey-towne; the inhabitants of it being all very Rich. This towne lieth upon the Maine, so that it is well wooded and watered; having a cleare and fresh Brooke running through the towne: Vp which although there come no Ale-wives, yet there is great store of Smelts, and therefore it is called Smelt-brooke.
"A quarter of a mile to the North-side of the Towne, is another River called Stony-river; upon which is built a water-mill. Here is good ground for Corne and Medow for Cattle: Vp Westward from the Towne it is something rocky, whence it hath the name of Roxberry; the inhabitants have faire houses, store of Cattle, impaled Corne-fields, and fruitfull Gardens. Here is no harbour for ships, because the Towne is seated in the bottome of a shallow Bay, which is made by the necke of land on which Boston is built; so that they can transport all their goods from the Ships in Boats from Boston, which is the nearest Harbour."

"Foure miles Northeast from Saugus lyeth Salem, which stands on the middle of a necke of land very pleasantly, having a South river on the one side, and North river on the other side: upon this necke where the most of the houses stand is very bad and sandie ground, yet for seaven yeares together it hath brought forth exceeding good corned, by being fished byt every third yeare; in some places is very good ground, and good timber, and divers springs hard by the sea-side. Here likewise is store of fish, as Basses, Eeeles, Lobsters, Clammes, &c. Although their land be none of the best, yet beyond these rivers is a very good soyle, where they have taken Farmes, and get their Hay, and plant their corne;

137

there they crosse these rivers with small Cannowes, which are
made of whole pine trees, being about two foote and a halfe
over, and twenty foote long: in these likewise they goe a
fowling, sometimes two leagues to sea; there be more Cannowes
in this towne than in all the whole Patent; every houshould
having a water-horse or two. This Towne wants an Alewife
river, which is a great inconvenience; it hath two good
harbours, the one being called Winter, and the other Suymmer
harbours, which lieth within Derbies Fort, which place if it
were well fortified, might keepe shippes from landing of
forces in any of those two places."

"Wichaguscusset (Weymouth), an Indian name: this as it is
but a small Village, yet it is very pleasant; and healthfull,
very good ground, and is well timbered, and hath good stoore
of Hey ground; it hath a very spacious harbour for shipping
before the towne; the salt water being navigable for Boates
and Pinnaces two leagues. Here the inhabitants have good
store of fish of all sortes, and Swine, having acornes and
clamms at the time of yeare; here is likewise an alewife
rever."

ASPINWALL
Ambrose/Aspinwall Family

Ambrose

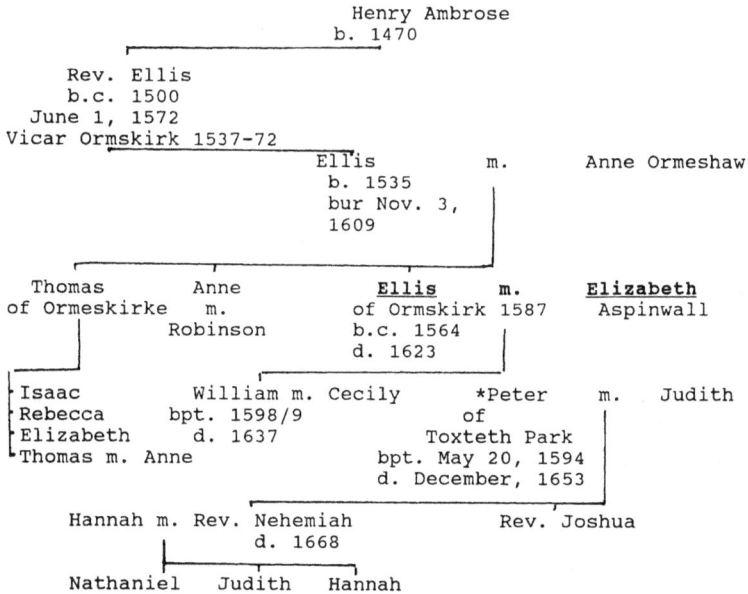

```
                         Henry Ambrose
                         b. 1470
    ┌─────────────────────────┘
  Rev. Ellis
   b.c. 1500
  June 1, 1572
Vicar Ormskirk 1537-72
                         Ellis          m.          Anne Ormeshaw
                         b. 1535
                         bur Nov. 3,
                         1609
  ┌──────────────────────────┘
  Thomas       Anne        Ellis     m.     Elizabeth
of Ormeskirke   m.      of Ormskirk 1587    Aspinwall
            Robinson    b.c. 1564
                        d. 1623
┌ Isaac          William m. Cecily    *Peter    m.    Judith
├ Rebecca        bpt. 1598/9             of
├ Elizabeth      d. 1637            Toxteth Park
└ Thomas m. Anne                    bpt. May 20, 1594
                                    d. December, 1653
     ┌──────────────────────────┘
   Hannah m. Rev. Nehemiah            Rev. Joshua
   │           d. 1668
 ┌─┴──────────────┐
Nathaniel   Judith   Hannah
```

*Peter Ambrose, an agent for "Sequestration" in Lancaster sent
two sons to New England. Joshua and Nehemiah both graduated
from Harvard in 1653. After their return to England, Joshua
became Vicar of Kirby, Lancashire, and Nehemiah eventually
became Vicar of Toxteth Park, Lancashire.

Aspinwall

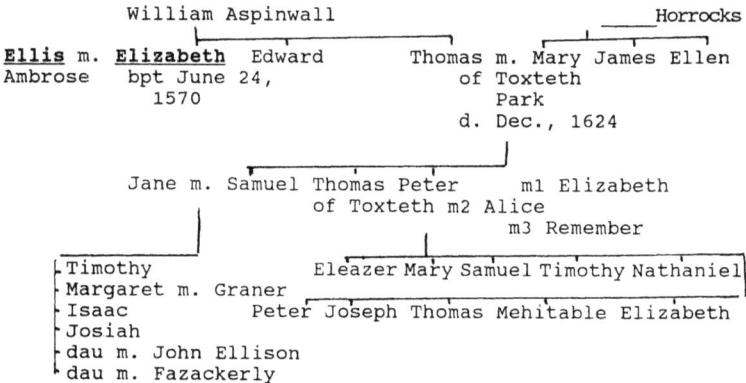

```
            William Aspinwall                        Horrocks
  ┌──────────────────────┴──┐      ┌────────────┴──────┐
Ellis m. Elizabeth   Edward     Thomas m. Mary James Ellen
Ambrose  bpt June 24,           of Toxteth
         1570                   Park
                                d. Dec., 1624
       ┌────────────────────────────┘
   Jane m. Samuel Thomas Peter      m1 Elizabeth
   │             of Toxteth m2 Alice
   │                        m3 Remember
┌ Timothy            Eleazer Mary Samuel Timothy Nathaniel
├ Margaret m. Graner
├ Isaac             Peter Joseph Thomas Mehitable Elizabeth
├ Josiah
├ dau m. John Ellison
└ dau m. Fazackerly
```

Will of Thomas Aspinwall

In the name of God, Amen. I, Thomas Aspinwall of Tocksteth Parke doe make this my last will and testament, ffirst be-taking myself into the hands of the faithful Creator and my Redeemer, whom I professe here to follow and with whom I ex-pect to live hereafter for ever, And then as to my worldly estate, besydes what i have otherwise hertofore don or have referred to bee further declared herein disposing and devising as following that is to saie; first I appoint my trusty and well beloved cousin Jirehjah Aspinwall and my brother-in-law James Horrocks executors. I will and desyre that my debts bee truelie discharged, wherof I have likewise caused and fathered a noate as nere as I coulde, I will that they be diligentlie and without overlong delaye required and in due manner looked for. And of my debts after they are received and of all my other goods and chattels unestated and not speciallie particularised disposed of and appointed heretofore or otherwise. After my debts and funeral discharged I will that my beloved wife have one third parte, my children all equally amongst them one third parte, and the last third parte after Legacies are deducted I will be divided equally amongst all my children saving him who shall have the tytle to the tenement in Toxteth nexte after my decease; And my will is that such of my child-ren as shall enjoye and have the estate and tytle of the tenement in Toxteth where I dwell next after my decease shall paye to everie of my younger children towards the increase of their potions if my executors and other friend to be named overseers of this my will do not see cause in them to the contrarie the sum of 5 pounds apiece. And if Samuel die with-out issue my will is that myne eldest son next to him shall suceed in this steed as of estate so of charge by mee given and imposed on him as to the said messuage and tenement in and by this my last will or otherwise. Moreover I give to the poor of Crosbie 13s. 4d. and to the poor of Birkbie 6s. 8d.

[Not signed by testator].

Richard Mather
Edward Aspinwall

The will of Thomas Aspinwall of Toxteth Parke deceased was proved 22 day of this month of December 1624, and adm. of his goods granted to the executors. An inventory to be exhibited before March 25th next.

Will of John Balch

The last will & testat of John Balch of Salem bearing date the
15th day of May, 1648.

I John Balch sick in bodie but in prfect memorie doe make
this my last will & testamt in manner & forme following - My
debts paid and Funeral expenses discharged those goods which
God hathe gyvenme it is my will to dispose of them as followeth -Imprimis I gyve unto Annis Balch my to be tilage and
also 4 Akers of medowe wth some pt of the barne to lay in Cowe
fodder & half of the great Fruit trees for and during the life
of said Annis.

Itm, I gyve vnto my said wife my best bed wth all Convenient furniture thereunto belonging & one fourth pt of all
my househould goods except the rest of my bedding & alsoe 2
Cowes by name Reddie & Cherlia & one yearling heaffer Further
my will is that so long as my said wife shall live my said
Sonnes shall sowe or plant 2 Akers of the aforsaid 4 akers for
my said wife for the term of 7 years and after that our sonne
shall do all himselfe. Item I gyve and bequeth to Benjamin
Balch my oldest sonne one half of my farm to him and his heirs
forever as alsoe two yoake of oxen i Cowe one third of my
young cattle & of the mare Coalt with one fourth pt of my
household goodes & half of the great fruit trees & after the
decease of my said wife my will is that the said Benjamin
Balch shall have them all himselfe. Item my will is that all
my Corne growing vpon the ground shall be equallie divided
into 4 equall pts amongst my wife & children Item I gyve vnto
John Balch my second sonne one fourth p't of my farm and one
yoake of oxen one third of my young cattell & mare Coalt one
fourth of my househould goods half of all the young aple trees
undisposed of and one Cowe.

Itm I gyve to Freeborne Balch my youngest sonne one
fourth pt of my Farme one yoake of oxen & one Cow I [bred] up
for him, one third of the young cattell & one third of the
mare & one fourth of my househould goods & half the young aple
trees betwixt him and his brother John equallie to be divided
& further my will is that Annis my wife & Benjamin my son
shall be executors to this my last will and tesamt my loving
friends John Porter & William Woodberrie (Woodbury) shall be
overseers of the same, in witness hereof I have hereunto put
by hand the day & year above written.

        Witness Peter
                Palfrey   Nicholas Paris
                            Jefferie Massey
                                        Palfrey

            The estate amounted to the "summe" of
                220: 13s 4d as pr inventory
                A true copy as on file
                            Atts Ichabod Tucker
    Clerk

Will of Thomas Gardner

Weighing the uncertainety of man's life I doe therefore in the time of my health, make this my laft will as followeth:

First I leaue unto my wife Damaris, all tha eftate fhee brought with her according to ower agreement: likewife I give unto her eight pounds, by the year during life, to be pd her by my fix fonns out of that ettate I shall leaue with them, which eight pounds I give on this condition that fhee fhall give up to them her right to the third pt of my houfing and lands during her life.

2-I give to my daughter Sara Balch: fifteene pounds.

3-I give to my daughter Seeth Grafton fifteene pounds.

4-I give to my daughter Miriam Hills (Hill) two daughters, Miriam Hill & Sufanna Hill to each of them five pounds to be pd to them, when they fhall accomplifh the age of eighteene yeares, or at theire marriagd:

I five unto my fons George & John Gardner that pt. of my salt meddow, lying on the weft fide of Capt George Corwin's meddow, which I value at twenty pounds.

I give unto my fonns Samuell and Joseph Gardner, the other pt of my falt meddow lying on the eaft fide of Capt. Corwin's meddow, wch I doe likewife value at twenty pounds.

My will is further that my houfeing with the feft of my lands & good & eftate with the medow before mentioned, fhall be divided into feaven equall pts: yt don with agreement or elce, the meddow before mentioned only excepted fhall be fould (& with the meddow as I have valued it) fhall be divided into feaven equal pts: which I doe give to my fix sons, as followeth: first I give to my fon Thomas two pts of ye feaven, he paying his mother in law forty-fix fhillings by the yeare, during her life.

2nd. I give to my fon George Gardner one pt of the seavewn, he paying to his mother-in-law 23 shill. by the yeare during her life.

3rd. I give to my fon Richard (as above) (also John, Samuel, and Joseph, have similare bequests in the order named.)

I doe appoynt my fons George & Samuell to be the executors of this my will & doe defire my loveing friends Mr. Joseph Grafton Sen and Deacon Horne to be my ouerfeers to fee this my will performed.

Robert Peafe (Pease / Rease)   Thomas Gardner
Samuel Goldthrite   The 7:10:68

"On the 29 March 1675: Robert Reafe (Pease / Rease) & Samuel Goldthrite came before the worshipfull Edward King Esq. and Maj. Hathorne Esq. & Hilliard Vern clearke of the court at Salem, being present & gave oath that the aboue written was affigned to & declared the laft will and teftament of ye sd Tho: Gardner & that ther is no latter will of his that they know of

                    Atteft Hilliard Veren clerk

Will of Robert Hull

-I Robert Hull, being in good memory of body and mind doe giue
to sonne, John Hull, my part of this house which was first
bylt, and the orchard or garden, with all opporttynances to
yt., and on lotte at muddye riuer, of thurty Accores, which I
promised to him at his marridge to giue at my death, and doe
make him my full executores of all oether goods, cattlells
after my death, and to see this my will to be performed, that
is to saye, I giue to my sonne, Edmund Quinney, [Quincy] that
porsson which is due to me by my wife, that 20 pound in goods
and corne, be yt more or less, and to his sonne, John Quiney,
on lote at brantrye which was my sonne, Richard Storer; to the
oether childrens, 12 pence a peece.   To Richard Storer, 9
pound, to be payed before or after my death, and to sonne,
Edward Hull, that peece of ground at the water mile and three-
[s]core poundes in money or goods.
Robert Hull.   20 of 3 persent, 1657.   [Recorded-Book I.
folio 511.
               [In the same file is a deed of gift, endorsed "Robt
Hull: my fathrs deed of Gifte vnto me 12 febr. 66." His son,
John Hull, "being now upon his marriage, being about the one
and twentieth yeare of his age," his father gives him as
follows: - "My dwelling House & garden, with all the fruit
trees and Appurtenances, bounded one the north, with the land
of Job Judkin; on the south, with the land of John Hurd; one
the east, with the Land of Ganaliel Waite; one the north west,
with the high way. As also my Lott of garden at mudy river,
given to me by the towne of Boston, of about 36 or 38 ackras,
bounded with Cambridg line one the North; vpon the south, with
the Land of Edward Belsher (Belcher); one the East, ptly: with
the Land of Robert Turner; one the west, with the Lotts of
Thomas Wheeler, Thomas Scottow & Isack Perry. As also A Lott
of 21 ackras, given by the towne of Boston vnto my sonn,
Richard Storer, & by me purchased off him, Lieing at Brantree,
by Manatticott river, betweene Mr Francis Loyall & Mr Ting
(Tyng). Said property, Robert Hull gave to his son, John,
reserving to himself during his life, the full enjoyment of
it.   Dated Dec. 15, 1646.
                           Feb. 12, 1666.   Power of
Administration given to John Hull to administer on the estate
of his father, Robert Hull, John being "his Eldest & now only
sonn."

Inventory of the estate taken, 4: 6: 1666, by Edw. Raynsford,
Robt Sanderson, Robt Walker.

Will of Radford Maverick

The Will of Radford Mauericke, Minister and preacher in
the Cittie of Exeter, 20 July 1622. My body to be buried in
the same Tombe with my wyffe in the parish church of S Mary
the More, with a sermon. To Radford Mauericke, my brother
John's son, my godson, 20 s, and I forgive him 20 s that he
oweth me. To John, son of my brother John, 10s. To my cousen
Sysell, my brother John's daughter, 20 s. To my kinswoman,
Robert Caddey's daughter, 5s.To Henrye Mauericke, my brother
Edward's so, 20 s. To my cousen Elizabeth, my brother Edward's
daughter, 20 s. To my cousen John Mauerick preacher one of
Zanchees works of the nature of god in lattyn, and to his son
Aron 20s. To my cousen Nathaniel Mauericke, my eldest bro-
ther's son, 10s. for a gold ring. To my brother-in-law Thomas
Brewer 5s., and to his son, by cousen Thomas Brewer, 5s. To my
cousen John Brewer his son and to his daughter Mary, my
goddaughter, 10s. apiece for a gold ring. To Joane Rackley, my
wife's kinswoman, my wife's best gown and beaver hat and band
with the trunk that they be in and one syld presse now at
Ilsington, a carpet which was her grandfather's, 20s. in
money, and 10 s. for a gold ring. To Mary, sister of said
Joane, 20s. To John Rackley a doublett and breeches. To his
wife Wilmote in respect of her attendance 20s. and a pair of
course sheets. To his son Martin Rackley 5s. at the end of his
apprenticeship. To his daughter Tamsyne 5s. To my wife's
sister's daughter, Mary Eastcott, 20s. To my cousen Anne
Rackley, widow a gown of cloth of sarge which lies at Gregory's Sopper's unmade, 20s. in respect of her attendance, and
a pair of old sheets. To her daughter Audrey 10s. To her
daughters Grace and Prisilla, 5s apiece. To my god-daughter
Dowsabell Sutcott 10s for a gold ring. To Mr. Gregory Soper my
saddle bridle and furniture and a Caliver. To my old servant
Cristover syvericke a sword, a shert, a pair of boots and
spurs, and 10s. To Mr. Lang my minister, one sarkett. To Mr.
Warren Vicar of Ilsington my free ...in a Tynne works, called
the Sanctuary, and to his successors forever Residuary
legatyee and executrix: Anne Rackley of the Cittie of Exeter,
spinster. Overseers: Mr. Clement Owlaburrow, Mr. Gregory
Soper, William Homes, Nicholas Somers, and John Parsons.
Witnesses: Clement Awlborow, William Homes, Nich. Somers, John
P sons, and Christover Syeurett.
     Codicil, made 27 November 1622, after a long sickness and
now in great weakness of body by means of a dropsy. Whereas I
have given divers gifts and legacies to sundey particular
persons of mine and my wife's kindred, I charge my executrix
that they hold good upon these conditions, that at the time of
my death I be of as good estate as I was. But seeing that it
hath pleased god to visit me sithence with a long and chargeable illness...and so expend the most part...she shall
proportionally deduct from them, but Joan Rackley, Docible
Southcott, and my cousen Anne are to have their legacies upon
my death, and as Anne Rackley was to have a gown which has
since meen made up for myself, I give her instead my wife's
cloak and 10s. Having about 200 (pounds) owing me, I desire,
if such debts are paid, that the money be divided among my
kinsfolk as follows: to Aaron my cozen John Maverick's son; to
my cousins, Radford by brother John Mauericke's son, his
brother John, and his sister Cicill, or to their children in

case of their decease; to Henry my brother Edward's son and Elizabeth his siter, or to their children in case of their decease; also a like portion to my wife;s kindred, Joane Rackley, her sister Mary, and her brother John Rackley, or to their children in case of their decease. Anne my executrix is to preserve to herself some portion of my lead work in Ilsington. Witnesses: Clement Owlborow, Edward Lang, and William Homes.

Will of Moses Maverick

The Will of Moses Maverick, on board the good ship Phaeneas and Margaret, 6 January 1678/9. To my landlady, Mrs. Elizabeth Downing. To Mr. Thomas Nelson. To Mrs. Deale and her two daughters. To my father and mother, brothers and sisters. To every officer in this said ship Phineas and Margaret. To Mrs. Ligh. To Robert Hall. I make my landlady, Elizabeth Downing, my heir and executrix and to see this will performed within ten days of the arrival of the ship at London. Proved 23 July 1679 by Elizabeth Downing als Dunning.

Genealogy of Mary (Gye) Maverick

Sources:
Weis, Frederick Lewis. Ancestral Roots of Sixty Colonists Who Came to New England Between 1623 and 1650. GPC. Baltimore. 1976.
Hunt, John G. The Ancestry of Mry Gye, Wife of the Rev. John Maverick. NEHGR. October, 1968.

10. Henry Fitz Roger
    b.c. 1344
    m. Elizabeth
    d. 1352, Chewton, England

9. John Fitz Roger
    b. betw 1344-1351
    m. Alice
    d. by 1382

8. Elizabeth Roger
    m1 Sir John Bonvyle (d. 1396)
    m2 Richard Stucle/Stuckley (d. by 1414) of Trent, Somerset
    d. 1414

7. Hugh Stuckley
    b. aft 1398
    sheriff - 1448; Devon County, England
    m. Katherine, dau of John Affeton of Afton, Devon County, England
    d. by 1459

6. Nicholas Stuckley
    m. Thomasine Cokeworthy

5. Sir Thomas Stuckley
    b.c. 1474
    m. dau of Thomas Wode/Wood

4. Margery Stuckley
    m. Charles Farrington/Farringdon

3. Ann Farringdon
    b.c. 1532
    m. Thomas Dowrish of Dowrish House
    d. 1590

2. Grace Dowrish
    m. Robert (b.c. 1531 d. betw 1604-1608), son of John (d.
    August 14, 1536; Plympton, Devon County, England) and
    Mary (Prowse) Gye/Guy/Gee/Geeye; c. 1555
    d. betw 1604-1608

1. Mary Gye
    b.c. 1580
    m. Rev. John Maverick; October 28, 1600; Islington,
    England
    d. aft 1666

Payne Family of "ffrythenden"

John Payn
    b.c. 1420; Frittenden, Kent County, England
    m. Joane, c. 1442
    wll dtd April 12, 1463
    Children
        Stephen (see below)
        Edmund
        Elizabeth

Stephen
    b.c. 1450; Frittenden, Kent County, England
    m1 dau of John Webb, c. 1478
    m2 Johane, c. 1488
    d. May 3 - October 21, 1505
    Children
        John (see below)
        Johanne
        Edmund
        James
        Thomas
        Stephen

John
    b.c. 1483; Frittenden, Kent County, England
    m2 _____ Buchorn, by 1526
    d. by 1526
    Children
        John (see below)
        Elizabeth
        Johane

John
    b.c. 1510; Frittenden, Kent County, England
    m. Jane, dau of Robert Coucheman (clothier); c. 1534
    d. betw 1549-1551; Frittenden, Kent County, England
    Children
        Nicholas (see genealogy in front of the book)
        Robert
        Elizabeth
        Margaret
        Cicely

Inventory of Robert Sharp's Estate

Inventory taken 19:11:1654, by Peter Olliver (Oliver), Edward Clap, Amt. 172.07.06. Estate indebted to Elder Colbrvn; debt yt was due fro Mr. Filbeame of Rehoboth; payd to Peter Aspinwall for so much of yt he lent ye said Sharp; to Robert Hake, Abraham Hoe, William Fugrame, for Labour; Mr. Gore, for goods; to Mary Read for seruice; to goodman Dunckin; Goodman Voysy; Capt Johnson of Rox: for a horse Coller; Edward Devotion, Tho. Clarke (Clark), Peter Olliver. Whole Estate, 172.7.6 Debts 83.06.08. The house & land, prized at 110, at the request of the widow & her friends set apart for the childrens portions, so farr as it goes, the rest the widow is to make good. Said land * house is bound over to the court for sd childrens portions, the Sonne paying his sisters theire portions; the house & land sd Robert Sharpe his father desyred is to be wholy his. 26 Jan 1654.

John Sharp's Agreement to Abide by Father's Will

I, John Sharp, sonne of the late Robert Sharp, of muddy Riuer, in the precints of Boston, bound to Edward Rawson, some 56 pounds; for the payment whereof I bind myself, wth my now dwelling house & land formerly ye dwelling house & land of my late father, in the some of one hundred and twenty pounds. Aprill 25, 1665.

If the above John Sharp pay vnto Abigaile & Mary Sharpe, his two sisters, the sume of 28 pounds apeece, as they shall attaine their seuerall ages as the Law prescribes, & also pay & sattisfy unto them or their guardians yearely duringe their minority the some of 50 shillings a peece, then this obligation to be voyd, etc.

                                        JOHN SHARP

In the presence of vs
     Richard Peacocke
     Paul Batt

A Ward Family Genealogy Circa 1500

Source: Visitation Circa A.D. 1480-1500

Les Armes de Warde saphir a vne crois patee toupace. Et sus son heauime la teste dune chiuere topace.

```
                       Dominus Simon
                        Ward miles
                            |
                       Dominus Simon
                        Warde miles
                            |
                     Dominus Iohannes
                        Warde miles
  _____|_____
  |           |              |         |              |        |
Iohannes  Dominus m. Nicholaus    Dominus      Willelmus nupta


     _____|_____
     |              |                 |                           |
  Iohanna    Catherina Beatris   Margareta D o m i n u s          |
                                                          _____|
  _____|_____|
  |            |         |       |         |           |         |
Iohanna      Simon    vna   alia       Dominus     Iohannes    Thomas
```

149

APPENDIX X   MISCELLANEOUS

Freeman's Oath

I (A.B.) being by Gods providence, an Inhabitant, and Freeman, within the Jurisdiction of this Commonwealth; do freely acknowledge my self to be subject to the Government thereof: And therefore do here swear by the great and dreadful Name of the Ever-living God, that I will be true and faithfull to the same, and will accordingly yield assistance & support thereunto, with my person and estate, as in equity I am bound; and will also truly endeavor to maintain and preserve all the liberties and priviledges thereof, submitting my self to the wholesome Lawes & Orders made and established by the same. And further, that I will not plot or practice any evill against it, or consent to any that shall so do; but will timely discover and reveal the same to lawfull Authority now here established, for the speedy preventing thereof.

Moreover, I doe solemnly bind my self in the sight of God, that when I shal be called to give my voyce touching any such matter of this State, in which Freemen are to deal, I will give my bote and suffrage as I shall judge in mine own conscience may best conduce and tend to the publike weal of the body, So help me God in the Lord Jesus Christ.

Inter-relationship of the
Allerton - Maverick - Tuttle - Ward Families

Isaac Allerton ———— Mary Norris
b. England,   b. Newberry, Berkshire,
c. 1586   England
m. Leyden,   d. Plymouth, Mass.
November 4, 1611
d. New Haven, Conn.
February, 1659

Moses Maverick ——————— Remember Allerton
b. England, c. 1610   b. Leyden, Holland; c.
m. Plymouth, Mass.   1614
June 6, 1635   d. Salem, Mass. betw.
d. Marblehead, Mass.;   1652-1656
January 28, 1685/6

Abigail Maverick ———— Samuel Ward
b. Salem, Mass.; by   b. Hingham, Mass.;
January 12, 1644   November 18, 1638
d. by 1682   d. by April 22, 1691

John Tuttle ——————— Martha Ward
b. Ipswich, Mass.;   b. Salem, Mass.; September
April 22, 1666   16. 1672
m. Ipswich, Mass.;   d. Ipswich, Mass.; August
December 3, 1689   17, 1723
d. Ipswich, Mass;
February 27, 1715/16

Winthrop / Dudley Feud

Winthrop and Dudley just could not get along. First Dudley was very critical when Winthrop moved his home from Cambridge to Boston. On August 3, 1632 Winthrop wrote in his journal that he had promised to reside in New Towne (Cambridge).

"The governor answered, that he had performed the words of the promise; for he had a house up, and seven or eight servants abiding inti, by the day appointed..." However, "seeing that the rest of the assistants went not about to build" Winthrop saw no reason to keep his promise. "The deputy, Mr. Thomas Dudley, being still discontented with the governor, partly for that the governor had removed the frame of his house, which he had set up at Newtown, and partly for that he took too much authority upon him (as he conceived)..."

Dudley also got upset because the governor had lent 28 pounds of gunpowder to Plymouth, given permission to Edward Johnson to set up a trading post on the Merrimac River, nor allowed Ratliff and Gray to stay in the colony after their banishment.

On the other hand, Winthrop made a number of accusations too. After Dudley gave some poor members of the congregation seven and one-half bushels of corn for the promise of receiving ten bushels in return after the harvest. Winthrop accused Dudley of "oppressing usury, and within compass of the statute." Dudley rebutted that it was "lawful."

Winthrop also accussed Dudley of expending too much public money on fancy "wainscotting and adorning his house". Dudley replied that it was of "little cost and that all he had done was nail clapboard to the walls to make the house warmer.

When Dudley resigned as deputy governor, Winthrop said he "could not leave his place, except by the same power which put him in."

To the credit of these two powerful men, Winthrop wrote that despite the bitter relations between Dudley and himself, they attempted to do their duties "without any appearance of any breach or discontent."

Colonists

Roger Conant

Roger Conant was born in 1592, the son of Richard Conant of East Budleigh, Devon, England. He spent time in Plymouth Colony (1623-1624), Hull, Cape Ann, Salem, and finally, Beverly, Massachusetts. At Cape Ann, he was made manager of the Dorchester Company fishing settlement because it was felt he could arbitrate a bad situation between Cape Ann and the Plymouth Colony and avoid bloodshed. At Salem, Conant and his followers were known as the "Old Planters".

Matthew Craddock

Matthew Craddock was a wealthy London merchant who was the first head of the Massachusetts Bay Colony. As governor of the Massachusetts Bay Colony in 1628, he defined his purpose for beginning the colony as "indeavoring to bring the Indians to the knowledge of the gospel." It was his July 28, 1629 proposal that transferred the colony's government from the company in London to the colony itself. Although he owned a plantation on the Mystic river, he never went to the colony.

John Harvard

Robert Harvard, father of John, was a butcher who owned his own shop, the Queen's Head Tavern, and several other pieces of property in the bawdy Southwark borough of London. Emigrants were pouring into the London area. In 1635, 338 aliens were reported living in Southwark. Most emigrants were weavers, tailors, dyers and other cloth-trade related occupation. The area retained a manorial status and were denied the right of electing its own Alderman and representation in the courts. Southwark inhabitants considered their situation tyrannical and became disgruntled.

The Harvards were well-to-do tradesmen and moderate Puritans. John Harvard was baptized in Saint Savior's Church (later Southwark Cathedral) in 1607. After Robert and four of his children died of the plague in 1625, the butcher business was sold and his wife remarried.

John, having inherited a good deal of money, was admitted to Emmanuel College of Cambridge in 1627. He received his B.A. in 1631/32 and M.A. in 1635. On April 19, 1636, John married Anne, sister of his friend John Sadler and lived in Southwark.

Puritan opposition was at its strongest in Southwark. In 1640, a public meeting on St. George's Fields in Southwark turned into a riot when apprentices, glovers and tanners celebrating the May Day holiday joined idle sailors and dockhands.

After living a little over a year in Southwark, they emigrated to the New World where they were admitted to Charlestown in August, 1637 and given a large allotment of land. On September 14, 1638, John Harvard died of consumption leaving half of his estate and all of his library towards the establishment of a college. After Rev. Thomas Allen of St. Edmund's, Norwich emigrated, the pious preacher married John Harvard's widow. In 1651 he returned to a Norwich parish.

Ancestry of John Harvard

Thomas Rogers, alderman and
cattle dealer of Stratford,
d. 1611

Robert Harvard m1   Barbara   Descyn m2   Katherine Rogers
Butcher of Southwark
d. August 24, 1625

Mary   Robert   John   Thomas   William   Katherine   Anne   Peter
bpt. Nov.
29, 1607
d. Sept.
14, 1638
m. Apr. 19, 1636 Anne Sadler m2 Rev.Thomas
dau of Rev.   Allen
John Sadler

Peter Hobart

Hobart was a powerful name throughout East Anglia and the Hobarts were of distinguished stock. Sir James Hobart was attorney-general and privy counsellor during Henry VIII's reign. Sir Henry Hobart, his grandson, was attorney-general in 1606 and Chief Justice of the Common Pleas Court in 1613. He did well and amassed a great fortune.

Younger sons, like Edmund Hobart of Holt, with little to lose were the only Norfolk men to participate in the war. Edmund was called by R.W. Kelton-Cremer "a member of the sole Royalist offshoot of that extremely Puritan Family."

Peter Hobart (Hubbard) was one of the sons of Edmund and Margaret (Dewey) Hobart of Hingham, Norfolk County, England. Peter was baptized there on October 14, 1604. He was admitted to Queen's College, Cambridge University on December 1, 1621; but moved to Magdalene College, the smallest and poorest college at Cambridge, in 1623. He received his B.A. in 1625/26 and M.A. in 1629. Ordained in 1627, Peter became curate at Haverhill until he emigrated with his parents and some of his siblings in 1635. The Hobart family and friends founded Hingham, Massachusetts where Peter served as pastor until his January 20, 1678/79 death. He was autocratic in his village and preferred the discipline of the Presbyterian Church. His sons, Joshua, Jeremiah, Gershom, Japhet, and Nehemiah graduated from Harvard. All except Japhet who may have converted to Catholicism, became clergymen.

The _Hobart Journal_ recorded over seventy-seven years of Massachusetts Bay Colony births, baptisms, deaths and burials. From circa 1637 through 1714, Hingham Massachusetts, and neighboring towns were well-documented. The diary was kept first by Rev. Peter Hobart and kept up after Peter's death by his son David Hobart. The small journal was passed down through the Hobart family and is now held by the Massachusetts Historical Society. The volume they have appears to be a copy since all entries are in the same, very legible handwriting, probably that of David Hobart.

Thomas Hooker, Jr.

Thomas Hooker, Jr., born circa 1586, was from Marefield, Leicestershire, England. He began his college education at Queen's College, Cambridge; but moved to Emmanuel College where he was scholar from 1604 to 1609, fellow from 1609 to 1618, and dean from 1616 to 1617.

He became curate at Esher, Surrey and lecturer at Chalmsford, Essex. In 1628, because of his militant beliefs, Thomas was called before Archbishop Laud, and in 1629 he was "silenced".

In 1630 he went to Holland where he became assistant minister under Hugh Peter at the English Church in Rotterdam. Wearing disguises to avoid the authorities, Hooker, Samuel Stone, and John Cotton boarded a ship for the New World in 1633.

He settled first at Braintree and then, along with Samuel Stone, he organized the church at New Towne (Cambridge). That church was eventually taken over by Thomas Shephard's followers when, in June, 1636, Hooker moved with his congregation to the wilds of the Connecticut River Valley. There was some indication that a disagreement with John Cotton was at the root of the move.

Hooker's children were Samuel, Sarah who married John Wilson, and Joanna who married Thomas Shephard.

Isaac Johnson

Isaac Johnson and his wife Lady Arabella, daughter of the Earl of Lincoln were probably the wealthiest and most prominent members of the Bay Colony. However, Lady Arabella died only two months after arriving in the colony and her husband died one month later. Winthrop described Johnson as "a holy man, and wise, and died in sweet peace leaving some part of his substance to the colony."

Thomas Morton

Thomas Morton arrived in the New World first between 1622 and 1624, and then returned to lead a settlement he named Merrymount. As an Anglican, his jovial antics were not appreciated by his conservative neighbors.

Thomas Morton's roguery at Merrymount (Braintree / Quincy) brought reprisals from both Plymouth and Massachusetts Bay. On September 30, 1630, Winthrop wrote "Thomas Morton adjudged to be imprisoned, tell he were sent into England, and his house burnt down, for his many injuries offered to the Indians, and other misdemeanors, Capt. Brook, master of the Gift, refused to carry him."

After banishment, Morton returned to England where he posed as a martyr and published the book New England Cahaan in 1637.
After conspiring with Sir Fernando Gorges in an attempt to have Massachusetts Bay Colony's charter revoked, Morton returned to New England. He was banished again for Massachusetts, roamed through Maine and Rhode Island, and returned to Massachusetts where he was imprisoned in 1645. He finally removed to Maine where stayed until his death.

William Pynchon

William Pynchon (b. Springfield, Essex, England c. 1590) of the Winthrop Fleet settled in the area to engage in the fur trade. He served as colonial treasurer from 1632 to 1634 and as magistrate in 1636. Pynchon was not in sympathy with the Puritan Rule and, as an amateur theologian, Pynchon published a pamphlet which was declared "heretical" by the General Court and was burned in Boston Public Square in 1651. His wife Agnes died the same year. He returned to England after being removed from his judge's seat.

Richard Saltonstall

Richard Saltonstall, son of Sir Richard and Grace Saltonstall, was baptized on October 1, 1610 at Woodsome,
Almondbury, England. He was admitted to Emmanuel College,
Cambridge University on April 28, 1627. Although father and
son emigrated with the Winthrop Fleet in 1630, Richard the
son, openly opposed the methods of Winthrop, Dudley and
Endicott. He was also vocal in his protest against the slave
trade. In 1635 he was listed as a resident of Ipswich.

Samuel Sewall

Born in Bishop Stoke, England in 1652, Samuel Sewall
became an influential landowner, merchant, and the Chief
Justice of Massachusetts.

Sewall emigrated on the "Prudent Mary" to Newbury, Massachusetts when he was just nine years old. His father had
traveled ahead to make way for the family. In 1667, he went
off to Harvard where he wrote his M.A. thesis on original sin,
but became a wealthy merchant rather than a minister.

He married Hannah, daughter of John Hull. Although he was
well-traveled, his diary showed the burdens of colonial life.
Only six of his fourteen children lived past childhood, his
wife had failing health, and he questioned his political and
religious affiliations.

Just eighteen years after the "Mayflower", the "Desire"
landed in Salem carrying black slaves. There were approximately 200 slaves in the Massachusetts Bay Colony by 1676. And in
1700, Samuel Sewall published America's first anti-slavery
tract "The Selling of Joseph: A Memorial". In it Sewall wrote
that all men were "the Sons of Adam, and Coheirs; and have
equal Right unto Liberty, and all other outward comforts of
Life."

Yet Sewall had also been a member of the courts that
sentenced nineteen witches to be hanged in 1692. However, his
shame for his role in the witchcraft trials was made evident
when , in 1697, he made a public confession of complicity. The
guilt he felt had plagued him for years.

In 1697, he published "Phaenomena quaedam Apocalyptica"
(phenomena concerning the apocalypse). He died in 1730.

Thomas Shepard

Thomas Shepard was born in 1605. As a student of John
Preston's at Cambridge, he turned his life to one of piety.
Then as a lecturer in Earle's Colne, Essex; Shepard angered
the archbishop with his preaching.

He was the youngest of the religious leaders who emigrated to New England. In the New World, he tried to explain his
reasons for leaving England with publications such as Defence
of the Answer, which he wrote with John Allen; The Sound
Believer; and "The Parable of the Ten Virgins".

He became a venomous prosecutor of Anne Hutchinson, but
was able to hold her in high esteem. That was probably due to
his integrity. He did not prosecute her because of hidden

agendas. Although he differed greatly with Hutchinson, she
realized the honesty of his beliefs.

John Tilley

John Tilley / Tilly of "Chilthorne Domer," Somerset
County, was not a pious Puritan in England. According to 1619
records of the Archdeacon of Taunton, Tilley was accused of
"living incontinently (lacking self-restraint) with one Marie
Hunt." A number of witnesses gave "detailed and sordid
accounts" of the relationship which lasted over a six or seven
week period.

The Archdeacon Court records indicated that in 1620, John
Tilley was accused of brawling with Nicholas Hunt (Marie's
husband or father ?) and others in a churchyard on several
Sundays.

When John was offered employment as overseer of fishing
at Cape Ann with the Dorchester Company in 1623, he could have
made a fresh start. But soon after arriving he was accused of
stealing salt used for curing fish.

He may have returned to England, but was soon back in New
England as one of the original Dorchester settlers. He became
a freeman in 1635. In 1636, while going down the Connecticut
River on a boat he was captured and tortured for three days
before being killed by Indians.

Henry Vane

Henry Vane, born in 1612, was the son of a diplomat and
statesman who took his young son on business trips throughout
Europe. Winthrop referred to him as "son and heir to a privy
counsellor in England" and a "gentleman of Excellent parts."

So it was a well-traveled, sophisticated Henry Vane
emigrated to New England forfeiting prospects and provoking
the displeasure of friends. His addition to the New World gave
the colony a importance and he soon became governor.

He only remained in America for a short time. His support
of Anne Hutchinson led to his defeat in his bid for re-
election. After only two years in the New World, Vane returned
to England.

During the time he was in New England he resided with
Rev. John Cotton in Boston. While there, he built an addition
onto Cotton's house which, according to Cotton's will, Vane
"by a deed gave ... at his departure to Vane's son Seaborne."

LITERATURE CITED

Balch, Thomas Willing. Balch Genealogica. Allen, Lane &
Scott. Philiadelphia. 1907.
Banks, Charles Edward. The Winthrop Fleet of 1630. GPC.
Baltimore. 1961.
Banks, Charles Edward. The Planters of the Commonwealth. GPC.
Baltimore. 1961.
Bardsley. A Dictionary of English and Welsh Surnames
Bell, Charles H. John Wheelwright; His Writings, including
His Fast-Day Sermon, 1637, and His Mercurius amerecanus,
1645; with a Paper Upong the Genuineness of the Indian
Deed of 1629 and a Memoir. Book for Libraries Press.
NY. 1970 repr of 1876.
Bodge, George Madison. Soldiers in King Philip's War. GPC.
Baltimore. 1967.
Browne, John. History of Congregationalism and Memorials of
the Churches of Norfolk and Suffolk. Jerrold & Sons.
London. 1877.
Burke, John Bernard. Prominent Families in America with
British Ancestry. London House. London. 1971.
Chamberlain, George Walter. Genealogies of the Early Families
of Weymouth, Massachusetts. GPC. Baltimore. 1984.
City of Boston. A volume Relating to the Early history of
Boston Containing the Aspinwall Notarial Records.
Municipal Printing Office. Boston. 1903.
City of Boston. Ninth Report of the Record Commissioners:
Births, Baptisms, Marriages, and Deaths, 1630-1699. Doc.
130. Boston. 1883.
Collections of the Connecticut Hist. Society. Hartford. Vol.
14, 1912 and Vol. 21, 1924.
Connecticut Nutmeggar. Connecticut Soc. of Genealogists, Inc.
June, 1985; Sept., 1985
Cowdell, Nellie. The Hotchkiss Family: First Six
Generations: Descendents of Samuel Hotchkiss (ca. 1622
-1663) of New Haven, Connecticut. Vol. 1. Gateway Press,
Inc. Baltimore. 1985.
Davis, William T. Genealogical Register of Plymouth Families.
GPC. 1975. Baltimore
Dow, George Francis. Everyday Life in the Massachusetts Bay
Colony. Benjamin Blom Pub. Boston. 1967.
Downing, John C. "British Russells: The Famous and
Infamous". Russell Register. 1980.
Ellis, Arthur B. History of the First Church of Boston 1630-
1880. Hall and Whiting. Boston. 1881.
Felt, Joseph B. History of Ipswich, Essex, and Hamilton.
Clamshell Press. Ipswich, Massachusetts. 1966.
Gardner, Frank A. "Thomas Fardner, Planter, and some of his
Descendants". Historical Collections of the Essex
Institute. v.37 no.3. July, 1901.
Galloupe, A.A. "Early Records of the Town of Beverly, Essex
County, Massachusetts". The Genealogical Magazine.
July, 1905. Vol. 1 No. 4.
Genealogical Guide to the Early Settlers of America
Graves, Mrs. Edward. Rev. John Russell of Massachusetts
Colony. Russell Register. np. nd.
Hansen, Ann Natalie. The English Origins of the "Mary & John"
Passengers. At the Sign of the Cock. Ohio. 1985.
Hart, Albert Bushnell. Commonwealth History of Massachusetts.

v.1.   States Historical Company. New York. 1927.
Hassam, John T. (comp.) Aspinwall Notarial Records, Liber X
    of Suffolk Deeds (Found Guildhall, London.
Heimert, Alan and Andrew Delbanco (eds.). The Puritans in
    America: A Narative Anthology. Harvard University Press.
    Cambridge, Massachusetts. 1985.
History of Hingham, Mass Vol. III
Hobart. Hobart's Journal
Holman, Mary Lovering. "Moses Paine of Braintree, Mass. and
    his Ancestry in England" American Genealogist. Warwick,
    R.I. January, 1945. Vol. 21 No. 3.
Holmes. Directory of the Heads of New England Families 1620
    1700. np. nd.
Hosmer, James Kendall (ed.) Original Narratives of Early
    American History: Winthrop's Journal "History of New
    England" 1630-1649. 2 Vol. Charles Scribner's. New York.
    1908.
Hotten, John Camden. Original Lists of Persons of Quality
    1600-1700. GPC. Baltimore. 1980.
Hull, Massachusetts. American Genealogist. Warwick, RI. Oct,
    1989
Hunt, John G.   "Some Passengewrs of the 'Mary and John' in
    1630". National Genealogical Society Quarterly. 1974.
Ketton-Cremer, R.W. Norfolk in the Civil War. Archeon Books.
    Connecticut. 1969.
Kuhans, Maude Pinney. The "Mary and John": A story of the
    Founding of Dorchester, Massachusetts, 1630. Charles E.
    Tuttle Co. Vermont. 1976.
Langston, Aileen Lewers & J. Orton Buck, Jr. Pedigrees of
    Some of the Emperor Charlemagne's Descendants. Order of
    the Crown of Charlemagne in the United States of America.
    np. 1974.
Lobdell, Julia Harrison. Nicholas Lobden (Lobdell) - 1635
    Hingham, Mass and some of His Descendents. Julia Harrison
    Lobdell. np. 1907.
Lower, Mark antony. English Surnames: An Essay on Family
    Nomenclature. John Russell Smith. London. 1875.
Marriage Records Before 1699. np. nd.
Massachusetts Historical Society. Broadsides, Ballands &c.:
    Printed in Massachusetts 1639-1800. 1922
Matthews, C.M. Place Names of the English-Speaking World.
    Charles Scribner's Sons. NY. 1972.
Mayo, Lawrence Shaw. John Endecott: A Biography. Harvard
    Univeristy Press. Cambridge. 1936.
Morison, Samuel Eliot. Builders of the Bay Colony. Houghton
    Mifflin Co. New York. 1930.
Morison, Samuel Eliot. The Founding of Harvard College.
    Harvard University Press. Cambridge, Massachusetts.
    1935.
Muddy River and Brookline Records 1634-1838: By the
    Inhabitants of Brookline, In Town Meeting. J.E. Farwell
    & Co. 1875.
Murray, Georgea Smith. John Russell of Charlestown & Woburn,
    MA. Russell Register. np. nd.
New England Historical and Genealogical Record. October,
    1856; April, 1852; January, 1854; April 1854; April,
    1861; January, 1879; July, 1886; April, 1887; July, 1893;
    July 1886; October, 1989; January, 1908; April, 1915;
    April, 1917; April, 1919, April, 1927; July, 1930;
    October, 1974; July, 1988; October, 1989.
New Haven Gen. Soc. New Haven Genalogical Magazine. np. nd.

Paige, Lucius R. List of Freemen of Massachusetts 1630-1691.
  GPC. Baltimore. 1978.
Pearl, Valerie. London and the Outbreak of the Puritan
  Revolution. Oxford University Press. Oxford, England.
  1961.
Pedigrees of Descendants of the Colonial Clergy. Society of
  the Colonial Clergy. USA. 1976.
Peel, Edgar and Pat Southern. The Trials of the Lancashire
  Witches: A Study of Seventeenth Century Witchcraft.
  Taplinger Pub. Co. NY. 1969.
Perley, Sidney. History of Salem, 3 vol. Salem. 1924-1928.
Phillimore, W.P.W. (ed.). Dorset Parish Registers.
  Phillimore & Co. London. 1909.
Pope, Charles Henry. Pioneers of Massachusetts. GPC.
  Baltimore. 1965.
Records of the Town of Cambridge (Formerly Newtowne)
  Massachusetts 1630-1703. Cambridge. 1901.
Richardson, Douglas. Nicholas Lobdell, Founder of the New
  England Lobdell Family. The American Genealogist. Jan,
  1978.
Roberts, Gary Boyd (ed.).   English Origins of New Eng-
  Families from The New England Historical and Genealogical
  Register. GPC. Baltimore. 1984.
Robey, Richard C. (ed.). Diary of Samuel Sewall 1674-1729.
  Vol. III. Arno Press. New York. 1972.
Rugg, Winnifred King. Unafraid: A Life of Anne Hurchinson.
  Houghton Mifflin, Co. NY. 1930.
Russell, George Ely. Founders of American Russell Families:
  Hon. Richard russell (c. 1611-1676) of Charlestown, Mass.
  Russell Register. np. nd.
Russell Register. Riverside, California. August, 1979.
  February 1980, November 1980, February 1981, May 1981,
  August, 1984, November, 1984.
Rutman, Darret B. Winthrop's Boston: Portraits of a Purtain
  Town 1630-1649. Institution of Early American history
  and Culture. Chapel Hill. 1965.
"Salem Quarterly Court Records and Files." Essex Antiquarian.
  Salem. 1901 & 1902.
Sasek, Lawrence A. (ed.). Images of English Puritanism: A
  Collection of Contemporary Sources 1589-1646. Louisiana
  State University. Baton Rouge. 1989.
Savage, James. Genealogical Dictionary of the First Settlers
  of New England. 4 vols. GPC. Baltimore. 1977.
Sewall, Samuel. The Seling of Joseph: A Memorial. University
  of Massachusetts Press. Massachusetts. 1969.
Seymour, George D. & J. Gardner Bartlett. "English Home &
  Ancestry of Richard Seamer. NEHGR. April, 1917.
Shurtleff, Nathaniel B. Records of the Colony of New Plymouth
  in New England. GPC. 1976 reprint of 1857.
Smith, Elsdon C. New Dictionary of American Family Names.
  Harper & Row, Pub. NY 1973.
Smith, Frank. Immigrants to America Appearing in English
  Records. Everton Pub. Utah. 1976.
Stewart, George R. American Given Names. Oxford University
  Press. NY. 1979.
Stone, Robert H.   A Stone Collection: The Origins,
  Migrations, and Growth of an Illustrious Family. Exposi-
  tion Press. NY. 1981.
Suffolk Co. Wills
Talcott, Alvan (comp). Families of Early Guilford, Conn. GPC.
  Baltimore. 1984.

Tepper, Michael. Passengers to America. GPC. 1978.
Torrey, Clarence Almon. New England Marriages Prior to 1700.
    GPC. Baltimore. 1985.
Vaughn, Alden T. and Francis J. Bremer (eds). Puritan New
    England: Essays on Religion, Society, and Culture. St.
    Martin's Press. New York. 1977.
Virkus. Compendium of American Genealogies
Waters, Henry F. Genealogical Gleanings in England. NEHRG
    Soc. Boston. 1901.
Weis, Frederick Lewis. The Colonial Clergy and Colonial
    Churches of New England. Soc. of the Descendants of the
    Colonial Clergy. Lancaster, Massachusetts. 1936.
Wies. Ancestral Roots of 60 Colonists who Came to New England
    between 1623 and 1650. GPC. Baltimore. 1976.
Winslow, Ola Elizabeth. Samuel Sewall of Boston. MacMillan
    Co. New York. 1964.
Winthrop. Winthrop Journal.
Woods, Harriet F. Historical Sketches of Brookline, Mass.
    Robert S. Davis and Co. Boston. 1874.

Index of Proper Names

Names in the text appear as they do in original documents and other sources. In this index, a person might be found under a number of different spellings of his name. For example, listings under Garden / Gardener / Garner / Gardner might all be for members of the same family.

A

Abbott 119
Adams 43, 50, 91, 108
Adkins 24
Affeton 145
Ager 85
Alke 81
Allen 12, 13, 34, 54, 119, 129-130, 155
Allerton 77, 128, 130
Alling 123-124
Alsop 100, 123
Ambrose 22, 25
Andrews 95, 110
Angier 29
Appleton 39
Aspenall 22
Aspeinwell 22
Aspinwall 9-10, 12, 22-32, 51, 86, 88, 100, 102, 111-112, 140
Atherton 26, 121
Austin 53
Awlborow 144

B

Backster 33
Bagster 33
Bailey 127
Baker 5, 14, 24, 33-36, 103, 121, 123
Bakere 34
Balch 6, 36-40, 55-56, 95, 141-142
Balche 37-38
Balchen 37
Balchin 37
Balcht 37
Balck 37
Ballamy 14
Balson 9
Balstone 30
Barbour 131
Barnard 54
Barnes 123
Bartholomew 59
Barlett 120
Bartlett 46
Bass 91
Batchelder 37
Batt 148

Baxster 33
Bayley 98
Beach 100, 123
Beal 127
Beauchamp 133-134
Bee 123, 125
Beeres 110
Beers 39
Belamy 70
Belcher 27, 108, 143
Bell 77
Bellomont 24, 27
Benison 91
Benson 73
Bent 117
Bewchamp 133
Bezbeech 90
Bickford 67
Bicknell 98
Billings 91
Bingham 71
Bird 22
Bishop 6, 40, 70, 89, 124
Black 6, 18
Blackstone 81
Blake 5, 7, 38
Blaxton 6-7
Bolch 39
Bonvyle 145
Bostwick 123
Bosworth 14, 73
Bowditch 88
Bowen 23
Bowles 50
Boylston 10
Bracket 93
Bradford 16, 77, 120
Bradley 100, 119, 120
Bradshaw 109
Bradstreet 10, 18, 58, 128, 130
Brandreth 132
Bratcher 29, 38
Breedon 112
Brett 96
Brewer 75, 144
Brewster 121
Briscoe 88
Brooks 103-104, 108, 154
Broughton 131

Brown 74, 117, 119
Browne 53-54
Bryam 98
Buchorn 147
Buckminster 111, 113
Buell 47
Bugby 29
Bull 79
Bunker 12
Bunn 14
Burges 85-86
Bursley 66
Burt 70
Burton 12
Buttolph 54

C
Caddey 144
Cane 128
Capen 6
Carr 83
Carter 21
Cartwright 83
Carver 53
Carwethan 81
Chaffey 14
Chamberlain 73
Chamberlyne 73
Chambers 106
Champney 103
Chandler 119
Chapman 46
Chester 105
Child 24
Choram 75
Chittenden 33
Clap 148
Clark 36, 77, 115, 124, 129, 148
Clasby 54
Cleare 92
Cleverly 124
Coddington 30-31
Coffin 53-56, 59
Coggeshall 30
Cokeworthy 145
Colborne 9, 112
Colbrvn 148
Colburn 26, 92, 112
Cole 41, 78, 82
Colledge 103
Collier 33, 35, 71, 91, 119, 121
Collings 43
Collins 7, 24, 41-48
Colljer 14
Conant 6, 14, 16, 36, 38, 56, 88-89, 132, 135, 151
Cook 43, 94
Coole 72
Cooper 62, 117

Corbet 105
Corning 6, 58
Cornwell 47
Corwin 18, 40, 142
Cory 67
Cotton 24, 27, 30, 153, 156
Coucheman 90, 92, 147
Cox 72
Crabbe 75, 79
Craddock 151
Cradock 5, 29, 44
Craft 111
Crofton 90
Cromwell 12, 18, 71, 74, 124-125
Crooke 49
Currer 101
Curruthers 42
Curtis 33, 130
Curwin 105
Cushing 12, 13
Cuttler 108

D
Dabyn 68
Darke 79
Daves 66
Davis 23
Davison 105
Davyes 108
de Douai 38
Deale 145
Dean 24, 27
Denison 16
Denning 37
Devotion 148
Dewey 153
Dingley 98
Dipple 33, 35
Dixwell 42
Dodge 6, 39, 94
Doliber 128, 130
Doliver 128, 130
Dollabar 81, 128
Downing 54, 145
Dowrish 76, 146
Drake 85
Draper 24
Druce 10
Dudley 9-10, 15-16, 61, 65, 128, 150, 155
Dunckin 148
Dunster 43
Durbar 120
Dyer 81, 85
Dysart 124

E
Eames 13, 129
Eastcott 75, 144
Eaton 103

Eliot 15, 27
Ellingwood 6
Emerye 96
Endicott 2, 4, 6, 16, 26,
  63, 82, 89, 95, 112
English 44
Ensign 35
Everett 9

F
Fairchild 88, 100
Fairfield 37
Farnham 66
Farrard 117
Farringdon 146
Farrington 146
Farrow 127
Fazackerly 22
Feake 3
Ferguson 78, 81
Filbeame 148
Firdler 128
Fiske 108
Folger 53-54, 59
Ford 98, 131
Foster 47
Fox 117
Franklin 15, 54
Frayre 53
Freeman 25
French 68, 80
Frier 53
Frisbie 124
Fryer 53
Fugrame 148

G
Gale 128
Gall 128
Gardener 49
Gardiner 49, 57-58
Gardner i, 6, 9-10, 16, 23,
  28, 36, 49-60, 88, 95, 113
Garner 49
Garnet 127
Garrad 117
Gaskell 53
Gaylord 66, 81
Gilman 78
Gleason 108
Goff 43, 120
Goffe 110
Gold 13
Goldthrite 142
Gordon 49
Gore 49, 148
Gorges 2-3, 19, 38, 134
Gorham 120
Gould 128
Grafton 54-55, 60, 78, 142
Graner 22

Graves 105-106
Gray 6, 14, 38, 61
Greeley 119
Green 55, 132
Groose 130
Gye 76, 80, 145-146

H
Hackham 88
Hake 148
Hall 47, 145
Hamlin 42
Hanford 33
Hansford 134
Harker 53
Harper 66
Harris 41, 76
Harrison 124
Hart 36
Harvard 11-12
Haskel 130
Haspineall 22
Hassard 79
Hathorne 55, 58, 94-95, 142
Hawkes 77, 81
Hawthorne 64, 94-95
Hayme 119
Haynes 10, 68, 105
Heard 67
Henfield 55
Herrick 6, 95
Hersey 13
Hill 5-6, 55, 117, 142
Hinds 81, 128
Hines 128
Hirst 61
Hobart 6, 12-13, 35, 64,
  68, 129, 153
Hobsin 47
Hoddy 7
Hoe 148
Holbrook 85
Holioke 105
Hollingsworth 18
Homes 144
Honchine 55
Hooke 79
Hooker 8, 10-11, 153-154
Hopcott 54
Horne 53
Horrocks 22, 25, 140
Horsmer 24
Hotchkiss 25, 124
Howe 117
Hubbard 56, 128, 153
Hubert 90, 108
Hulburt 42
Hull 7, 9, 14, 20, 61-69,
  98, 109, 124, 143, 155
Humphrey 16
Humphries 89

163

Hunt 156
Huntington 35
Hurd 143
Hurst 100
Hutchinson 7, 11, 20, 30-
   31, 155-156
Hyde 46

I
Ingersol 128
Ingram 88
Isles 131

J
Jackson 100
Jacobs 12, 44
James 12, 20
Jenkins 54
Jenner 105
Johnson 3, 21, 23, 56, 77,
   88 113, 148, 154
Jones 18, 66, 124, 129
Judkins 143

K
Keayne 7
Kettell 128
Kingsworth 46
Knight 14, 38
Kniveton 131
Knowlton 37
Kought 119

L
Lambert 18
Landon 74
Lane 33-34
Lang 144-145
Langley 76
Larkum 37
Lasher 72
Lathrop 6, 35
Lawrence 105
Leavens 23, 28, 102
Leavett 36, 70, 134
Leete 46, 48
Legg 81
Lendall 72
Lenthall 20
Lette 47
Leverett 7, 73
Levins 100, 102
Lewen 124
Ligh 145
Lincoln 113
Lindall 74
Lister 101
Litchfield 33
Lobdell 70-74, 119, 128
Lobden 72-73
Lobel 72

Lobell 72
Loomis 66
Loring 14, 33-34, 71, 73
Lothrop 39
Lovel 36
Lovell 56
Lovett 36
Loyall 143
Ludlow 3, 7, 68
Lydgate 106
Lyford 14
Lyther 96

M
MacKeever 114
Macy 53-54
Mallory 100
Mallott 36
Maltbie 124
Manning 67, 78, 81, 120
Marsh 34, 73
Marshall 134
Mason 50-51
Masters 10
Mather 7, 26, 44, 74, 140
Matthews 67
Maverick 7, 12-13, 18, 21,
   36, 75-84, 112, 128,
   130, 144-146
Meeker 100
Meekins 112-113
Merrill 23, 120
Merwin 66
Miller 105
Mitchell 66
Mix 46, 124
Moody 42, 44
Moore 42
Morgan 6
Morrell 23, 26, 53
Morrice 81
Morse 119
Morton 7, 8, 63, 154
Mosely 39
Moulton 37
Munroe 109
Munson 100, 124
Munter 88

N
Nash 20, 85-87, 98, 123
Neal 91
Nelson 145
Newcomb 120
Newgate 7
Newmarsh 36
Nicholls 83, 100
Norman 78
Norris 77
Nott 24
Nowell 3, 12, 114

Noyes

O
Oldham   14, 16
Oliver   7, 28, 148
Ormeshaw   22, 25
Owlaburrow   144-145

P
Paine   8, 61, 92
Palfray   88
Palfree   88
Palfrey   i, 6, 23, 26, 38,
   56, 88-89, 141
Palfreyman   88
Palfry   88
Palgrave   79
Palmer   103
Pares   91
Paris   141
Parker   77, 81
Parkman   55
Parsons   144
Patch   36
Paul   78
Payn   92
Payne   90-93, 147
Payson   111
Peacocke   148
Pease   43, 53, 142
Peck   12, 81, 123-124
Peirce   104
Penyon   18
Perkins   71
Perry   72-73, 143
Person   66
Peson   66, 67
Peters   18
Pettee   98
Phippen   66
Phipps   27-28, 52, 114, 129
Pickering   132
Pickman   88
Pierce   70-71, 73, 104
Piers   131
Pinney   66
Pitcher   127, 129
Pitt   105
Poole   119
Pope   44, 120
Porter   20, 34, 53, 55, 86,
   94-102, 141
Powell   124, 133
Pratt   20, 98, 134
Preston   7, 23, 28, 100-102,
   123
Price   39, 70-71
Priest   117
Prince   14, 119-120
Pritchard   100
Prout   9

Putnam   18, 95
Pynchon   3, 15, 82, 96, 112,
   154

Q
Quincy   91, 143
Quynby   37

R
Rackley   144-145
Ratliff   5
Rawson   148
Rayment   37
Raynsford   143
Read   72, 119, 121, 148
Rease   142
Reed   42
Replye   129
Reycroft   127, 129
Rice   42, 108, 117
Richardson   72-73
Roberts   77, 91
Robinson   33, 35
Rockwell   81
Roger   145
Rogers   81
Root   6
Rosman   81
Rossiter   67
Roswell   105-106
Rowland   132
Rowninge   120
Rudd   71
Rudge   132
Russell   12, 18, 21, 44,
   103-110, 119, 124

S
Saltonstall   3, 155
Sampford   9
Sanders   43, 55, 134
Sanderson   63, 143
Sanford   30, 92
Sargis   72
Savage   106
Schooler   7
Scottow   143
Scruggs   89
Seabrook   100
Sedgewick   12
Severance   54
Sewall   15, 61, 64, 155
Shaflin   56
Sharp   9, 23, 26, 105, 111-
   114
Sharpe   112, 148
Shattuck   53
Shaw   71, 98, 128
Sheafe   91
Shephard   11, 154
Shepard   155

Sherwood 77
Sholy 7
Simmons 85
Skinner 81
Skipper 76
Small 92
Smith 24, 50, 77, 85, 88
Smithson 47
Smythe 131-132
Somers 144
Soper 144
Sopper 144
Speare 119, 121
Spencer 31, 57
Springer 105
Squire 119
Standish 8, 16, 19, 71, 134
Stanley 29
Starbuck 53, 58
Starr 106
Stebbing 120
Stedman 72
Steele 72, 74
Stevens 23-24, 27, 46
Stilson 12
Stodder 14
Stone 6, 10, 14, 54, 115-118, 123
Storer 61-62, 143, 153
Stowe 117
Stream 85
Street 73
Stubbe 120
Stubbs 7, 14, 35, 72-73, 119-122
Stuckley 145-146
Sturges 86
Sturtevant 71
Sutcott 144
Swain 46
Swift 113
Swan 50
Syeurett 144
Symmes 12
Syvericke 144

T
Tainter 46
Taintor 46
Talemache 125
Talmadge 123-126
Terry 43, 70
Thomas 77
Thompson 78, 82
Tiddeman 67
Tilley 56, 156
Tilly 16, 156
Tolleemach 124
Tollemache 124-125
Tower 13, 119
Townsend 71

Trask 89
True 119-120
Tryer 53
Tucke 76, 79-80
Tucker 141
Tudor 1
Turner 55, 124, 143
Tuttle 124, 128, 130
Tyng 26, 112, 143

U
Underhill 9
Underwood 18
Usher 106

V
Vane 30, 156
Veazier 91
Veren 142
Vern 142
Vickars 70, 73, 129
Vickary 129
Vickery 129
Vinal 33
Vining 98
Vinson 86
Voysy 148

W
Wade 105
Wadsworth 51, 113
Waite 117, 143
Waldron 36
Walker 46, 92, 123, 143
Walters 128
Walton 77, 81
Ward 42, 70, 73, 78, 81, 119, 127-130
Warde 128
Warden 128
Ware 36
Warham 68, 81
Warren 79, 144
Waterhouse 28
Waterman 71
Waters 130
Watson 110
Way 71
Weaver 132
Webb 28, 147
Weld 55
Weston 18-19, 131-135
Wheeler 143
Wheelwright 30, 78
Whipple 115
White 23, 52, 55, 94-96
Whiting 41-42, 44
Wild 86
Willes 98
Willet 43
Williams 7, 17-18, 111, 114

Willis 105
Wilmont 110
Wilson 15, 128
Windsor 88
Winship 108
Winthrop 3-4, 7-17, 31, 54,
    62, 81, 112, 151, 154-156
Wolcott 43, 105
Wolfe 6
Wolford 11
Wolseley 131
Wood 68, 136, 145
Woodbery 89
Woodbury 6, 36, 141
Woodcocke 18
Woodman 78, 81
Woodward 58
Worth 54
Wright 9, 30, 56, 71, 95
Wyllys 105

Y
Young 90

www.ingramcontent.com/pod-product-compliance
Lightning Source LLC
Chambersburg PA
CBHW050715280326
41926CB00088B/3034